Bliss on Music

Bliss on Music

Selected Writings of Arthur Bliss
1920–1975

Edited by
GREGORY ROSCOW

Oxford   New York
OXFORD UNIVERSITY PRESS
1991

Oxford University Press, Walton Street, Oxford OX2 6DP

Oxford New York Toronto
Delhi Bombay Calcutta Madras Karachi
Petaling Jaya Singapore Hong Kong Tokyo
Nairobi Dar es Salaam Cape Town
Melbourne Auckland
and associated companies in
Berlin Ibadan

Oxford is a trade mark of Oxford University Press

Published in the United States
by Oxford University Press, New York

British Library Cataloguing in Publication Data
Bliss, Arthur 1891–1975
Bliss on music: selected writings of Arthur Bliss, 1920–1975.
1. Music
I. Title   II. Roscow, G. H. (Gregory H.)
780
ISBN 0–19–816222–7

Library of Congress Cataloging in Publication Data
Bliss, Arthur, Sir, 1891–1975.
[Literary works. Selections]
Bliss on music: selected writings of Arthur Bliss, 1920–1975/
edited by Gregory Roscow.
Includes index.
1. Music—History and criticism.   I. Roscow, G. H. (Gregory H.)
II. Title
ML60.B65   1991   780—dc20
ISBN 0–19–816222–7

Typeset by Rowland Phototypesetting Ltd
Bury St Edmunds, Suffolk
Printed in Great Britain by
Biddles Ltd, Guildford and King's Lynn

Preface

WHEN Sir Arthur Bliss died in 1975, it was as an elder statesman of English music or, as he humorously claimed, a *bon papa*. Half a century earlier he had been considered, with what now seems equal exaggeration, an *enfant terrible*. In between came not only the music on which his reputation rests, and in 1970 his autobiography, *As I Remember*, but a stream of articles, reviews, lectures, and broadcasts on a variety of musical topics. Such pieces are clearly relevant to an understanding of the man and his music, but they also provide a vivid commentary on twentieth-century music in general and on the 'English Musical Renaissance' in particular. Bliss travelled widely, held many important posts in musical organization and administration, and, in the words of a contemporary, received 'an aesthetic pleasure from the patterns of contemporary life',[1] a characteristic sometimes attributed to his American ancestry. From decade to decade his writings capture the spirit of the age. But whether from the pen of the *enfant terrible* or that of the *bon papa*, they exhibit the same vitality and generosity, the same insistence on sincerity and professionalism, and the same concern with the conditions in which music is made and enjoyed.

This volume contains everything of major interest that Bliss wrote between 1920 and 1975, with the exception of letters and of material that survives only in the form of notes. A particular consideration has been to avoid overlapping to any great extent with *As I Remember*, recently reprinted with additional chapters by Lady Bliss and Andrew Burn. Drawing on programme notes and similar brief descriptions, Bliss put much of what he wanted known about his own music up to 1965 into his autobiography, and I have accordingly limited myself to filling in gaps and including more detailed analysis of certain works.

Like much of his music, Bliss's writings are typically occasional, having been undertaken in response to a particular request or event and intended for a wide audience. His sense of an audience made him a particularly entertaining lecturer and after-dinner speaker. Examples will be found in the present volume; they are not necessarily the best, but simply those that are in continuous prose. It has been tempting to reconstruct others from the surviving notes, especially when coming across instances like the following, from a lecture on inspiration:

[1] H. E. Wortham, 'Arthur Bliss', *The Sackbut*, Apr. 1927, p. 255.

Preface

Coming up recently on the escalator at Leicester Square—in rush hour—a crowded queue going down, passing a crowded queue coming up, all in silence —only the metallic rhythm of the escalators. Suddenly the sound of a funeral march entered my consciousness. Caused by what? I used it for the funeral march to Churchill broadcast at his funeral.

In 1924 I visited the Observatory at Mount Wilson above Los Angeles—spread out in patterns of light below—in the clear velvety atmosphere I saw Saturn and its rings. I distinctly heard a vocal sound and noted it down. In 1956 I was asked to write an anthem for the Centenary of 'The Missions to Seamen' at Westminster Abbey. The words chosen came from the Book of Amos: 'Seek the Lord, seek him that maketh the Seven Stars and Orion.' My subconscious mind brought to the surface Mount Wilson thirty years before. I went to my notebook, found the phrase and used it.

The first example is the more typical. Interesting as such passages may be, however, the choppy prose of notes soon becomes tiresome; and reconstruction on a large scale is equally unacceptable. I have therefore omitted notes for lectures and speeches with some regret, but also in the knowledge that most of the ideas in them, if not the examples, appear elsewhere in the writings that are included.

While on the topic of what is *not* to be found in this volume, I must anticipate what some readers may regard as an accident of selection: namely, the sparing reference to composers, such as Walton or Prokofiev, with whom Bliss is often said to have an affinity. This is no accident. Bliss was always more forthcoming about those, like Schoenberg, whose aims and techniques were remote from his own.

The material in this volume is arranged chronologically, with brief biographical introductions to each chapter. Two pieces which do not fit comfortably into this scheme are included as Appendices. The chapter divisions are merely a convenience and are not meant to indicate phases of Bliss's life or musical development. The source of each item is noted after its title. As far as possible I have tried to keep the passing trail of the editor to a minimum. Spelling and some forms of punctuation have been standardized, generally in line with the usage in *As I Remember*. Misprints and occasional errors have been silently amended. Bliss made his wide reading very much his own in a functional spirit; his quotations are not always exact, or always attributed. I have checked those that can be traced and have indicated sources, without, however, giving the full scholarly treatment to what were designed in the main as popular presentations. Bliss's own notes are indicated by the abbreviation [AB].

The short title *Catalogue*, followed by a number, refers to entries in Lewis Foreman, *Arthur Bliss: Catalogue of the Complete Works* (London: Novello, 1980). Dates of musical works refer to the year of composition.

Preface

References to *As I Remember* apply to both the first edition (London: Faber & Faber, 1970) and the revised edition (London: Thames, 1989), since the pagination is the same up to the additional chapters. It is not within the scope of this volume to attempt analysis or assessment of Bliss's music or to provide a discography and critical bibliography; the latter are available in the recent and comprehensive compilation by Stewart Craggs, *Arthur Bliss: A Bio-Bibliography* (New York and London: Greenwood Press, 1988).

The proposal for this edition, which happily appears in the centenary of Bliss's birth, goes back several years. For her patience, and for much else, my greatest debt is to Lady Bliss, who gave me access to all her husband's material—now deposited in the Bliss Archive, Cambridge University Library—and provided every help and encouragement that an editor could wish for. I am grateful also to the following for help of various kinds: Stephen Banfield, Gordon St J. Clarke (BBS Sound Archives), Stewart Craggs, Eric Crozier, George Dannatt, Professor Vincent Duckles (University of California Music Library), Giles Easterbrook, Henry C. Haskell, Jacqueline Kavanagh (BBC Written Archives), Betty Lammin, Christopher Pike, Elizabeth Poston, Alison Smith, Barry Smith, Dr Dan Stehmann (Roy Harris Archive), Kenneth Thompson, and Philippa Thomson (Royal College of Music). Lastly, my thanks are due to all those, too numerous to mention, who shared with me their memories of the man and their enthusiasm for his music. His legacy of goodwill has made my task a pleasure.

G.H.R.

June 1990
Keele, Staffordshire

Acknowledgements

The publishers are grateful to copyright holders for granting permission to reproduce copyright material. Every effort has been made to contact all relevant parties concerned.

The illustration on the half-title page is of a book-plate designed for Arthur Bliss by Charles Paine; the illustration on p. 156 is a costume design by McKnight Kauffer for *Checkmate* (1937).

Contents

Contents

Contents

6. 1953–1963

7. 1964–1975

Contents

1920–1923

INTRODUCTION

ARTHUR EDWARD DRUMMOND BLISS was born at 'Hawthornden' in Barnes, London, on 2 August 1891. His mother, Agnes Kennard Davis, was an accomplished amateur pianist; his father, Francis Edward Bliss, who had come to England from Springfield, Massachusetts, was both a businessman and a keen connoisseur of art. If Bliss could trace his interest in music to his mother, it was to his father that he owed a talent for organization, a fondness for the visual arts, and, not least, a lifelong measure of financial independence. Two brothers born later also showed musical ability: Kennard on the clarinet and Howard on the cello. After Mrs Bliss's sudden death in 1895, the family moved to 21 Holland Park, Bayswater, where they were to live until 1923.

At an early age, encouraged by his father, Bliss determined on a career in music, eventually abandoning thoughts of becoming a concert pianist in favour of composition. One of his earliest works was a trio for himself and his brothers. He received a conventional education at Rugby and at Pembroke College, Cambridge, where, as a student of Charles Wood, he took degrees in History and Music in 1913. It was, however, his unofficial teachers who provided a greater stimulus: at Rugby the temporary music master who introduced him to the music of Debussy and Ravel, and at Cambridge the cosmopolitan musicologist Edward J. Dent, who quickened his interest in contemporary music. In 1912 he met Elgar, an object of adulation since boyhood, and they formed a lasting friendship. From Cambridge he went to the Royal College of Music as a pupil of Sir Charles Stanford, whose teaching he found less stimulating than attending the Diaghilev Ballets, especially Stravinsky's, with his fellow students Herbert Howells, Eugene Goossens, and Arthur Benjamin.

The outbreak of war in 1914 put an end to his studies. He enlisted immediately and served with distinction in France, first in the Royal Fusiliers and later in the Grenadier Guards. He was wounded in the Battle

1

"BLISS"

ONE-STEP

BY

ARTHUR BLISS

Price 2/- net each

F & B. GOODWIN Ltd.

LONDON

AGENTS   GOODWIN & TABB LTD 34 PERCY STREET LONDON. W

of the Somme, in which his brother Kennard died, and again later a
Cambrai, where he was mentioned in dispatches. Neither injury let.
permanent damage, but the emotional wounds were undoubtedly deeper,
as a single incident will suggest:

Just above Piccadilly Circus, a salvo had burst among a working party of the
Loyals. Blood and limbs seemed to be strewn about the road. Mangled bodies lay
silent or groaning. A memory of a coster's barrow spilt among the traffic and
splashes of fruit on the pavement shot into my mind. Arthur Bliss, very white and
resolute, was holding a man's arm which fountained blood, while its owner strove
to control the screams his torn body wanted to utter. [1]

When Bliss returned to civilian life in 1919, he was almost twenty-eight
years old and conscious of being a late starter. With a fund of energy that
impressed his contemporaries, he threw himself in the next two years into
every branch of musical activity: composing, conducting, lecturing, cham-
pioning the cause of new music in the press, seeking out Holst, Vaughan
Williams, and others for advice, signing manifestos, dreaming up new
projects with his friends, and making frequent trips to the Continent to
keep abreast of the lastest developments. In Paris he met Ravel and 'Les
Six', Cocteau and Picasso; in Salzburg, Schoenberg, Berg, Webern, and
Bartók.

Then, as later, Bliss drew many of his friends from the worlds of art and
the theatre—the designer Claude Lovat Fraser, the painters Wyndham
Lewis, Edward Wadsworth, and the Nash brothers—and his early projects included an arrangement of Pergolesi's *La serva padrona* (1918–19),
music for productions of *As You Like It* (1919) and *The Tempest* (1920), and
an orchestral evocation of the theatre, *Mêlée Fantasque* (1921), which he
later described as his first ballet score. But it was a series of experiments in
vocal and instrumental writing, all first performed in a twelve-month
period from June 1920, that earned him a reputation as the *enfant terrible*
of post-war English music: 'a semi-wild young man', the composer Joseph
Holbrooke remarked approvingly, 'who has perpetrated some singular
and comic music, which has shocked a lot of people—and also amused
many'. [2] The whimsical *Madam Noy* (1918), a 'witchery song' based on
nonsense verses on E. H. W. Meyerstein, was followed by a lyrical
Rhapsody (1919) for soprano and tenor vocalizing on the single sound 'ah'
to an orchestral accompaniment. In the carnivalesque *Rout* (1920), later

---

[1] Guy Chapman, *A Passionate Prodigality* (London, 1933, repr. 1965), p. 59. Bliss incribed his
copy 'The history of the 13th B[attalio]n Royal Fusiliers in the 1st World War with whom I served
from 1914–1916' and listed a number of pages, including the present one, for attention.
[2] *Contemporary British Composers* (London, 1925), p. 199.

re-orchestrated to provide interval music at the Diaghilev Ballets,[3] the soprano sings made-up words (e.g. 'ya ka da re mi no stun stan stun') to suggest the scraps of speech that might be overheard from an open window. For the Concerto for piano and tenor voice, strings, and percussion, Bliss provided words 'of such an abstract nature that they convey no *mood*'.[4] One might add 'or sense', for it is as if Bliss distrusted conventional meaning and was turning his back on a language and a lyrical idiom made bankrupt by war. In *Conversations* (1920) he avoided words altogether, offering instead instrumental evocations of such situations as 'The Committee Meeting' and 'In the Tube at Oxford Circus'.

With these 'experiments in sound', Bliss made a name for himself in the fashionable London salons as a daring but accessible innovator. He was not, however, tempted to continue in the same vein indefinitely. Early in 1920 Elgar had invited him, along with Herbert Howells and Eugene Goossens, to write a new work for the Three Choirs Festival of 1922. He responded with a full-scale symphony. Known at first simply as Symphony in B, it was subsequently (and controversially) entitled *A Colour Symphony*, reflecting his chance reading of the symbolic associations of colours in a book on heraldry.

Bliss gave the first performance of the symphony, under unfavourable conditions, at Gloucester Cathedral in September 1922, and more successfully in London in March 1923. A few days after this second performance, he delivered a lecture to the Musical Association (pp. 33–42 below). It was to be Bliss's last public platform in England for some time and, like the symphony, the lecture marks the end of a phase. Three months later he was to leave for America.

---

[3] In the season 26 May–30 July 1921 at the Princes Theatre. Bliss later orchestrated the *Polonaise* from his Suite for piano (1925) for similar use in the season 14 June–23 July 1926 at His Majesty's Theatre.

[4] Quoted in an interview by Katharine E. Eggar, 'The Orchestral Work of Arthur Bliss', *The Music Student*, 13 (Sept. 1921), p. 674. Although the text is now lost, an example is given in this interview: 'Man can endure . . . Incisive factors of the mind . . . Conceptive images . . .'

═══════

STRAY MUSINGS IN AMSTERDAM

In the spring of 1920, Bliss joined a party of musicians led by Adrian
Boult to hear Artur Nikisch conduct in Amsterdam. *RCM Magazine*,
16, 3 (1920), pp. 17–20. An extract appears in *As I Remember*,
pp. 57–9.

Holland is inhabited by a people that believe implicitly in a policy of
'thoroughness', whether in tulip growing, painting, financial business, or
gastronomy. It is said that you can judge the character of a nation by the
food it consumes, and if that saying has some psychological truth in it, then
my opening words contain more sense than I had dared to hope. For are
not wienerschnitzels and cheese washed down by beer a 'thorough' recipe
for an empty stomach?

The musical life of the country is no exception to this, but is on a level
with its other activities. In Amsterdam, for instance, the famous symphony orchestra is subsidised by the state, which grants almost unlimited
rehearsals, and actually sets aside several weeks of the musical year for the
sole purpose of perfecting orchestral technique—assuredly a veritable
paradise for conductors, who are thereby enabled to rehearse the strings,
the woodwind, the brass, each in turn! One was aware of the result of this
careful preparation at the first concert at which I heard the orchestra, the
occasion being the annual performance of the *St Matthew Passion*, in the
Concertgebouw.

Every concert hall develops its own peculiar personality. The Queen's
Hall, I feel, radiates a happy holiday humour, is out to enjoy itself,
overlooks mistakes, and applauds with indiscriminate relish; the Salle
Gaveau, on the other hand, wears an air of brilliant snobbery, anxious not
so much for its musical traditions as that the society it has invited shall not
demean themselves by an excess of enthusiasm; lastly, the Concertgebouw disports a serious mien, as though within it sat a conclave of
prosperous shareholders about to meet their chairman, conscious of his
promise of a 10 per cent dividend, and withal determined to meet this
expected prosperity with due moderation and respectability. There are
no late-comers—the soloists appear—Mengelberg[5] descends in silence
—the baton is raised—the *Passion* commences.

---

[5] Conductor of the Concertgebouw Orchestra 1895–1941.

I have met such a personality before, in less happy times, in days gone by when one was but a marionette whose head, legs, and arms danced at the bidding of a powerful and all-compelling personality, to wit, the drill sergeant at Chelsea. I smiled to myself as I thought that the eminent flautist could no more phrase a passage as he felt it than could I have marked time in triplets against my neighbours' twos, that no fiddler could there use a down bow in defiance of the rest, any more than I dare turn left consciously instead of right; uniformity of bowing, of phrasing, of dynamic force was absolute, and the result achieved was magnificent. And yet in spite of one's admiration for a well-nigh perfect rendering, there would intrude this thought: 'If only our Drapers, our Brains, and our James's[6] were here, just to show this orchestra the effect of several finished musicians infusing the general interpretation with their own individualities.' Mengelberg may be a superb musician, he may be a superb conductor, but he has not got the same gift of awakening enthusiasm in an orchestra that one gentleman has, who came several days later—Arthur Nikisch.

Meeting Nikisch was like being confronted with some giant of the past, of whose titanic exploits one had read, but whose personal existence one felt sure must be a myth founded on legendary lore. I am certain I shall feel no greater surprise when faced with Plato, King John, or Blondin. A little older, a little greyer, a little sadder maybe, he is still the leader of indomitable fire and energy, the inspirer of enthusiasm and loyalty. The preparation for his concert, which was to contain two symphonies, the *Eroica* and the Schumann D minor, preceded by the *Euryanthe* Overture of Weber, was interesting. First, two three-hours' rehearsal with the band, then a dress rehearsal, to which the public were admitted on the payment of a small tax, and finally, the concert on the following evening.

To gauge accurately one's impression of a Nikisch concert needs an abler pen than mine; suffice it to say that he goes for the broad interpretation of the whole, rather than for the perfection of any detail, and he appeals to the imaginative faculty rather than to one's faith in historic tradition, and that he has a way of purposely over-emphasising points of dynamic interest and change of time at the early rehearsals of the work, which naturally fall into their proper proportion to each other and the whole by the concert performance. His great knowledge of men, founded on his many years' experience of orchestras throughout the world, was surely never shown so vividly as in the manner in which he chose to end his first rehearsal with the orchestra—the first for twenty years or more. If you look at the

[6] Three families of English musicians: the clarinettists Charles (1869–1952) and Haydn (1889–1934) Draper; the horn players Alfred (1885–1966) and Aubrey (1893–1955) Brain; and the bassoonists Edwin F. (1861–1921) and Wilfred (1872–1941) James.

miniature score of the *Eroica*, page 176, you will see a pause, and it was on that pause, held long with a mighty crescendo on the violins, that the rehearsal came to an end. You could see the band, like so many Oliver Twists, asking for more, if only for an additional three bars or so.

Before I quit the question of music in Holland, there is one mysterious phenomenon on which I should like to lay stress, and that is the reverence they have for Gustav Mahler, culminating the other day in a great festival in his honour. Mahler appears to be in Holland what Ravel is in France, Stravinsky in Russia, Vaughan Williams and Holst in England: a powerful medium of contemporary musical thought. If that really is the case, his is but the bleating of a sheep in an assembly of lions. If you insert a Mahler symphony into a programme that contains, for instance, *Daphnis and Chloé*, *Le Sacre du printemps*, the *London Symphony*, and *The Planets*, for all its noise produced by a thousand players, it would be well-nigh inaudible. Why the apparition of the Albert Memorial should conjure up in my mind the shade of Mahler, I know not. It may be the figment of a diseased brain, but I am conceited enough to think that that is not the plausible reason.

You need not go as far as Venice to enjoy the beauty of moonlight on a system of canals: it is enough to cross to Holland. Amsterdam is a lovely city by night, with its brilliantly lighted Kalver-Straat, through which the youth and beauty of the place stroll careless of traffic, its shady pensive canals, shadowed by tall buildings, its busy little trams, that look like lighted worms, moving slowly and noisily through narrow streets and over bridges, and its fine houses, many in the brick style of the seventeenth century. It sinks in one's mind like some harmonious nocturne, and typifies the sense of contentment and restful ease that seems such a characteristic of the place and which is reflected in the works of so many Dutch painters, like Vermeer, Pieter de Hooch, and Jan Steen. From the feverish activity of London, may I often be transported to the tranquil canals of Amsterdam!

UNEXPLAINED SUPERSTITIONS

THE CULT OF THE DEAD

Musical News and Herald, 23 April 1921, p. 523.

It is not good, in one sense, for a creative artist to be alive—he is *ipso facto* of no account. To be dead is to be exalted. If ever a desire for inflated success comes upon me, which the gods forbid, I shall die straightway and achieve it. That death with its attendant mystery can completely alter the status of an individual in the eyes of others is a curious but none the less prevalent superstition. Hence the veriest scribbler that ever defaced manuscript paper is patronisingly forgiven, while the genius who has suffered most neglect when living is presented on his death bed with a public passport to the assembly of the great.

No one hears with envy panegyrics on dead musicians. To write them is a task as congenial as it is safe; but when it is at the direct expense of the living, who need it still more, I for one tap the culprit on the shoulder and say, 'Enough, my good sir, put away that telescope you are wielding so dangerously: do you not see that you are regarding the dead through one end, and the living through the other? Come, let us attain to a true perspective and look at both with the naked eye.'

We have living today, in Europe, several musical minds that an unprejudiced posterity will rank as high in musical achievement as Haydn, Weber, Mendelssohn, Berlioz, and Schumann. To avoid vague generalities I will mention four who are regarded by some as still of the younger modern school (as though 'young' were a question solely of age, and 'modern' evoked a sight of the future): Holst, Ravel, Stravinsky, Vaughan Williams. In spite of the known work of such men, for every one performance of a Holst we have ten of a Mendelssohn, and for every one of a Vaughan Williams a host of Schumanns.

We are incorrigible worshippers of the dead. They assume for us today an unaccustomed lustre. A tawdry work of Sullivan heads a concert on 'Warriors' Day'. An English conductor flies like a whirlwind through Italy and leaves *The Planets* behind for Scriabin. As in so many other phases of musical life the defect lies in the imagination. Once you obliterate the prejudice that because Holst, living in Hammersmith, can be seen daily for a modest twopenny bus ride, he must, therefore, be as ordinary a mortal as Vaughan Williams, who is actually a professor at the Royal

College of Music, you can then pass to performing his works as often *now* as you will when he has gone to places whither it will tax all your ingenuity to follow him.

I am tired of the line of thought—'A dead Englishmen is better than a live one, and if you must have a live one, have a Frenchman.'

London is so obviously the centre of musical activity that we are necessarily the dumping ground of much that is inferior in mentality and craftsmanship. Early works by Casella, Prokofiev, and Schreker occur to my mind, bringing remembrances of additional rehearsals and instruments, and giving the public a totally wrong standard of talent by the simple method of excluding the works of our own contemporary composers from such important concerts.

The Eternal Rhythm[7] of Goossens, the *Spanish Phantasy* of Berners, the tone-poems of Bax would, in vulgar parlance, put the lid on these other works pretty effectively.

I abhor the narrow provincialism that performs English works simply and solely because they are English; it is judging by a wide cosmopolitan standard that I affirm that it is here in England that we have the surest signs of musical enlightenment, as far apart from the neo-Chaminade school in Paris as from the neo-Strauss school in Berlin.

To a certain extent the Press has aided this superstition, devoting so much space, as it does, in those lucky papers that welcome musical articles, to the dead. It is assuredly good to examine critically the great masters of the past (we cannot always live in the present), but I fail often to find adequate space given to subjects like the recently-completed opera of Vaughan Williams,[8] Goossens' newly-published Piano Quintet, Milhaud's experiments, and to the many signs which mark this as a period of very special creative activity.

Gentlemen of the Press, I implore you to wipe from your vocabulary the words 'young' and 'promising' which have followed so many English composers from their birth onward, only to be swallowed in the paean of praise which, already written, greets their mighty decease.

Vivent les vivants!

---

[7] A symphonic poem (*c.* 1913), later withdrawn.
[8] *The Shepherds of the Delectable Mountains* (1921–2). Bliss conducted the first performance at the Royal College of Music in July 1922.

RECENT WORKS OF IGOR STRAVINSKY

Musical News and Herald, 14 May 1921, p. 625.

Certain of Stravinsky's later works, restricted for the most part to the smaller musical forms, have raised more discussion and controversy than perhaps the composer had foreseen; I refer to the *Three Children's Tales*, the *Four Russian Folk Songs*, the two ragtimes,[9] and the *Three Pieces for solo clarinet*. Relatively unimportant, and mostly of humorous import, these works are akin to the pencil and charcoal sketches which serve artists as essays and tests for their larger canvases, and it is as unfair to judge Stravinsky on these works as it would be to condemn a painter on the stray drawings in his portfolio, which were but a preliminary to the final conception.

To many composers, of course, these 'trials' are unnecessary, but where the technique is experimental, and the mode of expression individual, they are justified, and we should feel gratified at being admitted to his workshop and allowed to peep at his methods.

To an interested observer of Stravinsky's progress these small works reveal a growing strength in contrapuntal devices, a keener sense of rhythmic changes, and his constant delight in simplification of texture. I should like to call attention specially to the *Four Russian Folk Songs*, possessing as they do a lyrical charm which shall commend them to any singer who wishes an introduction to Stravinsky's vocal works, and to the *Three Pieces for clarinet*; the last of these, played throughout in the high register of the instrument, has a rhythmic vigour that is most stimulating.

Two other works on my desk by the same pen do not belong to the above category, namely, the piano score of the ballet *Pulcinella* after Pergolesi, and the Suite from *L'Histoire du soldat*, arranged for clarinet, violin, and piano.

The grafting of a Stravinsky on a Pergolesi is a bold horticultural experiment, but the resulting fruit is tasty. The tunes and clichés of the eighteenth-century Italian are maintained, but the technical and imaginative treatment savours plainly of contemporary Russia. Sometimes, indeed, Stravinsky with a brusque gesture sweeps his older companion

---

[9] *Piano-Rag-Music* and *Ragtime* (both 1919). Bliss conducted the first English performance of the latter on 27 Apr. 1920 at an Aeolian Hall concert that included his own Piano Quintet.

somewhat bluntly aside, but on the whole theirs is a harmonious alliance.

L'Histoire du soldat suffers necessarily by its reduction from a chamber orchestra, the piano having to combine the duties of brass and percussion, but let us be thankful for it in such a convenient form. The suite consists of a series of dances: a crisp march, a vivid tango, a graceful waltz, a fierce ragtime, and so on. The scoring could only have been written by Stravinsky—note, for instance, his predilection for the low double stopping on the violin—and the interest of the whole is heightened by the fact that the three players must be eminent musicians as well as brilliant executants.

In closing let me mention the setting of the *Volga Boatmen's Song* for wind, brass, and percussion, a useful variant to the well-known arrangement by Glazounov.

RECENT WORKS OF ARNOLD BAX

Musical News and Herald, 21 May 1921, p. 652.

Bax is perhaps the most spontaneous of any living composer worthy the free gift of that appellation. Music flows from him as readily and easily as words from an experienced orator; and it is perhaps for that very reason that an hour spent with his music is so refreshing a tonic, after the dry perusal of much stuff that is devoid of spontaneity.

I have heard it said that Bax's music is diffuse, lacking in conciseness, is strung out, not well knit, and so on in the journalistic way. This may be true of Bax the student—I do not know him—but of Bax of today, in the strength of his creative maturity, I maintain that if his ideas run to length they do so with such a wealth of invention that the fault, if it be one, is readily condoned. When one remembers the amateurish works that drop dead in the second bar of their meagre existences, one welcomes a professional and accomplished musician who can think in big lines and fill to overflowing big conceptions.

The most important works on my table are his Quartet for strings in G major and the *Elegiac Trio* for flute, viola, and harp. There is no doubt about the mastery of Bax's technique. A simpleton can see that he knows, to state it prosaically, his business full well. Whether he writes for strings, harp, or woodwind, the scoring is invariably certain of effect, supple, and instrumentally successful. I hope the quartet will be played everywhere.

It is quite easy in the hands of good musicians. I heard it murdered once, but that will not affect its life.

The *Elegiac Trio* is very characteristic. No one else but Debussy would have brought into association three such instruments, though to compare the language of Bax with that of the French master, as some uninformed American critic has done, is verily one of the silliest musical statements of the year.

A wealth of songs and piano works is issued, besides the folk song for cello and piano dedicated to Felix Salmond, and a welcome addition to the romantic literature of that instrument. It is impossible to deal with them all separately, but I should like to draw especial attention to the free arrangements of *Traditional Songs of France*. The whole five are gems. Bax's songs are not for the lazy type of singer. Like all individual thinkers, his technique is personal, and has got to be assimilated. His songs should be sung as I have heard Anne Thursfield and John Coates sing them, so that the difficulties of the vocal line sound perfectly easy and natural.

A word—in secret—to the public pianist.

I am going to tell you for nothing how to do something incredibly daring. Cut out your Chopin group at your next recital and substitute a Bax group. It means a little more work, but you will be thought no end of a pioneer. His works are just as interestingly written for the instrument, they are just as varied in style and mood, and—between ourselves—they are sometimes of better material. Let me suggest a group:

Toccata
Mediterranean
What the Minstrel Told Us
The Slave Girl
Burlesque

I want to close on a note of admiration for the firm of Murdoch, Murdoch, and Co., who are publishing most of Bax. Such enterprise is a compliment to the best English music, and stands as a shining example to firms who prefer to keep the taste of the public low for commercial reasons.

REFLECTIONS ON THREE WORKS OF EUGENE GOOSSENS

Musical News and Herald, 4 June 1921, p. 721.

Three important compositions by Goossens have lately seen the light from the house of J. and W. Chester, Ltd., namely a Violin Sonata, a Pianoforte Quintet, and a group of *Three Poems* for pianoforte. The oldest in years is the Violin Sonata, a work in three movements, each of which bears a well-defined character.

I remember listening to a fine performance of this sonata given by Albert Sammons and the composer some years ago, but since that time I have not had an opportunity of hearing it again till quite recently. À *propos* of this fact, I have come to the conclusion, after serious thought, that violinists are by nature timid. I feel certain many of them possess a long list of works for their instrument, neatly arranged in order of popularity. Topping all, of course, comes *The Devil's Trill*, and as you descend the list these unhappy works become more and more interesting, and more and more unpopular, until at the bottom cluster a little devoted band representing the best contemporary thought, but (unpractical dreamers!) not drawing a brass farthing into the house. Here, of course, we come across the Goossens sonata.

The better-known the violinist is, the less can he afford to risk anything by the inclusion of such a work. The attitude is not a very fine one. Just imagine a musician like, for instance, Vaughan Williams saying to himself: 'I do not get enough people to come and listen to my *Sea Symphony* and my *London Symphony*. I will straightaway sign a contract with some firm of balladmongers, and supply them with fifty such a year; and when my name is known at the end of every pier on the South Coast I shall feel the satisfaction that only comes with success well earned.' You, violinists, would not think much of composers who adopted such methods, so do not be surprised if their verdict on you, as they watch you clinging so desperately to the popular favourites, is 'guilty of timidity'.

This particular work of Goossens is unfortunate in another way. Being revived, as I have mentioned, after a premature burial, it was peremptorily dismissed in more than one paper as 'interesting'—damnable word. (How often do you not whisper it at dinner parties as you turn to your neighbour, just as she has finished retailing a long personal anecdote that you have not quite heard, and the point of which you have unfortunately missed!) All music is interesting, however old, just as all criticism is interesting, however off the mark. This sonata, with the animated grace of its first movement, the lyrical pensiveness of its second, and the robust vigour of its third, is enlivened with a wealth of ideas, and permeated with that characteristic elegance of thought that distinguishes Goossens from many of his English contemporaries. The one miscalculation, to my thinking, is the inclusion of a folk song. Its entry is too self-conscious, which makes me think that Goossens is no more in tune with the spirit of English folk music than—well, than I am.

The Pianoforte Quintet, in one movement, is altogether a bigger work, whether viewed from the imaginative or the technical standpoint. It is in the form of a 'fantasia', the whole conception germinating from the melodic line of the first few bars. The 'one movement' form, comprising, as it must, the varying moods of a larger work of several movements, is a difficult problem, and Goossens proves his exceptional musicianship by the sure grasp he shows of the two chief difficulties—continuity of thought and symmetry of outline.

Here again I can only remember one performance. I think possibly the Royal College and Royal Academy of Music may welcome such a work into their repertoire. Good piano quintets are rare, and it is a pity that the Schumann, which, in spite of good tunes, is poorly written for the instruments, should serve students so continuously as a model for that particular combination of instruments.

In his latest works for the piano, Goossens has gone to nature for inspiration, and has labelled his *Three Poems* with the sub-titles 'Awakening'—'Pastoral'—'Bacchanal'. These labels are somewhat misleading, as the composer views nature from a different vantage ground to Debussy. Whether he is emphasising the dawning of the world from darkness and night, the stirring of spring with its blossoms and flowers, or the revelry and madness of the midday heat, he gives us, not an atmospheric impression, but a clear-cut personal opinion on the great secrets of nature. These are unquestionably the best works he has yet written for the instrument, and were one of the three works I sent to Germany a few months ago at the request of a friend there who wanted an introduction to contemporary English piano music. (The other two works were the Ireland piano sonata and two pieces by Bax.) Moiseivich has been awarded the dedication, and no doubt the pianist has returned the compliment to the composer by a performance of them in America. We have not heard them yet in London, but probably we shall in due course. They need not only a pianist with facile technique, but one who is as imaginative, as subtle, and as daring as the composer who penned them. A criticism that has been levelled at us from Paris is that our compositions are not blessed with 'style'. This is false, like most generalities—the subject of this article alone disproves it.

———

WHAT MODERN COMPOSITION IS AIMING AT

A lecture to the Society of Women Musicians on 2 July 1921. An abridged version appears in *As I Remember*, pp. 248–55.
Musical News and Herald, 23 July 1921, p. 90; 6 August, pp. 138–9; 20 August, pp. 189–90.

At any given period in the course of musical history you can witness the spectacle of two distinct and antagonistic parties operating one against the other. Seldom has there been a time when there has not been a dispute worth contesting; if there has been a respite, it is only because there has been no music worth fighting about, and as soon as a new champion comes into the field the battle rages again with undiminished force, generally indulged in by musician and layman alike. The fighters on each side have had the same banners, the same passwords, and the same weapons; they possess certain characteristics which serve to distinguish them. Ranged on the one side are those whose ideals and traditions have already passed safely into history; they may have had to contest them in their youth, but as soon as their views were accepted as established laws, all they had to do was to tighten their grasp on them with a view to developing them to their logical conclusion. Most of them were probably born at the end of an epoch, during which some new trend of thought had been sifted and probed, broadened and enlarged to the fullest possibility. Their sole aim now is to make use of the stable popularized structure as a prop for the expression of their own personalities. They may not be old in years; in fact, there are many young folk among them.

Facing them in this Homeric struggle are those whose temperament reacts against well-worn formulas and existing traditions, who descry in most of the music of the day the threadbare *clichés* of some dead master's achievements served up anew. They may not be very young; in fact, there is generally a sprinkling of grey hairs on this side.

Musical gladiatorial shows were the rage very early in history. A notable one occurred in 1594, the year that Palestrina died, when several poets and musicians, tired of the severe style of vocal church music of the times, met together in a nobleman's house in Florence and breathed the magic word 'opera' to each other. You should have seen how the Venetian

Guardian thundered against the Florentine *Musical News*, and how the Genoese *Observer* vowed he did not know which side was right.

Again, towards the latter end of the eighteenth century, when the polyphonic period had culminated in the glorious works of Bach, the young Mozart arose, who set music adrift on entirely new seas, developing the origin of the orchestra, of chamber music, and of that beauty of architectural form which Beethoven was to carry to its highest point. A tempestuous period this, as 'La Guerre des Bouffons'[10] was in full swing in Paris, with Gluck attacking the conventions of the Italian opera.

Later still arose the vexed question of the association of music with the sister arts, chiefly with literature. The older composers followed by instinct the ideal of producing beautiful sound for its own sake. Music, they said, was made to listen to, and the ear should be the only critic; realistic suggestion, literary association, programme music, were to them anathema. Now, however, we find Berlioz giving literary interpretations of works, Schumann starting a paper, Wagner madly pamphleteering.

A new spirit was abroad, the spirit of romanticism. Probably the age which produced a succession of men like Victor Hugo, Goethe and Schiller, Wordsworth, Byron, Shelley, and Swinburne was to a great degree responsible, but at the root of the movement lay a natural reaction against the long period of abstract music, against which we in return are reacting now.

Finally came the national opposition to the overpowering German romantic tradition of the latter end of the last century, an opposition which manifested itself under many different guises. Dvořák sprang up in Bohemia, Grieg in Norway, Moussorgsky, Borodin, Rimsky-Korsakov in Russia, later Debussy in France, and Vaughan Williams in England. In most cases these composers set themselves consciously to express national traits of mind, using melodies akin to the folk music of their countries, employing rhythms suggestive of their national dances, and so on. Debussy stands apart, a lonely pioneer, whose antagonism to the German romanticism is not shown in the exploitation of national tendencies so much as in the perfecting of an individual technique, as far removed from the machinery of his contemporaries as is the rapier from the cudgel.

And thus to our own period, perhaps the most striking in all the world's history. It is always cheerful to think that the age in which we live scintillates above all others, towers in genius and talent over the years that

---

[10] 'The War of the Comedians', a dispute about the relative merits of French and Italian opera. The controversial performance of an opera by André-Cardinal Destouches in Paris in 1752 was followed by an equally controversial performance of Pergolesi's *La serva padrona* by a company of Italian comedians. Gluck was too young to be involved in the quarrel.

have gone. We are, perhaps, too near the achievements of our own time to view them in their proper perspective, but assuredly this is an exceptional era, containing many great names on both sides, comprising those who are closing an epoch as well as those who are opening a new one. Both are equally important in the growth of sound, but as the subject of this paper restricts me to future developments in music, I will pass to a brief survey of the latter.

Gaze round Europe and cast a glance on those who are in the forefront of the new Development; look not at America, for she brings in little. In Italy two potent forces have arisen, in the persons of Casella and Malipiero. Both are men whose thoughts soar futurewards. To those who sickened under the fear that Italian opera is summed up in *The Girl of the Golden West*, the *Setti Canzoni* of Malipiero must come as a healing medicine. These bear the sub-title 'dramatic expressions' and are composed of seven alternatively tragic and comic scenes, based on short dramatic incidents where the action is reduced to the mere element of contrast, contrast of environment, of character, of mood. They follow each other without interruption, with an easy change of scenery. Hating the operatic style of singing, he has expressed himself through a medium of absolute simplicity, and he is directly opposed to the commonplaces and paddings of the conventional drama.

Casella, some of whose works have been heard in England, notably *Le Couvent sur l'eau*, is an experimentalist in technique, daring and certain, who, along with Tommasini and Respighi, is a very active member of the Italian musical community. These latter two are chiefly known to the English public by their respective orchestral treatments of the Scarlatti and Rossini ballets.

In France Ravel stands apart by himself, the reincarnation of the seventeenth-century spirit under a modern habit, combining as he does an audacious harmonic scheme with classic clarity of style.

Behind him move the so-called 'Group of Six', who indeed pretend to react against what they term Ravel's over-refinement, but who pay him often the compliment of imitation. They have been treated somewhat unjustly over here, I think, being judged on their group output rather than on their several individual efforts. Personally I think Milhaud and Honegger the most promising. Both have written much, both have healthy imagination and technical equipment, and both are too far removed temperamentally from the enervating Parisian salon to deteriorate into fashionable jokers. But whatever be our personal opinion, the Six truly stand as a body for vitality and simplicity in music, and express hatred of the humbug and pomposity attributable to their neighbours across the Rhine.

In England many names shine forth, of which the most conspicuous are Vaughan Williams, Holst, Goossens, Bax, Ireland, and Berners. One of our national characteristics is the distrust of musical cliques; we do not band together mutually to protect common musical ideals, and in some ways this disunion is a healthy sign. Such an alliance as the invincible band of Russia or the Parisian Six is foreign to our nature, with the result that every side of musical progress is represented here. Vaughan Williams, with his strong adherence to modal counterpoint, and love of national folk song, is in direct communion with Purcell, as Ravel is with Couperin. Holst the mystic, Bax the romantic, Ireland the rugged, Goossens the exquisite, Berners the satirist, all add their quota to the stream of national music that looks like flowing with nobler current than that of any other country.

In Spain we have men like de Falla, with his sincere portrayal of Andalusian melodies and rhythms, and his individual orchestral colouring, sufficient to grant him a special niche in the European movement.

In Budapest there is Bartók, in Amsterdam Schoenberg. We have not had a chance to estimate the value of these two men; except for the *Five Orchestral Pieces* we know little of Schoenberg's later developments. These certainly made a deep impression by their almost brutal frankness, and raised him high above the composer of the *Chamber Symphony* and the String Sextet,[11] both of which works show only too plainly the professor of detestable memory.

Finally, we come to Russia, the birthplace of the most remarkable musician of the time. Stravinsky, the composer of *Petrouchka, Le Sacre du printemps*, and *Rossignol*, is too well known over here to need any description from me, and abler pens than mine have written dissertations on his methods. I take my hat off to him and to the others whose names I have mentioned, not only for what they have created, but also for what they have killed, for their effective exposure of pretentious nobodies as well as for their contribution to the world's musical wealth.

Let us take toll of some of their victims.

1. The oratorio composed especially for the provincial festival on the lines laid down by the Canon and Chapter.

2. The symphonic poem *à la* Strauss, with a soul sorely perplexed, but finally achieving freedom, not without much perspiring pathos.

3. The pseudo-intellectuality of the Brahms camp followers, with their classical sonatas and concertos, and variations, and other 'stock-in-trade'.

4. The overpowering grand opera with its frothing Wotans and stupid King Marks.

[11] *Verklärte Nacht.*

What Modern Composition is Aiming at

Give me such works as *Le Sacre du printemps, L'Histoire du soldat*, the *Sea Symphony* and *Savitri*,[12] *The Eternal Rhythm* and *The Garden of Fand*,[13] the Ravel Trio and de Falla's *Vida Breve, L'Heure espagnole* and the *Five Pieces* of Schoenberg, and you can have all your Strauss *Domestic* and *Alpine* symphonies, your Scriabin poems of Earth, Fire and Water, your Schreker, your Bruckner, and your Mahler.

You may ask what constitutes this new development; is there any sign by which we can see it? And any criterion by which we can judge it? Tread softly! We are on dangerous ground; every composer has his own particular fetish, his own plan of attack and defence against the other side. I can but tentatively throw out some general hints; we can, for instance, say that the majority are continually striving towards a state of simplicity. It is not that the musical mind is becoming less subtle, but that, in translating thought into terms of sound, the mode of expression arrived at is a far more direct one.

There is abroad amongst them now a hatred of padding, a contempt of laborious super-texture; they are, in other words, anti-Mahlerites. I fear I cannot say a good word of German music: it is to me anathema, not because it is Teutonic, but because to my mind it is at the same time ponderous and trivial, or, in the jargon of present-day science, boundless, yet finite.[14]

This desire for simplicity assumes many forms; Vaughan Williams, for instance, prunes his work until it is reduced to the most concentrated essence of expression. He never makes a pompous remark, and he seldom utters a redundant statement. Holst, again, even with an imagination that likes a large canvas in his mature work, avoids an over-elaboration. His score of *Savitri*, a drama on the great subject of Love's triumph over Death, consists of three singing parts, an orchestra of 12, reinforced by a small female chorus, and takes but half an hour to perform. He has painted a poignant scene with the fewest possible strokes, and the very simplicty carries with it an overwhelming conviction. So many contemporary composers, if they had the necessary breath, would preach 'Down with the type of music that Strauss upholds in his *Tod und Verklärung*, down with his doping of the uncultured with a mighty subject, and then feeding them with a sentimental and pretentious hymn-tune.' Rather would we have the

---

[12] Bliss had recently (June 1921) conducted performances of Holst's one-act opera at the Lyric Theatre, Hammersmith.

[13] A symphonic poem (1913) by Arnold Bax.

[14] A view Bliss always maintained: 'I do feel that when I listen to the big Mahler *Symphony of a Thousand* there is a certain vulgarity about it, and vulgarity as described by Aldous Huxley . . . it's blowing a thing which should be that size into *that* size . . . and when I hear a work of that kind I long to go back and put on a record of a delicious masterpiece like *L'Après-midi'* (from an interview by Michael Chanan, recorded in 1974 for the Granada Television Historical Record archive).

other extreme, Milhaud's tangos in *Le Bœuf sur le toit*, and Stravinsky's three clarinets in *Les Berceuses du chat*. Let the latter speak for himself and others on this subject of simplicity: 'I want neither to suggest situations nor emotions,' he says, 'but simply to manifest, to express them. Though I find it extremely hard to do so, I always aim at straightforward expression in its simplest form. I have no use for working out in dramatic or lyric music. The one essential is to feel and to express one's feelings.' There you have in a nutshell the profession of faith of many on this subject of elimination of all but the essential—straightforward expression in its simplest form—feel and express one's feelings.

With this clear inspired goal in view they do not bother with 'metaphysical preoccupations, with emotional hysteria, with pseudo-intellectual effusion'. They are determined to set a stern face against extramusical associations. Stravinsky sums up his sound theories with one gigantic conception of *Le Sacre du printemps*. Let it be judged as an aural sensation alone.[15] Listen to it, if you can, unprejudiced. I appeal, I am sure he would say, not to the professional, steeped in music, but to the man who can come to listen with his imagination only awake, and his other faculties in subjection. It is the child to whom the work makes the strongest appeal, who is attracted at once by the simplicity of its message and the convincing sincerity with which that message is conveyed. I am afraid the fine ladies whom I see applauding it so vigorously have neither the one nor the other characteristic, but only find in it a sensation all the more delicious for being totally incomprehensible. While I am on the subject of this work, let me remind you it was written in 1912–13. It is, therefore, eight or nine years old. The magnitude of it will be more readily grasped if you can bring yourselves to reflect for a moment on most of the other works written at the same time by contemporaries. The other day I believe a learned professor[16] actually hotly debated whether fifths should still be licensed or not, and often I hear the whole-tone scale discussed as if it were a phenomenon remarkable and daring, whose continuance threatened the actual existence of composition. Poor Debussy, with whom alone that scale is to be associated, is dead, and to spend time on either of those two chestnuts is as reprehensible as to debate with Einstein as to whether Isaac Newton be not the most daring figure in contemporary science. The general mental attitude of the day, which, as I have said, is to condemn musical camouflage and dope, and to aim at sincerity and simplicity, reacts immediately on the technique of the composer.

15 On 7 and 23 June at the Queen's Hall, Eugene Goossens had given controversial performances of *Le Sacre* as a symphony.

16 Sir Charles Stanford, Bliss's *bête noire* since his student days at the Royal College of Music. See 'Some Aspects of the Present Musical Situation', pp. 39–40 below.

The concentrated directness of thought is allied to an equally direct and forcible method of expression. There are several indications of this attitude. Firstly, with regard to the orchestra, there has arisen a keen desire to investigate more fully the individual timbre of each instrument, to explore its most extensive expressive capacity. Again, it is Stravinsky who has been the pioneer, although Holst and Goossens in England, and Milhaud in France, have exploited the tendency. As an example of this 'particularization' recall the opening of *Le Sacre*, where Stravinsky gives the long initial phrase to the bassoon, in spite of the extreme high register in which it has to be played. The peculiar timbre obtained plants one as immediately in the atmosphere intended as does the opening sentence in Shakespeare's *Hamlet*: 'Who's there—nay, stand and answer!' There is no preamble, you are in it, or, as his detractors affirm, in for it.

The custom of the moderns to make instruments function in the most independent way possible has given rise in late years to the growth of the chamber orchestra, an orchestra of 10 or 12 players, shall we say, all soloists, in the texture of whose ensemble the particular timbres stand out like coloured threads in a variegated carpet. Great sonorities of tone can be obtained by the judicious use of a few instruments, and the concerted effort produces a richness and diversity impossible to obtain with the old method of mass treatment.

Stravinsky's *Ragtime*, which I performed several years ago[17] at the Aeolian Hall, is scored for two violins, bass, flute, clarinet, horn, cornet, trombone, percussion and cymbalum. His *Pribaoutki* is scored for voice and eight instruments, his suite from *L'Histoire du soldat* for seven: violin, double bass, clarinet, bassoon, cornet, trombone, and percussion. Both these works were presented by M. Ansermet last summer at the Wigmore Hall, and the sonorities obtained were remarkable. Relatively speaking, Mahler's last symphony, with its required 1,000 performers, is a confused mezzo forte. Of course, all those who are using the chamber orchestra do not make their various instruments balance, as, for instance, the four strings of a quartet balance. How can a trombone balance a violin? The idea of the instrumental groups in the classical orchestra is done away with, and the composer uses instruments that are widely incongruous in quality and dynamic value, just as Wyndham Lewis, Wadsworth, or the Nash brothers create a picture with tones that are of varying density. This preoccupation with the timbre of instruments and the resulting mass sonority obtained by the combination of them has brought two phenomena in its wake.

Our old friend 'abstract music' has cropped up again. I dwelt briefly on

[17] Apr. 1920 (see n. 9 above).

the inverse reaction which was brought about by the literary music of romanticists like Liszt and Berlioz, which supplanted the abstract music of a Bach or a Mozart, and mentioned that I suspected that the union of music with literature would soon be severed in the divorce court of criticism on the grounds of incompatibility of ideals. We are helping to divorce it now. We are tired of the music that can only be appreciated by having a knowledge of the philosophic association which envelops it. Must I bring in Nietzsche to save the face of Strauss? Music has nothing in common with the other arts. It stands aloof and mysterious. It can no more convey a philosophic truth or literary epigram than could Schopenhauer play the double bass, or Wilde (Shaw, I almost said) deliver a musical criticism. Walter Pater was searchingly exact when he prefaced his essay on 'The School of Giorgione' with the words: 'It is the mistake of much popular criticism to regard poetry, music, and painting as but translations into different languages of one and the same fixed quantity of imaginative thought, supplemented by certain technical qualities of colour in painting, of sound in music, of rhythmical words in poetry. A clear apprehension of the opposite principle—that the sensuous material of each art brings with it a special phrase or quality of beauty, untranslatable into the forms of any other, an order of impressions distinct in kind, is the beginning of all true aesthetic criticism.'

To the consequent ridding of sound of all its obligations to non-musical elements, this study of timbre and mass sonority has largely contributed. We have been too long distracted with bygone associations. If we hear a phrase we are at once on the *qui vive* for its rhetorical development. We are so prejudiced that we cannot truly listen with the pure emotion evoked by sound alone. Debussy was right when he exclaimed, 'Give me the note of the shepherd's pipe!' What is the use of sitting in a chair over a score and pretending that because you can inwardly hear the tune and general harmonic basis of it, being, thank God, an educated musician, you are realizing the composer's intention and extracting a more pleasurable excitement thereby than if you sit in the concert hall and actually drink in the resulting sound with your ears? With abstract music it is all tomfoolery. Crouch in front of a *pêche Melba* and see how far imagination and gastronomic associations carry you. Contemplation of still life is placidly pleasant, but ask Tantalus his feelings when the horn of plenty is actually within his reach. Similarly, perusal of non-abstract music like Max Reger's might conceivably while away ten minutes, but to study a Stravinsky score except from a technical curiosity is to display an abysmal ignorance of the very source of its inspiration. We are entering an age where emotion in music will be studied by the purely musical. When next Ansermet plays the Stravinsky symphony for wind instruments, I beg of you all to go with mind lightened of any past prejudices and try to listen to the sound *en masse*, a symphony, in fact, as Leigh Henry puts it, conceived as an orchestral entity moulded in sound substance.

One more point and I have finished. I have tried to show that we are reaching an age of simplicity and vitality in expression, and that the very sincerity of our emotion has driven out all the tendencies culled from other arts, which serve only to obscure the issue of music—an issue wrapped in the word 'sound', and sound only.

Lastly, I want to dwell on an evolution in music that derives its source from these two movements—an evolution which emerges as a distrust of all existing sound combinations. If I am to judge by my ears alone—do I like the result obtained from a violin and a piano, from a piano and full orchestra, from two violins, viola and cello? Have we got so fixed, like flies in treacle, that we cannot revise our impressions in this direction? I ask you to bring this point, amongst others, to the forefront in the ensuing discussion. Do you not think that the Holst song with violin alone,[18] the proposed quartet of Stravinsky for three violins and bass,[19] Milhaud's Sonata for two violins and piano, Bax's Trio for flute, viola, and harp,[20] are not very definite steps in the required direction? The advent of the pianola, again, brings a most capable and original recruit into our army of sound. It is, of course, no converted or developed form of piano, but an entirely new sound-producing mechanism, more adapted for the unequal battle with full orchestra than any piano could be.

We live in rapidly moving times—many mentalities are at work who are not afraid to explore every avenue, who are desperately anxious for progress as contrasted with growth, a subtle distinction that Edwin Evans has enlarged on. Do not be led away by vapid phrases like 'music of the future', 'ultra-modern developments', and such like. That talk springs from the fountain of fear. The progress I have described is a contemporary one, is bang in the midst of us. It is those who dub it futurist who are themselves clinging desperately to the past. Some musicians I meet are contemporaries of our Victorian grandfathers. It always remains a mystery to me why they will entrust themselves wholeheartedly to the taxi, the aeroplane, the tube, and the telephone—all products of our time—and yet in music shrink back mentally dismayed into the well-marked era of the stage-coach and Puffing Billy. Do not, on the other hand, be persuaded by those rapidly moving gentlemen who cry 'Parci' before the work in question has had enough performance to be digested. A useful member

---

[18] *Four Songs* for voice and violin (1916–17).

[19] An unrealized project. Stravinsky is said to have disliked the sound of unaccompanied strings after his *Concertino* (1920) and did not write for them again for some years.

[20] *Elegiac Trio*.

of my village cricket team used to shout 'How's that?' before even the ball had left the bowler's hand. A keen and useful partisan of his side, I never checked him, but not an authoritative player of the game of cricket.

A powerful society like this can do a world of good in critically and wholeheartedly standing by the music of their time. I doubt whether you realize what a wonderful season this last has been. London is so primarily and clearly the hub of the world's musical wheel that going along the spokes to America, Holland, France, Italy, and Switzerland is like a prolonged provincial tour. The brilliance of the past few months is not accounted for by the presence of so many distinguished foreign guests, but by the exploits of our native musicians. I will give you three instances alone, as I hate ambiguous generalities: Goossens' performance of *Le Sacre du printemps* and of his own *Eternal Rhythm*, the unique series of Bach recitals given by Harold Samuel, and the perfection of ensemble attained by Messrs. Albert Sammons, Lionel Tertis, Felix Salmond, and William Murdoch of the Chamber Music Players. Moreover, the atmosphere of London has been made peculiarly congenial for the continuance of fine work, both creative and interpretative, by the intelligent and critical sympathy awarded to the best by the gentlemen of the musical press. I am sure that there are individuals there who are as much in the forefront of musical progress, and as largely responsible for the results achieved, as are the composers and executants themselves. It is a rare but refreshing sign that there are actually critics holding important positions who are not afraid to say: 'Go on, get a move on, do not stick', and the result is (I whisper it for fear they may be here) we all do go on with redoubled energy and encouragement.

I fear I have made many digressions from the main paths of my paper, but I shall feel no qualms if I have thereby started hares that will excite a fierce and successful pursuit. The subject was 'What Modern Composition is Aiming At'. I should have preferred the title 'What Contemporary Composition has Already Achieved', to which I reply—a triumphant and enduring success, with an ever widening future before it.

A SHORT NOTE ON STRAVINSKY'S ORCHESTRATION

Musical Standard, 30 July 1921, p. 43.

In using the word 'orchestration' as the heading of this article, I am sure I hit the precise term in dealing with Stravinsky. He does not answer to the name 'instrumentator', applicable to one who thinks first in melodic outline or in architectural form, and then transfers that conception into the varieties of colour obtained by orchestral instruments. He does not say to himself—'Now, on what instrument can this particular phrase best be played?'—but rather 'What phrase on this particular instrument (say, bass flute or bassoon) can best convey the colour that this passage of mine demands?' His melodic ideas, as Henry Prunières[21] states, come to him readily imbedded in a definite atmosphere of sonority. This is orchestration as opposed to instrumentation.

The composer's conviction of this truth is shown by the fact that when for convenience sake he issues works of orchestral mould in the restricted form of a chamber or piano score, he invariably thinks of the labour as entailing not an arrangement but an entirely new work—the conscious effort of rethinking in the new sonorities at his disposal.

His earlier work naturally reflects the influence of his master, Rimsky-Korsakov, and in *L'Oiseau de feu* he employs the carefully adjusted balance of instruments and the exploitation of traditional colour effects that characterizes the older man. But in *Petrouchka* he takes a step forward in the direction that led him to the realization of *Le Sacre du printemps*—treating his various instruments as individuals, whose particular timbres could be investigated to the full, not solely as members of a family who worked in collusion for harmonic effect. The result was a richness and a kaleidoscopic variety comparable only to the Oriental rays whose general colour scheme is all the more daring for the brilliant strands that stand out in isolated distinction. Just as the colour scheme determines the pattern or design, so does the 'orchestration' deliberately define the musical idea.

It is in *Le Sacre*, in which Stravinsky uses an enormous orchestra

---

[21] French musicologist (1886–1942).

—employing five of certain instruments of like timbre—that this particularization reaches its height, and throughout the work much harmonic and contrapuntal cacophony is only made of effective brilliance by the sure touch that the composer displays in building up his mass sonorities. In the hands of lesser men, many of the conglomeration of notes would have resulted in confused turgidity. Since then Stravinsky has turned his attention to the smaller combinations, and has projected *Ragtime, Les Berceuses du chat, Pribaoutki*, and *L'Histoire du soldat*. This last, the most important, perhaps, is typically scored for violin, bass, clarinet, bassoon, cornet, trombone, and percussion. Here, of course, there is no balance judged by a string quartet standard, but an effect comparable to a canvas that is compiled of 'tones' of various density. The whole trend of these miniatures is towards the goal of pure sound, to that Utopian hour, when we shall listen to music with our ears and imagination stirred, and our all too academically controlled intellect asleep.

HENRY PURCELL (1658–1695)

Bliss had recently completed a *Set of Act Tunes and Dances* based on
the music of Purcell, and had conducted its first performance at the
Wigmore Hall on 11 June 1921.
The Chesterian, 17 (1921), pp. 13–15.

In this age when lovers of music are insistently engaged in sweeping over the treasures of the past, many of which have gathered undeserved dust, and while sifting out what is of less value are enshrining that which has withstood the Spartan test of time, it is only just and right that the masterpieces of Henry Purcell should be welcomed with an ever increasing admiration.

It was not till the formation of the Purcell Society in 1876 that a systematic edition of all his compositions was given in handsome volumes to the world. These have given proof of such original beauty and versatility that this generation, which has profited thereby, looks up to their composer as a shining ornament of an age itself remarkable for music. In England, indeed, the time was ripe for much music-making. Far too long had the Puritan domination suppressed the wonderful church music of Byrd and Gibbons, going so far as to proclaim instruments in churches as 'profane, pagan, popish, idolatrous, dark, and damnable', so that with the Restoration a natural reaction set in, which Charles materially aided by his re-opening of the Chapel Royal and inauguration of court festivities.

Purcell therefore grew up in an atmosphere very congenial to the furthering of his musical abilities. Nor was he likely to meet discouragement at home, for did not his father hold the honourable post of 'Marshall of the Corporation for Musique in Westminster'?

He found himself sitting at the feet of one Captain Cooke, 'Master of the Children of the Chapel Royal', among the other 'children' being Michael Wise and John Blow, and ere long felt the inspiring influence of Pelham Humfrey, fresh from his visit to France. Very often must the young Purcell have listened with ready ears to the stories of the gay dances and ballets performed at the French court and the doings of giants like Lully and Molière.

All through his life—alas, a short one—he had a happy facility for pouring out music of every kind, now for the theatre, now for the solemn Abbey service, now for the intimate enjoyment of chamber music players. Hardly any other composer, with the exception of Mozart, has shown such an abundant genius for the expression of pure beauty. It seemed to them both so easy and natural a pleasure that neither had laboriously to carve out a special path along which to pursue a fickle inspiration. Both were so richly endowed with the gift of melody that they poured it out unaffectedly for the enjoyment of their listeners. Neither propounded a theory, neither flirted with a philosophy.

Purcell did not hesitate to learn from foreign sources, and indeed in his first printed compositions, *Sonnatas of III. Parts: 2 viollins and basse: to the Organ or Harpsichord. Composed by Henry Purcell, Composer in Ordinary to his Most Sacred Majesty, and Organist of his Chappell Royale*, he deliberately sets out in his preface that he 'faithfully endeavoured a just imitation of the most famed Italian masters.' It is, moreover, probable that the massive choral effects, quite new to English music, which he obtained so simply, arose from his study of Italian models.

And why not? What he wrote was his own and sprang naturally and unconsciously from his English environment. Moreover, he had the glorious tradition of the Elizabethan madrigalists and lutenists fresh in his mind, and it would have been but affectation to have embellished his post at the Abbey with the airs and graces of a French *monsieur*. In the year 1680, when Purcell succeeded Blow as organist of the Abbey, began the long series of dramas in which music played an important part. Two of these, by the way, have had distinguished performances quite recently. At Cambridge *The Faery Queen* was staged with every sign of success and to the evident enthusiasm of large audiences. Here in London Mr Holst gave two imaginative performances of *Dioclesian*.

During Purcell's lifetime it was the success of this latter work that won for the composer the friendship of Dryden, resulting in the joint production of *King Arthur* and later the 'operatic' version of Howard and Dryden's *Indian Queen*.

During his short life he wrote incidental music to more than fifty plays and produced one real opera, *Dido and Aeneas*—an astounding sign of fertility, though this prodigious array of compositions is appreciably lessened when one realizes that often a song or dance was his own contribution to the play.

Alongside these flowed a constant stream of odes, including the famous and immortal *Ode on St Cecilia's Day*, a style of work that inaugurated the choral concert with its secular-cantata form that has persisted in England up to the present day.,

Though his early death robbed the world of many noble works, he left an inheritance rich enough to establish him as our last great English composer for two hundred years.

It is this fact, and no mere love of scholarly labour, that has contributed to the revival of interest in Purcell. With the ever increasing faith in the renaissance of English music has come the deepening pride in our great musical ancestors, and the thought that the gap from the end of the seventeenth century to the end of the nineteenth century has been one record of foreign domination in English music, has led us to turn our gaze back to Henry Purcell.

With the exception of Boyce, Arne, Sullivan, and Parry, we have been content to supply the audience from the foreign composer. It has shown us in no ungenerous light, has enabled us to judge broad-mindedly, has given us a criterion on which to base our judgments. It has given us more: it has supplied us with all the technical machinery, which, with our characteristic national aptitude, we mould and alter to our own uses—but till recently it has not given us a composer to carry the mantle of Purcell. Many think that the day has arrived when the words with which he prefaced *Dioclesian* no longer apply: 'Poetry and painting have arrived to their perfection in our own country. Musick is yet but in its nonage, a froward child, which gives hope of what it may be hereafter in England, when the masters of it shall find more encouragement. 'Tis now learning Italian, which is its best master, and studying a little of the French air to give it somewhat more of gayety and fashion. Thus being farther from the sun, we are of later growth than our neighbour countries, and must be content to shake off our barbarity by degrees.' If the day *has* arrived, we have bridged the gulf between ourselves and Purcell.

━━━━

LONDON LEADS IN MUSIC

Daily Mail, 20 October 1921, p. 6.

One of the many surprising results of the upheaval of the last few years has been the sudden change effected in the leadership of the world's music. Before the war a man who expressed the opinion that London was 'the musical forum' of the world would have been gaped at as blankly as if he had attributed to Siam the pioneer work in popularizing football. 'Go to Germany!' was the cry. 'Go to Vienna, go to Paris, go anywhere, but do not stop in London, for we are an unmusical nation.' It seems so long ago that I do not remember whether that advice contained truth or no, but in this year, 1921, it is emphatically a superstition now moribund.

To start with, all European nations are equally musical or unmusical; there must always be a majority who are entirely impervious to sound other than the hoot of a motor or the click of a golf ball, and a minority who are mentally alert and enthusiastic for music and who embody constructive opinion. I do not think the ratio varies very greatly anywhere; what is an inconstant factor is the degree of enlightenment that this minority possesses.

In Germany today isolation has necessarily produced an ignorance of all music but its own, and its own flows as sluggishly as a stream in the drought. Of what avail are state-subsidized opera houses, endless rehearsals, tradition-bound performances of great exactitude where the comtemporary outlook is so circumscribed? *They have machinery in abundance for making music, but not enough raw material with which to feed it*.

Paris, our other rival, seems at this moment to be suffering from a musical anaemia. They are not, indeed, ignorant of the music of their neighbours, but on seeing it shrug their shoulders with the air of saying, 'To become catholic is to lose our splendid exclusiveness.' If this continues I fear we shall have to borrow the microscope to see them at all.

London escapes both these evils. We welcome all music here; we are, indeed, too generous. Foreign artists are beginning to swarm back, many with no other qualification than that of playing third-rate stuff faster than all competitors or singing fourth-rate arias an octave higher than other rivals. But we *do* provide them with an audience eager to hear, discuss, and compare, and out of it all is growing the steadily increasing admiration for our own musicians, creative and interpretative.

29

With the exception of two or three outstanding figures in Europe, the heart of musical creation beats in London—Elgar and Bax in Hampstead, Vaughan Williams and Ireland in Chelsea, Holst and Howells in Hammersmith, Goossens in Bayswater. It is such personalities that have largely contributed to the growth in importance of musical London, and now that we hold the leadership it will need another such upheaval to cause us to detach our grip.

THE SHANTY BOOK

A review of *The Shanty Book*, Part I, edited by R. R. Terry (1921).
Queen, 12 November 1921, p. 6.

One of the many romances that has met its death at the stern approach of machinery and the factory is the spirit of the 'shanty'. Time was when all forms of work implied hard manual labour, and fortunately it is a primitive instinct throughout the world to ease that work with song. So the spinner sat at his wheel, the weaver at his loom, and in like fashion the seaman at his windlass and capstan. But with the advent of mechanical labour, the need for manual toil gradually died, and with it the labour song. A great pity—for the practice gave to music a dignity, lifting it out of the status of a mere recreation, and imparting to it a much-needed universality, making it at once an inspiration and a necessity.

The labour song naturally declined first on land, lingering on at sea in the form of the shanty, as all work aboard a sailing vessel was performed by hand, but eventually the donkey engine and steam winch held sway over the hand-worked appliances, and the old spirit that inspired the shanty gave out in spontaneity. Here and there no doubt one can come across an old mariner who can remember a snatch of a tune or two current in the eighties, but what a pale ghost of the song whose chorus would be roared by thirty lusty seamen hauling 'hand over hand' to the solo singing of a specially appointed shantyman! Take away the labour and you destroy the whole lift and swing of the song. They can only be saved for us landlubbers in the form of a collected edition, such as Dr Terry has compiled, and our gratitude is due to an enthusiast who has laboured to catch and preserve with accuracy and discrimination the nautical flavour of these healthy bygone days.

The words themselves are quite a joy. They unconsciously, strange to say, lead us to recall to mind the songs shouted and whistled by marching troops in France during the war. In both cases there is the stereotyped opening of one or more verses, followed by improvised words relating chiefly to personal topics, such as the quality of the food, the peculiarities of the officers, the longing for shore and home.

This edition cannot, of course, compete with the intricate nature of the shantyman's improvised wit, but it gives enough to show that a Rabelaisian good humour and a salubrious 'grousing', not forgetting a curious delicacy, stamped the typical singer at his 'short pull' and 'sweating up'. There are numerous references to Napoleon—*e.g.* the halliard shanty, 'Boney was a Warrior'—and to the curious Mexican president, Santa Anna (no one quite knows why); also the mysterious mythical heroes, Ranzo and Stormy, and famous ships like *Flying Cloud* and the *Victory* were celebrated.

The tunes are equally interesting, showing, as many do, traces of the strange and varied lands for which the sailor found himself bound: a good example is 'Johnny Comes Down to Hilo', which is plainly of Negro origin. Some again of the shanties are clearly modal, others apparently have been converted into the modern key system during the course of their history. The editor has taken great pains to distinguish and treat accordingly the different characteristics of the tunes, and the understanding of the atmosphere in which they thrived has contributed largely to the pleasure which a mere landsman like myself finds in playing them over.

These romantic relics of an age less material than our own are astonishingly pleasing. One opens the volume, and one feels the spray on one's face, and the exhilaration of the sea breeze in one's lungs. Dr Terry receives the welcome thanks of all jaded musicians.

———

THOSE DAMNED FILMS!

Musical News and Herald, 18 February 1922, p. 220.

I must have sat through hundreds and hundreds of films, and of late I have left their 'gorgeous palaces' more and more convinced that the art directors responsible for the accompanying music know not their job— little blame to them, for in the kaleidoscopic world of the moving picture theirs is a particularly difficult one. Long ago, when it was first realized that to show a picture in silence was to court disaster, the primeval managers viewed the necessity of including music with the same complacency as did the restaurant proprietor. In the eyes of both, it was but a gentle stimulant to the imagination, lulling the critical faculties to sleep, so that a faulty picture would pass muster as easily as a poorly served cutlet. It was to be an additional security against any undue exercise of the intellect, for—let me state this as the first cinematic axiom—the picture house is no place for those who feel the need of a mental stimulus.

It is primarily for the inert, the exhausted, the feeble-minded, the unimaginative, and those who have not seen LIFE. That is why we all go. Have you ever floated down the rapids tucked up on an iceberg or felt the grip of the hangman's rope while your best friend raced his car against the train that carried the governor and your pardon? If you have—you will flee the cinema—it is too painful. We have not, and therefore throng there.

Once inside, the proprietor says: 'Thou shalt not think', and sure enough, think we can't. He does it all for us. If there is any likelihood of a situation flashing unexpectedly on us and jolting the mind with delicious thrills, the danger is averted by a wordy explanation that interrupts the sequence of events for quite a minute. If again, a girl carelessly, as it were, drops her wedding ring, we are assured of the existence of gravity by seeing it actually strike the ground and remain there, magnified to more than life size. Nothing is left to chance, nothing is left to thought.

To provide suitable music for this doping of the brain brought us by the films is comparatively simple. There is much music that produces no thought and does not bear thinking of. But soon the directors become more ambitious. They conspire together to raise the music, which had hitherto served but to drown the twittering of the operator's lantern, to the artistic level of the picture it accompanied. They took the 'don't think' policy one step further. You were not only to be *told* what was happening and then *see* it happen, but, luxury of luxuries, you were to *hear* it happen.

You could now explain more definitely (say) the contrast between the wife dancing at the night club resplendent in tiara and osprey feather (ragtime, 'My Coal Black Mammy'), and the husband, a literary gent, in the garret, poisoning himself with cheap cigarettes while he completes his masterpiece (*Unfinished Symphony* by Schubert). This was immensely thrilling, but carried in its wake one great disadvantage.

In the case of the films you are dealing with pale impersonalities—they are not flesh and blood, but rather creatures of some exquisite fairy land—that explains the hysterical triumph that greets their one live appearance here. We feel by watching them so often that we have really created them. We know the artistic joy—let us say no more.

But with music that has solid pretensions to greatness you are face to face with definite human emotions; you are at grips with something infinitely greater and more inspiring than the paltry tangle of incidents on the screen. The result is that the music in these cases compels all the attention, distracting willy-nilly the interest from the films and compelling the imagination to focus on itself. An analogous case is found in many portions of *The Ring*, where the vocal line, together with the words declaimed, are of no importance compared to the symphonic ideas embedded in the orchestral writing.

There are only two alternatives before the future music director of the films. Either, if you are of a conservative disposition, choose music that is not expressly written for the picture, but which is neither too good to overweight the film, nor too bad to hurt your dignity as a musician; neither too inappropriate to be absurd, nor too realistic to be inappropriate, neither too long nor too short, too slow or too fast, too soft or too loud—either, in fact, spend all your spare time hunting for the right tune, or—and here we speak *ex cathedra*—get some composer to collaborate with the producer and write those special cinema noises which I hope to enlarge on at a later date.[22]

What a proud day it will be for some of us to be featured as the sound-producing experts on a real live million-dollar movie!

———

SOME ASPECTS OF THE PRESENT MUSICAL SITUATION

A lecture to the (now Royal) Musical Association chaired by Percy Scholes, the musicologist and critic who had persuaded Bliss to give
A Colour Symphony its title.
Proceedings of the Royal Musical Association, 49 (1922–3),
pp. 59–77, which includes a transcript of the discussion following the lecture.

I find that it is advisable amongst musicians to speak the truth at the outset, otherwise they are liable to mistake fiction for fact; so let me say at once that this short paper contains no matter that has not already been sifted and probed, no criticisms that have not been adequately capped, and no suggestions that are not practically commonplaces to all present in this room. For if, as has been said with unction, there is nothing new in art, then obviously there is nothing new to be said about it, though a million pens splutter and a myriad tongues wag. Always the same music rises to the same accompaniment of chatter, and indeed we are so inured to reading and talking about it in preference to hearing it, that we are often enabled to combine the three functions simultaneously, digesting as we do

[22] There is no record of a further contribution to this topic.

our analytical programmes and forming our considered judgments there-from, actually during the performance of the music to which they refer. So what tones of quality can be superimposed on this bedrock of sound to season the appearance of the new in music, which as we are told is but the reappearance of the old, bidding us the prima donna's everlasting farewell?

Like political situations, which recur as automatically as phases of the moon, and to ease which different remedies are applied by each succeed-ing generation, so do musical developments follow each other with mathematical precision, hand in hand with comments thereon, recording similar situations of twenty, fifty, a hundred years before, and we probably are not logically wrong when we maintain that the musical critics of today, amongst whom, for the moment, I belong, are but reiterating—perhaps indeed with more point, perhaps with less unconscious humour—yet reiterating the diatribes, commonplaces, and eulogies, of, shall we say, Mr Davison[23] and his confrères thirty years ago; which is a flat, stale and, I am told, unprofitable proceeding, but still at this gathering a natural and pleasant duty.

And yet, forsooth, I am in quite another department to the musical critic and historian, for the would-be composer looks at music from a very different vantage point, utilizing as it were the telescope, to scan the harmonic field through the reverse end. As an individual, he is necessarily narrow-minded, leaning solely towards those composers of any age who have expressed, or are expressing, a similar personality, and looking with little sympathy on those whose aims are antagonistic, much as he may admire details in their technical equipment. He collects and assimilates only what can strengthen and crystallize his point of view, letting through his sieve or net all alien or superfluous matter that concerns him not. In short, he looks at all music in relation to himself, while the critical mind, functioning objectively, regards each facet of the art in relation to its opposite or adjacent fragment.

The giraffe, who in the course of centuries is busily engaged in elongat-ing his own neck so that his food may be more easily accessible, has no sympathy for, and but little interest in, the mole, who has lost the use of his eyes from the perpetual fear of appearing above ground. Here in the giraffe we see the true creative artist, a persistent seeker after new means of expression. The historian, on the other hand, who sits down to write a treatise on evolution, is not concerned so much with the giraffe's neck, or

---

[23] J. W. Davison (1813–85), music critic of *The Times* 1846–79.

the mole's eyes, as is the animal itself, but sees both in relation to other phenomena like the leopard's spots, or the donkey's ears.

That is why the views of all composers on contemporary music should be discredited as serious statements and why the erstwhile utterances of, for instance, Sir Charles Stanford, who read a paper here in 1920,[24] and Mr Hamilton Harty,[25] who spoke his views in 1922, should be received with all due caution. If such criticisms as these come from them as composers, they are narrow-minded but natural. If, however, they speak *ex cathedra* as teachers and conductors, they are not only narrow-minded, but unnatural. For the interpreter whether in the college room or in the concert hall should hesitate to impress upon a broad-minded audience a less broad-minded utterance.

We are acquainted frequently with the statement that it is the amateur who is the backbone of British music, as is the non-commissioned officer that of the British army, and moreover, that we can tell the height of the musical barometer by studying the pressure of the amateur on its surface. On this count then today is a favourable atmosphere in which to let music thrive: countless folk fiddle, sing, dance and play; in every village choral societies are in active operation; in many places amateur orchestras are springing up, proving once and for all that making music is a very popular and natural and English way of taking pleasure. Was it not the same 250 years ago, during our golden age of music? It little mattered then, any more than now, whether they played with perfection and brilliance, if only they brought to their playing, love and care; and, that then too, there were existing plenty of enthusiastic but bad performers, is proved by many references in Pepys' diary, himself no mean executant on the flageolet. On the 1st May 1663 he writes: 'I went to hear Mrs Turner's daughter play upon the harpsichord, but lord! it was enough to make any man sick to hear her; yet I was forced to commend her most highly.' In both generations, his and ours, there was a great company of music makers; most of the great houses had their museums of instruments, which were used by the guests, or by professional musicians hired to come in and play; and it is curious to find the same reluctance on the part of the inviter to reward with grace the skill of the invited. In another letter, for instance, Pepys naively remarks: 'Only the musique did not please me, they not being contented with less than 30/-.'

But a new portent has arisen in our times, a hybrid has appeared —amateur in accomplishment, though professional in intention—a fearsome creature, which though known as a sheep by musicians, is often

---

[24] On Some Recent Tendencies in Composition', *Publications of the Royal Musical Association*, 47 (London, 1920–1); reprinted in his *Interludes, Records and Reflections* (London, 1922).
[25] Irish composer and conductor (1879–1941), notably of the Hallé Orchestra 1920–33.

mistaken for a wolf by the public. The true professional is he who tries to make his living by attaining the highest possible level of efficient inspiration in his particular line, thereby setting a standard for others. This new quasi-amateur, however, simply loses money in the effort to persuade himself and his friends that he is gaining an *entrée* into the ranks of the professionals. The clear line between one and the other is fast disappearing; for every one true professional player and singer, at London recitals, you may get ten bungling, well-meaning amateurs. Of course everyone has the perfect right to think themselves musical, and to go as far as to express themselves in music; but few, surely, earn the privilege of indulging in this self-expression in public, charging for this revelation high prices, and putting themselves *ipso facto* in competition with the greatest. Most of them think that the divine law of compensation justifies their exhibitions. Do we not know those who atone for faulty intonation by the skilful wearing of a pretty dress, or even variety of dresses? Others too, of a subtler turn of mind, exploit their mentality at the expense of their technique, putting forth an interesting and seldom-heard programme, on the chance of escaping the otherwise inevitable comparison. It is a curious paradox, that the greater the technician, the smaller the mind, so that you rarely get standard performances of great modern works, the necessary technical skill that causes superficial difficulties to vanish, combined with the wide imaginative outlook needed to make the work intelligible, being lacking in the same personality. If one, for example, has heard Busoni play Bach, does one care about hearing Miss Smith, we will say, perform the same work? It is surely more pleasurable to muddle it through by oneself, or pedal it out on the pianola. As a matter of fact, that is what we all do; we refrain from troubling about Miss Smith. If she is indeed our friend, we sneak into the concert as a dead-head, and behave like a hypocrite in the artists' room afterwards, but if she is not our friend we turn our back on the hall that day. No result accrues from the recital except a financial loss, coupled with the complete disillusion felt by the stray two or three folk who wander in to hear her on the chance, and who, thereupon, register a vow not to go near a concert again for the rest of the month.

Now a vast number of fledglings fly from the nests of our musical colleges and academies, every year. Where do they go to roost? A certain percentage, of course, go straight into orchestras of some description, and immediately find work. I am not referring to those who at once justify their existence. One of the reasons why our orchestras have a world-wide reputation for skill in reading and musicianship in performance of new works after but few rehearsals, can be traced to the large number of young expert players who fill their gaps as they occur. Nor am I speaking of the large class which flow into our organist and school posts. They get a special

training such as they require, and though music in the parish be dominated by a vicar who does not know the difference between Purcell and
Spohr and music in the school be at the mercy of the headmaster who
thinks enthusiasm for Bach un-English, the results are generally surprisingly good. I speak entirely of the multitude, who aspire to be interpretative artists and who feel that at the outset of their career, some such
course as the immature London recital must be faced.

Now an immature attack in music is just as fatal as an immature attack in
the field. Unfortunately, in music such an enterprise does not convey you
to the hospital; instead it takes you to the provinces, where with a carefully
expurgated press notice, you sweep along, scattering wrong notes, flat
chest tones, exaggerated personalities, in fact all the symptoms of a
wrongly-acquired metropolitan superiority.

Well, how can we deter Miss Smith and her fellow amateurs from
encumbering the musical profession with further mediocrities? No one is
ever convinced by argument—so argument is useless. Experience too is
expensive and does harm to the musical community; think by analogy of
the disastrous result to the public of flooding the world of plumbers with
amateurs. No leaky cistern could be considered safe, after being repaired
by such a one. Similarly this periodic deluging of the musical community
with amateurs, merely to find out whether they are destined to land on
their feet eventually as artists, would simply result in the destruction of
what little public there is left. No—the axe must be laid at the very root of
the trouble, and crooked, weak, half-dead, and unpromising branches
lopped off early. I suggest that our great colleges and academies should
have two distinct systems of training—one suitable *for amateurs, aiming
at giving them sufficient technique* not to shame themselves in the drawing
room, after dinner, and still more at implanting in them a taste that is
impeccable and a love that is lasting. This will obviously be an impossibil-
ity unless the teachers themselves qualify in the matter of taste and
enthusiasm. Then there should be a second curriculum, devised specially
for the training of professional musicians, based on quite different principles—for the boxer who is training for his career necessarily undergoes
an intensive preparation, which for the ordinary man, who punches a ball
ten minutes every morning, to keep fit, is a waste of energy and time.
These professionals should be kept apart musically as far as possible, and
during their years of training, live a life as beneficial to the growth of music
as was the atmosphere of Rembrandt's studio for the ripening of pictorial
art. At the end of their studentship they could be wished 'God speed' with
the certainty that they need not fear the competition of those who could
be recognized at once as not belonging to their category.

But for all this accomplishment one great asset is required—a fountain-head of taste—and where shall we find that? Some of our most responsible men have quaint lapses into quite the reverse. On every bookstall, for instance, I find a magazine nicknamed 'The World's Best Music'. Quite a number of us buy it because quite a number are anxious for a modest sum to get into touch with the best in art; but we know perfectly well that, in spite of several good articles, the music it contains is very far from the world's best. At the best, it is the world's most popular music; but a joke at which the gallery shout in a body is not necessarily a standard for the world's wit. To be as charitable as possible, we must surmise that those who run it have for the moment failed to discriminate between what is the best, and what is the best-seller. The scheme of the paper, like similar schemes, may have arisen from the erroneous notion that it is the public who are to be educated. Let us leave the poor public out, I pray—it is we musicians who are in need of education. If, in every musical post in England, there were men whose outlook was generous and catholic, and whose discrimination for the best music of all periods was acute, the result would be overwhelmingly more sudden than that obtained by herding the public into one room, and feeding them up with musical food, sauced with condescension. No—let us tune our own pianos before we complain of the street bands outside.

There is, however, one hopeful sign that a great number of people wish to read about music, and do actually do so—and that sign is the large space devoted to music in the press. I do not mean so much the critical accounts of concerts, which are of course very considerable in number, but rather the variety of articles dealing with more general subjects, such as are found, for instances, in the *Times* and *Telegraph* on Saturday, the *Post* on Wednesday, and in several of the Sunday papers every week. No country I am told has such a musical grip on the press, and I cannot believe that any editor would insert articles from altruistic motives. They are put in to be read, and presumably they are read. The public should realize though that it is mainly the composer who is responsible for the enlightenment of the critical faculty of today, for the more the composers broaden the basis of music, driving therein the wedge of tolerance, the more the critical mind expands and aspires. The critic is the rudder of the big liner of public taste—he does not drive the vessel but is subtly driven, and although he appears to be the agent of direction, he is so only at the guidance of the composer at the wheel. But let not the composer take to himself any conceit for this independence. The pilot is at the mercy of his passengers' pockets, and directly influenced by the decision of his board of directors. Most composers, whether they will or no, are acutely susceptible to the influence of audiences, and in much of the music today will appear a reflection of that world convulsion we have all been through so lately, which has left so many with nerves tingling and senses dulled. For instance, one potent influence on contemporary music is exerted by the realization of the general listlessness of today's audience. You find it in the attitude of the public towards every art. Go in to any picture exhibition —stand at the corner of a room and watch the in-comers. See how they saunter in and either go straight for some painting that is more startling than the rest, in subject or treatment, or even more often just amble round the four walls with a nod for an acquaintance here, and a cut to an enemy there, and so out to the next room, carrying away but the barest recollection of a blaze of colour—nothing else. In just such spirit does the twelve o'clock occupant of a Sunday pew listen to the preacher's voice, hearing but a holy sound and often not retaining its logical continuity.

Similarly with our concert audiences. Anything that depends on clear concentrated listening is anathema to many of the delicate ladies of the audience for whose neurasthenia doctors have prescribed no mental activity; and for the flowing screamers in the gallery, independent young slaves of modernity that they are, every bar must jolt and jar like a French express run on German coal, or the music is but passive and dull. They are like the carcasses of frogs, which, stimulated by electricity, still exhibit signs of life even in the absence of brain cells. Is it strange then, that we jigger them with rhythm, and explode them with reiteration? Is it unnatural that we tend towards works that are short and lack development, that are incisive and pointed? Our audiences are against us. 'But', you say, 'that is all very interesting, but what have they to do with our music? You should write for yourself alone, regardless of your audience.' 'Sir,' I reply, 'we are the audience. In our writing for ourselves we are but writing for them. What gives them pleasure is also our amusement and our interest.'

I was very glad to pick up Sir Charles Stanford's paper, read to this Association over two years ago, and published now in his book *Interludes*, in which he puts the case against much of the new music. Coming from one of the greatest European teachers, his arguments are potent and weighty, and yet, as a member of a new generation, I feel I have the right to reply, even if only on the ground that, being Irish, he will not resent an honest antagonist. Like the nigger, related in Walter Page's *Life and Letters*,[26] he may even welcome a hit back. You remember the old nigger that wished to pick a quarrel with another old nigger. Nigger No. 1 swore and stormed at Nigger No. 2. Nigger No. 2 said not a word, but kept at his work. Nigger No. 1 swore and stormed more; Nigger No. 2 said not a word. Nigger No. 1 frothed still more. Nigger No. 2 still silent. Nigger No. 1 got desperate and

---

[26] *The Life and Letters of Walter H. Page*, ed. Burton J. Hendrick, 3 vols. (London, 1922). Page was the American ambassador to Great Britain 1913–18.

said 'Look here, you kinkly-headed, flat-nosed, slab-footed nigger, I warn you before God, don't you keep giving me more of your damned silence.' So here goes.

The first sign he sees of the retrogression of modern music is the, according to him, prevalent love of writing fifths consecutively. This writing of fifths is a bugbear that haunts the musician in his cradle, dogs him at all his examinations, and often leads him to any sort of stilted contrapuntal passage in order to avoid them. We are a people who love tradition; that is why we take to our hearts Handel, Mendelssohn, Brahms, and Ravel. We find ourselves doing so many things mainly because our forefathers did. We even wear our appendices, although told by science that they are useless and dangerous. Centuries ago the Bank of England was attacked. Ever since then, although it has been fortified to stand a most vigorous siege, and actually moved from its old site, we still send a small handful of soldiers every night to protect it from assault. In the time of the plague, court houses were decked with a pot of herbs to keep away contagion. I am told to this day, the epoch of inoculation, the old custom still survives. And so with consecutive fifths. Some acoustical authority declared they were ugly; the avoidance of them became a rule, and it is still cherished, although the ear has so developed (thanks to the composers) that it delights in consecutive seconds, sevenths, ninths, twenty-firsts, in fact in anything that it can conceive will further adorn any particular passage. Every master broke this rule at the bidding of his own ear and so will every master continue to break it, besides which when you speak of consecutive fifths the phrase means nothing; it depends on what consecutive fifths. Do you refer to trombones or strings or piano or voices or combinations of each, and on what part of your scale are you using them? Some are obviously less beautiful than others. Of course, if you are learning to write vocal music in the manner of Palestrina for a severe disciplinary exercise, it would be a breach of style to employ them, but if you are expressing yourself in the terms of your own day, don't be such a fool, is my advice, as to restrict yourself to any such boundaries. The first car that went on the road was preceded with a man with a red flag. Where are the red flags today? Some people see this subject of fifths as a dark shadow covering all modern music; actually there is only one composer that I know of who makes of them a fetish, and that is Vaughan Williams, not for any puerile love of breaking rules, nor from any desire to be ugly, but for the sole reason that the simplicity and purity of the resulting sound is in accord with what he wishes to express. With most others it is but another weapon in their armoury, the avoidance of which does not any more enter their heads than does the red flag the equipment of a modern racing car.

The same misapprehension is felt by Sir Charles with regard to the whole-tone scale. He need not feel any fear, in spite of his saying that the increasing tendency is to worship and enlarge on the whole-tone scale, making for impurity of intonation. Even before his words were written, the greatly lamented Debussy was dead, and with him the whole-tone scale, its employment as the basis of tonality being a personal cliché. Others indeed experiment with it, but no one before or since has used it as a principle as he did, and with his death the whole-tone scale died out, leaving behind it a legacy of special effect, applicable to certain phases of emotion, but certainly nothing to terrify the older generation into labelling the epoch 'retrogressive'. How well I remember the savage delight with which our master would rend us as imitators of Debussy, if we innocently placed three major thirds in succession. No matter what the mood, no matter what the context, those little thirds did the trick; we were thereafter followers of Debussy.

This trick of labelling English composers and of pigeon-holing them, each with a ticket stamped with a foreign name, has led another Irishman to say that there is no English music of the present day. It is all copied from abroad, and, so I understand, is ugly and bad. But what are Mr Harty's credentials for passing judgment on English music? He is an Irishman who picked up Richter's baton at the Hallé concerts, and whose programmes do not show a great knowledge of contemporary work, but in fact reflect the conservatism of the stronghold in which they are given. He is in short an eminent conductor who is carrying on the German Classic tradition in Manchester with great success, and whose exuberance, of not a very venturesome order, leads him to composition of a charming nature not unlike that of his great model, Arthur Sullivan. But he must not condemn all other composers for not being like Arthur Sullivan. We can't all be as serious as the Sullivan of *In Memoriam* and *The Golden Legend*, and as for the Gilbert and Sullivan operas, well! where is the Gilbert of today?

To return to the more serious opponent, Sir Charles. He mentions in addition to consecutive fifths and the whole-tone scale the tendency to overcrowding modulation. But what does he mean by that? Modulation presumes a basis of key system, and generally throughout Europe we find the principle of polytonality or atonality superseding the old key system. We can point to the Schoenberg school in Vienna, the Busoni school in Berlin, the Stravinsky and Milhaud school in Paris, not to speak of Goossens and Berners in London. What on earth has modulation got to do with it? His statement leaves one as aghast as if Copernicus appeared to the Royal Astronomical Society and accused them of thinking the earth flat. Half the folk who condemn the new music cannot have heard it. They come and speak against it, wasting their time and ours in the tiring pursuit of fighting shadows. Taking Sir Charles's obviously true statement that music springs from two elements, rhythm and melody, there will be little in contemporary thought that escapes the appellation of music. In rhythm we have developed out of all recognition, due largely to the popularity of Slavonic music, but also traceable to the study of the supple stress and rhythm of our own Elizabethan writers, while in melody, every year brings fresh fields for exploration, the only difficulty being that certain ears resent the term 'melody' as applied to contemporary music. One critic has truly said that a tune is simply a succession of notes to which our ears have become accustomed; for instance, you go to the piano and improvise on the black keys, and do what you will, you cannot help making tunes, simply because our ears are so familiar with the pentatonic scale. As your sense of hearing develops, the more melodic utterances will you find in the works of all ages. When a critic writes, 'There is no melody in this symphony', he really means, 'My ears are not yet sufficiently trained to retain any succession of notes in this score, so, I fear from ignorance, it appears to me to be without tune; I confess I am hampered too in my effort to concentrate, by the knowledge that I have to tell the world, this evening, what it is all about.' That would be a modest and true statement of fact, but of course he cannot make such a confession because he is paid to be dictatorial, rather than truthful, and I can well remember the storm that broke out on an honest and very well-equipped critical head, which had the audacity to say that its owner did not understand a particular work at first hearing, and therefore would not presume to express an opinion. And if a composer cannot fathom another composer's intentions, during the first performance, surely no critic can pass a lasting judgment. I fear we shall soon have a footman telling the chauffeur how to drive.

Personally I look at this great burst of mental activity in England as far from being an ugly or retrogressive movement. Perhaps, being in closer touch with it than members of another generation, I can appreciate the impulses that direct its energies, and although in such a mass of music there is bound to be much that is relatively unimportant and occasionally trivial, there are also numerous indications that out of it will come the greatest epoch in English music for 250 years. No cavilling generalizations made against this effort will do any more harm than that caused to the sides of the *Aquitania* by the wash of a cross-channel steamer.

May I finally express my cordial thanks for having been given this opportunity of addressing such an historic body as the Musical Association, and to ask their indulgence for a somewhat rambling paper. All I hope is that I have started several hares that will be immediately and successfully persued.

1924–1934

INTRODUCTION

BLISS's father had remarried in 1918, and in 1923 he decided to return to America with his new family. Bliss accompanied them, though not to take up permanent residence. On his departure he claimed to be 'running away, before England, which is the most critical country in the world, finds me out', and he mentioned also

a wish to carry out in practice my theory that films should be written to music instead of music to films. An emotional concerto, full of colour, pathos, and humour ought to suggest ideas to an imaginative film-producer like D. W. Griffiths. My idea would be a round-table conference between caption-writer, producer, scenario writer, and composer, at which suggestions would be made by each specialist in turn. Modern music is as young as the film industry, and there should be a great future for the alliance of the two. A man I certainly intend to open negotiations with at Los Angeles is Charles Chaplin. He would make an excellent subject for musical treatment. Many people do not realise how far it is possible to produce essentially humorous music[1]

Despite this early interest, however, he did not write his first film score until more than a decade later.

The Bliss family crossed the continent to settle in Santa Barbara, California, a wealthy community in which Bliss was soon a prominent figure in the arts. He spent the winter of 1923 in New York, travelling to Boston and Philadelphia to hear their orchestras under Monteux and Stokowski, the virtuosity of which made a lasting impression. Returning to Santa Barbara, he began reviewing for the local newspaper, arranged concerts, wrote music for a play, *King Solomon* (1924), and took the leading role in a play opposite his future wife, Trudy Hoffmann. They were married on 1 June 1925 and shortly afterwards returned to live in London,

[1] 'From "Colour" Symphony to Charlie Chaplin' (interview), *Musical Mirror*, Apr. 1923, p. 104.

MASKS

BY ARTHUR BLISS

at first in a studio flat in Redcliffe Square and from 1929 at East Heath Lodge in Hampstead.

With the sound of the great American orchestras fresh in his mind, Bliss wrote two orchestral pieces, *Introduction and Allegro* and *Hymn to Apollo*, in 1926. For the remainder of the decade he was occupied principally with works for voice and orchestra. Elgar, who had kept aloof since *A Colour Symphony*, responded more favourably as the dedicatee of *Pastoral: Lie Strewn the White Flocks* (1928): 'I could judge that your work is on a *large* and *fine* scale, and I like it *exceedingly*.'[2] Inspired by a trip to Sicily, this was the first of many choral works which Bliss based on an anthology of poems from a variety of languages and historical periods, as if to suggest the universality and timelessness of human emotions. It was followed by a swashbuckling *Serenade* for baritone and orchestra (1929), written for his wife, and the great choral symphony *Morning Heroes* for the Norwich Festival of 1930, in which he paid tribute to his brother 'and all other comrades killed in battle'. In the same year he presented the Gold Medal of the Royal Philharmonic Society to Vaughan Williams. Having exorcised memories of the war[3] in a large-scale dramatic work, Bliss turned to chamber music, a Clarinet Quintet appearing in 1931 and a Viola Sonata in 1933. In 1932 *A Colour Symphony* was performed in a revised version.

Throughout these years Bliss made frequent trips abroad—to America twice, and frequently to the Continent to attend music festivals—and continued his advocacy of modern music, though no longer as a fervent apologist. His writings reflect a wider interest in musical conditions in the country as a whole, and especially in the effects of broadcasting. By 1934, the year in which Elgar, Delius, and Holst died, he had two small daughters and was having a house, Pen Pits, built in the Somerset countryside, with a small detached music room in the woods nearby. This was to serve as a summer home until 1939.

[2] From a letter of 9 May 1929 (quoted in *As I Remember*, p. 95).
[3] For many years after the war he was troubled by persistent nightmares and in particular by a fear of being 'doomed to fight on till extinction' (ibid. 96).

BERNERS AND BAX

Modern Music, February 1924, pp. 26–7.

Though contemporaries, Berners and Bax represent two extremes in English music. Berners, it might be fancifully said, is most at home in the salon, whose rather languid brilliance he lights up with epigram and sally—he passes from one guest to another, picking the guard of each and lightly mocking the exposed weakness—a sometimes awkward but always salubrious visitor. Among the victims that have felt his satire are the sentimental German *lied*, the blustering English folk song, and the Spanish dance.

His broadest laugh is heard in the *Three Funeral Marches* where the heir to the rich aunt bemoans her sudden decease with such rich unction; and his subtlest gesture is in the waltzes, whose sentimental associations he dismisses with good-humoured chaff.

In a world of unconscious musical humorists, is it not a prize to find one who wears the cap and bells by royal patent?

Bax is the romantic weaver of dreams—no gilded smartness of a salon for him, nor bustling city either. He might have stepped out of a fancy of Barrie's[4] brain, and his music has just the same quality of 'fey'.

A visit to Russia and his love for the legendary Celtic lore have been the two predominating influences in his musical inspiration. More prolific than any of his age in England, Bax has gradually reached a more incisive and direct utterance, of which stage the Piano Quartet is nicely typical. Robust and even provocative in theme, it is the concentrated expression of what in an earlier Bax would have reached three separate movements.[5] There is a great deal to be said for the age of the telegraphic code.

[4] J. M. Barrie, author of *Peter Pan*.
[5] The quartet is in a single movement.

LIBERTIES WITH *CARMEN*

From November 1924 to March 1925, Bliss contributed music
reviews to the Santa Barbara *Morning Press*. The two recalled in
As I Remember (p. 81) are reprinted here.
'Farrar's Liberties with Carmen Amazing', Santa Barbara
Morning Press, 8 November 1924, p. 5.

Last night a large audience witnessed Miss Farrar's[6] representation of
what Richard Wagner called the most perfectly conceived of the operas.
Bizet, who wrote the music, and Mérimée, who devised the book, would
have surely turned in their graves if an echo of last evening's performance
had reached them on the radio. They were present, indeed, on the
programme in microscopic type, but otherwise they had nothing to do
with the show.

Miss Farrar evidently thinks their dramatic genius out of fashion; that,
indeed, the opera must be pepped up some, and that in the optimistically
termed 'modern revised version' she is endowing the operatic stage with
new life and new ideals. So she contrived a delightful evening's entertainment, compounded of extravaganza, revue, and burlesque, in which the
word 'Carmen' is heard bandied about like a joke taken from another
source.

Mérimée, to begin with, made Carmen a poor cigarette girl, whose
fortunes led her into many romantic environments: lonely mountains, for
instance, with the gypsies, and the crowded precincts of the bull fights.
Miss Farrar performs her gay role in front of what looks like a linear
representation of the Einstein theory of relativity, and in order to make
things hum, Persian-clad girls vie with gentlemen who have walked
straight out of an Oscar Straus operetta, and the unfortunate Toreador,
whose first song should take place in an inn amidst gay conviviality, is
compelled to give tongue by a damp Venetian canal.

Well, let us not be too particular. Obviously it was not meant to be the
opera of Carmen known to the civilized world—there was no chorus, or
logical sequence of dramatic effects, and Miss Farrar herself must have
looked back with some humour to her triumph in the part at the Metropolitan some years ago, when she was content to act and sing superbly

---

[6] Geraldine Farrar (1882–1967), a popular soprano whose most famous operatic roles were
Madam Butterfly and Carmen.

without being at the same time librettist, composer, and producer. But, I hope, this is not going to start a precedent. I should hate to see Tristan in a tuxedo or witness Lohengrin buzz in in a Ford.

CONCERTO FOR TWO PIANOS AND ORCHESTRA

This was the first performance of a rewriting of the Concerto for piano, tenor voice, strings, and percussion (1921); the soloists were Guy Maier and Lee Pattison, with Koussevitsky conducting the Boston Symphony Orchestra. This rewritten version was itself revised in 1925–9 and again in 1950. The concerto was arranged for three hands in 1968, making it the most frequently revised of all Bliss's works.
Programme note, Boston Symphony Orchestra, Symphony Hall, Boston, 19 December 1924.

No explanation is really needed for the comprehension of this concerto, as it is intended as music in the abstract without any extramusical association. There is no literary programme attached to it, nor does it seek to convey any particular atmosphere or paint any mental image. It is to be regarded as sound and nothing else, and the total impression it aims at cannot be explained by the help of any sister art.

I have eschewed the string tone in this work, from the rooted conviction that strings and pianos are unpleasant to the ear. I have never liked violin or violoncello sonatas, or piano trios, from the point of view of a listener, however beautiful the material written for those instruments, so I determined to concentrate on a pianistic combination that was blended with woodwind, brass, and percussion, but no string instrument.

The concerto is in one movement and follows a very geometric design. As an Oriental Print is often developed from one small and seemingly inconspicuous pattern, so the form of this work is knit closely together by the development of a two-bar theme that makes its appearance in the second bar. The pianos are not used as in the classical concerto, where they fill the role of star performer to a background or chorus, but are of an equal integral part of the whole composition, and can be regarded as two great arabesque-making machines. Both piano designs are conceived for virtuosi pianists or pianola players.

MYRA HESS CONCERT

Santa Barbara *Morning Press*, 11 March 1925, p. 3.

A very fine artist came to Santa Barbara last night in the person of Myra Hess. Until recently, the musical world was inclined to adopt a patronizing attitude to the fair sex who strive for honours on the concert platform, in spite of such outstanding figures as Dame Ethel Smythe, composer; Renée Chemet, violinist; Suggia, cellist; and the pianist last night.

But I vouch for the fact that not only is Myra Hess the best woman player I have yet heard, but she comes near to being amongst the few really great living players of either sex. She is a very quiet and contained person; she does not make any attempt to startle by technical display, or even cause an occasional excitement by over-emphasis or indeed an exaggeration of any kind. After hearing her play, you are left with a vivid impression of great beauty conveyed by the most spontaneous and natural means. In other words, Myra Hess is a musician born with a great love and reverence for her art, and not made so by any amount of time, toil, and trouble, let alone advertisement.

There are several occasions in a concert-goer's life when he feels he hears a particular work played as perfectly as he could ever wish to hear it, when, as it were, he sees the author's mind portrayed for the first time, clearly and authoritatively. Such a moment I realized when I heard Arthur Nikisch play the *Freischütz* Overture in Amsterdam, and when I listened to *Figaro* under Strauss in Vienna, and coming to lesser but no less beautiful things in themselves, a Negro spiritual sung by Roland Hayes. There occurred such a magical instant last night, when Myra Hess played a sonata by Chopin. I cannot imagine a more beautiful interpretation, and to a mazurka by Paderewski and a valse by de Pachmann,[7] I shall now add a sonata by Myra Hess—one of the high points in one's musical remembrance. There were so many lovely things on the program: three preludes and fugues by Bach, to start with—no ordinary program this, with but one distinctive piece by the great John Sebastian. After the Chopin came *Papillons* by Schumann, oh! so daintily and refreshingly played, then a more modern group from Spain and France, and as an encore, a tit-bit from Italy, that gladdened the ear like a cork drawn from a champagne

---

[7] Vladimir de Pachmann (1848–1933), Russian pianist.

bottle. Those who were not there missed some of the finest playing of their lives.

MUSIC IN AMERICA: AN IMPRESSION

The Sackbut, September 1925, pp. 30–1.

America gives at this moment the impression of unexampled musical activity—as if some hundred-headed hydra were, after many years of fruitful voice-training, to lift each of its young voices in lusty song: the fact that some of the throats emit a distinctly foreign intonation does not affect the general exuberance, wherefore it is no small wonder that the ensuing chorus bids fair to drown the husky and ageing voice of Europe, gradually enfeebled, as it is, by the economic pressure on its windpipe.

It is hard on one's sense of patriotism, but in America lies the future of music. On the west side of the Atlantic are found more and finer orchestras, larger audiences, countless more clubs for the study of music, infinitely more schools, and withal every sign of still further development. Hardly a year passes without its crop of new orchestras and musical institutions, into which European artists are being continually absorbed —a process which in time will inflict the Old World with pernicious anaemia.

One feature of this growth struck me forcibly—it is almost exclusively the professional element that sustains the interest; of amateur choral societies similar to the English ones, of amateur chamber music organizations, so prevalent on the continent, there are few signs. Almost always the clubs rely for their entertainment on their own or visiting professional artists, to which attitude I ascribe the fact that the American audience is most swayed by the heart, and little by the head. They have not yet learnt to make music in the true amateur spirit—for the love of it—and the constant dependence on others has kept their critical instinct in a somewhat primitive state. Hence, in America, personality and the glamour of an anecdotal private life have a dangerous advantage over mere musicianship. As soon as for every paid symphony orchestra there spring up two purely amateur orchestras, and for every paid choir, three amateur choral societies, I prophesy a great change for the better in the critical attitude of audiences.

As it is, they possess a vitality for the absorption of music far exceeding ours. It is almost awe-inspiring to scan the list of concerts advertised at the beginning of each season in New York alone, and to gauge thereby the appetite of the average concert-goer. It is well-nigh impossible to get a seat at any orchestral concert in Boston or Philadelphia, and although symphony concerts in New York are as numerous as divorces, they are invariably as well-attended. In Chicago and farther west, one finds the same demand for orchestral music, and if bulk alone counted in audiences as in other essential commodities, the scales would undoubtedly tip in favour of the Stadium in New York and the Hollywood Bowl.

There is one distinctive feature about American audiences. They have not yet had time to acquire deep prejudices, judging rather by a simple criterion as to whether a work interests or moves them, irrespective of whether it is what their fathers and grandfathers would have termed 'music'. If it be a new and unfamiliar piece of music, the audience, as well as the composer, will have the undoubted advantage of knowing that the presentation will take place under the best possible conditions. I have heard composers say that they never realized what a performance of a new work could be until they heard the Philadelphia Orchestra play it, for with that, as with other fine orchestras there, they could rely on a plethora of rehearsals and a conductor who would direct with the conviction that a new work was more worthy of a fine rendition than a familiar one. It would seem that with these many advantages some truly American school of composition would arise, either a group having some technical and imaginative points in common, and in contrast to European methods, or individuals representing strongly the districts in which they lived and worked —why not, for example, the New England school, the Middle West and Pacific Coast composers! With all wish to illustrate this attractive prospectus, one must admit the truth that, so far, there is no American school of composers as such.

The majority working in America so obviously bring the traits of their original country with them that for many years no distinctive school can grow up—until, indeed, the country has absorbed its foreign blood and welded a characteristic style out of the fusion. At present the country is in danger of becoming Europeanized. In addition to the swarms of artists who conduct, play, and lecture, some distinguished composer is sure to arrive who sets his stamp on the students of the country. One year it will be Casella, last year Stravinsky, next year Bartók, later Honegger or Schoenberg, and each time some trick or mannerism from Europe is absorbed.

Most of the really living music in America draws its inspiration from outside the country, *viz.* Eichheim from the Orient, Loeffler from the inspiration of the Schola Cantorum, Bloch from the traditions of his own race, Carpenter from Paris.

I heard an American composer trace the musical stream of his country to the twofold sources of 'jazz' and 'Negro spiritual'. Personally, I think he was unjust to his music.

Jazz has been grossly overpraised, and when the experiment was tried of supplanting this hot-house flower from the dance hall to the rarefied regions of the concert platform it withered to boredom as would the slapstick suddenly introduced into a sparkling Sheridan comedy.

As for the beautiful Negro spirituals, in any other form they appear to me but barely disguised interpolations for effect, the conscious dressing up of folk song in symphonic guise, of which we have seen so much, with the difference that the former tunes belong to an entirely different race from that of the composers who make use of them.

At present there is nothing in American music comparable to the architecture of the country, which has all the impulse of a new creative effort. Only Varèse shows something that may prove the American uncut diamond meet to be polished by others who come later. But even he lives in and reflects New York—and is that not now the most cosmopolitan city in the world?

―――

WELCOME TO SCHOENBERG!
A COMMENTARY ON THE *GURRELIEDER* AND ITS COMPOSER

Musical News, January 1928, p. 12.

In a few weeks now, Arnold Schoenberg will arrive in England to conduct a performance of his *Gurrelieder*—the first in this country, if I mistake not. It is an event of considerable importance, not only because the work in question can be said to be one of the landmarks in German music since Wagner, but also because it will give musicians generally a rare chance to make up their minds about a composer who has been the centre of controversy for many years. I say a rare chance, because it is curious that while his name is so well known—in any musical discussion it is seldom long out of the argument—his music is but little played.

In this respect perhaps he resembles his contemporary Einstein, whose 'relativity' is bandied about like the latest toy, but whose real mathematical achievements may be realized by only a few score experts in Europe.

In the case of the musician, it can be proffered that the extreme difficulty in the execution of his works lies in the way of their frequent performance. To give his latest quartet, for example, the Kolisch Quartet devoted something like forty rehearsals. The meticulous care insisted on by Schoenberg in the shaping of every phrase, and in the dynamic value of every chord, makes it clearly impossible for an amateur organization to attempt the playing of it—and, in the case of the professionals, where have they the time for such detailed devotion?

This is a misfortune, for it is only by constant hearings, and by the expenditure of great concentration, that the student can grasp the meaning of what he hears. It is not the so-called revolutionary methods of Schoenberg which present the difficulty—in fact, the actual sounds he makes, with their at first disturbing absence of tonality, are very soon assimilated by the ear—but behind these sounds lies one of the most complicated and powerful brains in today's music.

He is the Alekhine[8] of musical aesthetics, and in pursuing him through the tortuous mazes of his thought one is reminded of watching some game of chess by a master, who with infallible logic arranges his pieces to bring about the inevitable win. It is, in fact, the close texture and economic complexity (no fat, no stuffing, little lean, and a lot of bone) which keep the listener at a distance, sometimes irritated, more often, I fear, bored. A masterly cerebration given in place of a more facile emotion is displeasing to those who regard music as a rest cure or mental relaxation. To comprehend Schoenberg, we must give almost as hard a thinking and as prolonged a concentration as he gives us.

One side of musical composition he makes comparatively easy for the student—and that is the form in which he casts his works. Herein we find a process purely classical. You can direct a composition of Schoenberg as you can one of Beethoven; if the mould of a Beethoven quartet is intelligible to you, so will be a quartet by this twentieth-century classic.

He simply carries on and elaborates a tradition, and his contrapuntal devices, his developments, the proportion of his movements, though more complex, are unmistakably founded on the practices of his predecessors. In this connection it is interesting to note that as a teacher —and a great one he is!—he relies entirely on the discipline to be gained by a close study of the great masters. Many a budding revolutionary who has sought out Schoenberg in Berlin must have been surprised and slightly abashed to be set down to the study of a Bach fugue or a Palestrina motet instead of, as he had hoped, being quickly and illuminatingly shown a method of quick initiation into the 'New Music'.

---

[8] Alexander Alekhine (1892–1946), Russian chess-player, world champion 1927–35 and 1937–46.

It is perhaps fortunate that the public will hear an early and comparatively easy work like the *Gurrelieder* rather than one of the more forbidding examples of his later thought. The *Gurrelieder* comprise a vast setting for solo voices, male choruses, mixed chorus, and colossal orchestra, of a love story based on poems by Jacobsen. It consists of three parts, and tells of the love of King Waldemar for Klein-Tove, with numerous episodic characters introduced. A large part of the work deals with the portrayal of nature, and is a direct offshoot from the Romantic legacy bequeathed Schoenberg by his older contemporaries. Schoenberg was a young man when he conceived this great project, being no more than twenty-six years old—and though the score was not completed till some years later, the mastery over so great a canvas at that age compels admiration.

It was in March, 1900 that Schoenberg began the work which, some twenty-seven years later, he will conduct in London. To get the right perspective in musical events, it should be mentioned that this was two years before the production of Debussy's *Pelléas et Mélisande* and three before the appearance of Strauss's *Symphonia Domestica*.

Practically all that Schoenberg composes is written in an incredibly short space of time. He told me that his last quartet, for instance—a work lasting some forty minutes, in four movements—was written in less than a month. Everything is thought out clearly beforehand, the shape and scope of the work, the proportions secured, the details devised, and then, and not till then, is the work committed to paper, fluently and with lightning speed. It is as though the brain were in a state of incandescence during those moments of translating thought into the musical code, so definitely and clearly is every part related to the whole.

This colossal mental activity is typical of the man, who with his piercing and roving eyes, and mobile lips, reminds one of nothing so much as a globule of mercury.

He is not a stranger to England, since as long ago as 1912 he came here at the instigation of Sir Henry Wood to conduct his *Five Orchestral Pieces*. But we are now perhaps less hostile than we were then to the new and unfamiliar, and it is to be hoped that the performance of the *Gurrelieder* will foster in the hearts of English musicians a respect for what Schoenberg stands for, and a desire to become better acquainted with his work—for, whether we like it or not, all must admit that he has stamped his personality indelibly on the music of his period.

MALIPIERO, LOVER OF ANIMALS
A THUMB-NAIL SKETCH

Bliss had met Malipiero on a visit to Venice in the autumn of 1927 to
attend a festival arranged by the American patron of music,
Elizabeth Sprague Coolidge, for which his Oboe Quintet
had been commissioned.
Daily Telegraph, 28 January 1928, p. 7. Reprinted in
The Chesterian, 69 (1928), pp. 166–7.

To appreciate more fully the musical outlook of Malipiero, one of whose works was played at the Royal Philharmonic concert on Thursday, it is perhaps helpful to know something of the man.

This is not too easy, for he lives a very retired life in the beautiful village of Asolo, just north of Venice, seeking no notoriety but preferring isolation. He very rarely travels thence, travelling being with him a laborious project, only to be undertaken with much disliked preparation; for, whither he goes, his beloved animals go too.

These include a large assortment of dogs, cats, and birds of all sorts. I saw a salamander in his study, asleep on the desk, where he works, and, most treasured of all, two aged owls, who live on short poles in the kitchen, and who, to my great amusement, danced a slow, dignified saraband to the singing of their master.

Malipiero is a keen scholar and lover of the music of his own country. He is bringing out a limited and beautifully-engraved edition of the madrigals of Monteverdi, with little vignettes of his own devising—a complete edition, that will be authoritative. His admiration, too, for Domenico Scarlatti is unbounded, of whose bold and felicitous invention he is never tired of speaking.

Like most Italians, Malipiero feels at home in the theatre, but in a theatre—let it be added—of his own invention, for his stage works have all been a protest against the current conventions of grand opera.

There is a curious mixture of tragedy and comedy in Malipiero's personality. In his music passages of a gloomy irony alternate with great bursts of laughter. His sense of the comic is very acute (some of his comments on contemporaries are gems), but there is another side to the man, portraying a somewhat sardonic pessimism often peculiar to those who live so persistently in the sun.

Though an aristocrat by lineage, Malipiero feels a strong bias towards the more popular types of old Italian folk music. In his quartets and operas I find that he dignifies with restoration the street-song forms of rispetto, stornello, and strambotta.

I did not know the particular work played on Thursday, but some of his orchestral music is decidedly difficult to the ear. It is music that must be coaxed to sound well. Malipiero is a very assiduous craftsman, and it is perhaps this very polishing and perfecting that results in a certain obscuration of the original thought.

Musical Italy, like other nations, stands today on the bridge between the achievements of the late nineteenth century and the possible achievements of the near future. To this difficult transition Malipiero brings the mind both of a scholar and of an explorer. He has, as it were, for his motto, the words of Goethe—'An old foundation is worthy of all respect, but it must not take from us the right to build afresh whenever we will.' To know Malipiero is to have a great affection for him personally, and for his music the respect one always pays to absolute sincerity.

———

INSPIRATION

Untitled contribution to a symposium on inspiration by contemporary composers. 'Opinions', *The Chesterian*, 28 (1928), pp. 109–10.

You have set me a very hard task in asking me to commit to paper concrete facts about so elusive a subject as Inspiration—'twere easier to bottle a cloud effect or define a south-westerly gale. Like electricity one is well aware of its presence, though hazy as to its source. Perhaps you will agree with me that in one sense it is a condition granted to all artists whatever their medium—that at rare infrequent moments there flashes through a personality not only the vivid imaginative thought but also the creative ability to pin it down in a final and flashing setting: that everyone at one time or another is granted that trembling delicate and snail horn perception of beauty.

The trouble is, of course, that such moments are so intermittent and irretrievable with most of us that they only suffice for a few bars' thought, a turn of phrase, a few strokes of the brush, an instant modelling of a muscle.

We have all experienced those clarifying moments when a phrase stood out, as it were, in bas-relief, inevitable, as though it had been presented to us suddenly, brought to truth complete, Minerva-like. These are times of the greatest receptivity, when all the senses are alive and responsive to a marked degree. One is living in a state of inward harmony and vitality, as in a white intense light wherein objects impinge on the retina with remarkable clarity. One sees a table for the first time, or senses the pleasure the Chinese has in handling jade, or grasps as with a fist a clotted bunch of notes hitherto dangling evasively.

It is in fact a state of clairvoyance in which abstraction from one's environment and everyday life is momentarily complete.

Fortunately or unfortunately, the secret of prolonging these states of mind over a long period, keeping them afloat, as it were, is known only to one or two in a generation. To sustain a long flight over an extended area requires the sort of volcanic creativity that Wagner possessed so abundantly. There are many today who can use their wings to drop gracefully into the next field, but no one living has spanned a continent.

Without inspiration, however good 'the labour of the file', a work is of little value. Cleverness can be picked up dirt cheap nowadays, and as for technical pyrotechnics—are they not sold on every travelling showman's booth?

The madness from the gods alone keeps alive a work in the world-wide museum of still-born eccentricities.

MORNING HEROES

'Arthur Bliss's *Morning Heroes*', *Monthly Musical Record*,
October 1930, pp. 289–91.

Dear Mr Editor,

I am giving you a short account of my new symphony, as you asked me to do—it is no more than that.

I have not given any kind of musical analysis, because that would entail unwinding the threads of the tapestry again—a perfectly intelligible process for a Penelope, but surely unnecessary when morality is not at stake! Moreover, do you not agree with me that so-called programme notes of the quasi-musical order are so misleading and so often unreadable that it remains a sheer surprise that audiences do not gently lynch the author of the nonsense they are humbugged into buying?

It is pleasant no doubt to have musical examples to play over, but we both know that they bear as little reference to the whole work as do two or three pinches of salt to an alderman's lunch. But—well, I have given you a few, but please print them all together at the end; they will look better there, and I shall not have to point out their why and wherefore.

Arthur Bliss.

Morning Heroes is a symphony in five movements, lasting an hour and written for a large mixed chorus, full orchestra, and an orator. As the name suggests, it is a symphony on war and bears the dedication:

> To the memory of my brother, Francis Kennard Bliss,
> and all other comrades killed in battle.

I make no defence of my choice of this subject, as I have no political views to put forward, no moral prejudices to air, no theories indeed of any kind to expound. I have been guided entirely by my aims as an artist, for whom other considerations than the aesthetic do not exist. My choice of an orator as soloist was determined by my wish to achieve a greater dramatic intensity than seemed possible through any other medium. The words, for instance, I have chosen for him are not suitable for singing but are eminently adapted to the dramatic declamation that I require of the orator, who must use every variety of colour and pitch. In relation to the music which accompanies him his words are the principal strand in a symphonic texture of lightly scored sound.

I. HECTOR'S FAREWELL TO ANDROMACHE

The orchestra opens with an extended prelude, immediately imparting to the audience the tempo and colour of the whole work. One sudden outburst alone breaks the continuity of the mood and prepares for the orator, who starts with the following narration taken from the Sixth Book of the *Iliad*.

So Andromache met Hector now, and with her went the handmaid bearing in her bosom the tender boy, the little child, Hector's loved son, like unto a beautiful star.

Then follows her appeal to him to stay and his heroic reply, after which Hector prays to Zeus for the glorious future of his son, kisses him, and takes a farewell of Andromache, who departs to her home 'oft looking back and letting fall big tears'.

II. THE CITY ARMING

Without a pause the full chorus breaks in with the words from Walt Whitman's *Drum Taps*, beginning:

Morning Heroes

First, O Songs, for a prelude.
Lightly strike on the stretched tympanum, pride and joy in my city,
How she led the rest to arms—how she gave the cue,
How at once with lithe limbs, unwaiting a moment, she sprang;
O superb! O Manhattan, my own, my peerless!

III. VIGIL

The slow movement of the symphony is in two parts. The first, for women's
voices, is a setting of a Chinese poem (Li-Po). The tragedy of the watcher is
here summed up in the fewest possible words:

The warrior's wife is sitting by her window. With a heavy heart she embroiders a
white rose on a cushion of silk. She pricks her finger! The blood falls upon the
white rose and turns it red.

Swiftly her thoughts fly to her beloved one, who is at war, and whose blood
perhaps reddens the snow.

She hears the gallop of a horse. Has her beloved come at last? It is only the
tumultuous beating of the heart in her breast.

Lower she bends over the cushion, and with a silver thread embroiders the
tears that have fallen about the reddened rose.

For the second part of this movement I have set for men's voices
the words of Walt Whitman, beginning:

By the bivouac's fitful flame
A procession winding around men, solemn and sweet and slow.

The thoughts behind this contemplative movement are obvious, and
they need not be put into any further words.

IV. ACHILLES GOES FORTH TO BATTLE

The scherzo depicts the exploits of Achilles the shining hero, his wrath
over the death of Patroclus, his arming for battle, and his setting forth at
the head of the Greeks. I have used Chapman's translation of the
Nineteenth Book of the *Iliad*:

The host set forth, and pour'd his steel waves far out of the fleet,
And as from air, the frosty north wind blows a cold thick sleet,
That dazzles eyes, flakes after flakes, incessantly descending,
So thick helms, curets, ashen darts, and round shields never ending,
Flow'd from the navy's hollow womb.

An extended coda is composed of the roll call of heroes of both sides,
sung with elation by the chorus.

V. NOW TRUMPETER FOR THY CLOSE

The finale brings with it the only reference to the Great War. It opens with the orator declaiming a poem by Wilfrid Owen (killed just before the Armistice) and called 'Spring Offensive'. Its first stanza is as follows:

> Halted against the shade of a last hill
> They fed, and, lying easy, were at ease
> And, finding comfortable chests and knees,
> Carelessly slept. But many there stood still
> To face the stark, blank sky beyond the ridge,
> Knowing their feet had come to the end of the world.

This leads straight to a choral setting of 'Dawn on the Somme' by Robert Nichols, from which the symphony gets its name. The poem ends:

> Oh, is it mist or are these companies
> Of morning heroes who arise, arise
> Toward the risen god, upon whose brow
> Burns the gold laurel of all victories,
> Hero and heroes' god, the invincible sun?

I cannot as an artist express war except in a general (timeless) sense. Achilles is THE hero, whatever humbler name he may suggest in the minds of us who live now; the parting of Andromache and Hector is the last glimpse that ANY wife catches of her husband; Manhattan epitomizes ALL 'teeming and turbulent cities'.

Only in my reference to the Somme do I describe the particular (particular to us at any rate) and so approach more nearly the memory of him for whom this requiem was chiefly written.

FROM FIRST MOVEMENT

Morning Heroes

FROM SECOND MOVEMENT

Alla marcia

The tear – ful part – – ing. _____

FROM THIRD MOVEMENT

Andante sostenuto

etc.

FROM FOURTH MOVEMENT

Allegro con fuoco

FROM FIFTH MOVEMENT

Andante molto tranquillo

61

WHAT BROADCASTING HAS DONE
FOR MUSIC

The Listener, 16 November 1932, pp. 704–5.

The BBC has grown in ten years[9] to be the greatest music-making machine, by a very long chalk, that has ever existed; so immense indeed has it become that only a comparison with some great industrial concern producing its thousands of tons of steel or gallons of oil can give any idea of its varied and tentacular existence.

Its important music section, of which I am writing, has to prepare for one year a sum total of programmes that is absolutely staggering. Here is a bare survey of some of its divisions of labour, with which in a twelvemonth a listener can become acquainted: eighteen public symphony concerts, twenty-four Sunday studio concerts, the regular Promenade season every night for two months, to which has recently been added a further season of two weeks after Christmas, a series of public chamber-music concerts, eight contemporary music concerts, as well as (here we come to the bulk of the work!) three hundred and fifty orchestral programmes given by various sections of the orchestra, one hundred and fifty by military band, one hundred by special theatre orchestra, one hundred and fifty by wireless singers, one hundred chamber concerts, and innumerable solo programmes, not to mention operatic performances, educational series, and the many hours devoted to dance music.

It is appalling to consider the problems involved in this mass-music organization, in the laying out of a schedule that shall run to plan for a year. It is even more alarming to dwell on the human contacts involved, the cubic content of the musicians themselves, taken in bulk, who urge their claims to perform all this music. In face of real difficulties it must be admitted that the music branch has done its work admirably and courageously. Courageously, I certainly think, for it cannot, however much it may wish, act entirely autocratically. It administrates in a public concern supported by a ninth of the population, listened to and criticized by more nearly a fourth; consequently, in theory at any rate, it has to give that fourth just about what it wants, or get out.

Now in practice it works slightly differently, insomuch as the BBC

---

[9] The British Broadcasting Company was formed in 1922 and in 1927 became a public corporation, receiving its revenue from licence-holders.

rightly makes use of its official aloofness as a corporation to withstand the attacks of isolated shareholders. If a citizen here or there attacks, for example, the policy of giving Bach cantatas, he is in the position of a man fighting shadows; there is no substance concrete enough to hit—it is like poking a pond with your umbrella. Even if a daily newspaper levels its spearhead against the same annoyance, the target is only quietly removed, to appear later a little further off. This is just as it should be. The BBC must be governed by a beneficient oligarchy, otherwise it would lose all personality. It has obviously decided rightly and with subtlety to bridge any gulf between the public and itself by enticing the said public to creep up to its own level of taste, hoping that sooner or later complete harmony will result. It calls the tune in fact and is paid for it as well—a most happy state of affairs.

And what is its standard after ten years' growth? Unquestionably a high one in music. A serious listener can in a year become acquainted with the best symphonic and chamber music of all periods performed sometimes superbly, at all times adequately. It is the equivalent, in painting, of a year's tour round the most famous galleries of the world. No one can fairly ask for anything better, and no one in any other broadcasting centre of the world can hope to get as much.

But this does not quite end it. The listener is not only provided with a foundation of experience which would without the radio most likely take him years of study and travel; he is also initiated into the musical language of his own day—and that is important, for even lesser works of talent of our own period often speak or should speak with more force and intimacy to us than masterpieces of other generations. The music branch is definitely conservative—it, perhaps, has to be—for is not England itself the most conservative of nations, and proud to hold up 'Safety First' as the passport for life? In spite, however, of this national stale blanket characteristic, the number of controversial works that are slipped in is considerable, and this is where the music branch has the advantage over other sections. It does not have to appeal so often to the grown-up child. It need not cut, prune, bowdlerize, prettify or tame a symphonic work, until it means just nothing, and then offer it with assurance to a crowded audience of middle-aged Peter Pans. It is a question of take it or leave it in musical matters, and it is vastly to the credit of the musical programme committee that it does say in so many cases, 'Just take it!'

It has quietly and, as a matter of course, set a standard of programmes much higher than the majority of its listeners thought they could stand. It is, in fact, achieving on a national scale what Sir Henry Wood has done with his Queen's Hall audiences—unostentatiously raising the level of musical appreciation. There are unmistakable signs that it has succeeded in its policy, and this, the general high and catholic outlook on music, is one of the main causes of the prestige the BBC holds in other countries.

Naturally all this endeavour would be useless without a convincing presentation, and here again the BBC has to its credit a very definite accomplishment. To take two instances, it has formed a symphony orchestra[10] for its own concerts, trained by its own conductor, Dr Boult, which is reaching a potential virtuosity hitherto unknown to any English orchestra. It has again collected a large chorus of picked voices, trained by Dr Boult, which can be relied on without nervousness for the most exacting performance.

The special quality of both chorus and orchestra is a precision of an almost mechanical kind. I believe this to be right. The personal character-istics of a conductor are quite valueless over the air, and what is judged is the scale of perfection to which careful rehearsing has brought the orchestra.

In an era when the conductor looks like usurping the traditional role of the prima donna, the very limitations imposed by broadcasting supply a healthier and necessary corrective.

This wireless age applies a peculiar acid test to certain conductors, which sometimes they are not over-anxious to challenge—and not to conductors only. It necessitates also a firm discipline in an orchestra, without which it is a mere rabble of camp followers suddenly confronted with the enemy.

Till recently there was no money, and therefore no time to rehearse, and unfamiliar works had to be got through as best they could, generally maimed in the process, sometimes killed. This work-slaughter has greatly diminished, now that there is time for sectional rehearsals, for attention to bowing and detail, that a few years ago would have been impractical. Once again the BBC has set a standard of playing high enough to cause a perceptible stiffening and liveliness in other orchestras, which is as it should be. Having reached their powerful and consolidated position, it is difficult to foresee where this strength and power will lead it. One of its most useful attributes is a certain mercuriality—it is continually present-ing a new face to the air. The BBC has perhaps taken for one of its mottoes La Rochefoucauld's words 'aussi différent de moi-même que des autres'. In any case prophecy is futile. It may be that with music on a mass production basis, works will become so familiar as actually to turn the stomach (music critics know this nausea), or possibly in the welter of sound even music itself may be irretrievably destroyed.

We might easily reach a saturation point, when a month's silence will

[10] The BBC Symphony Orchestra was formed in 1930 under Adrian Boult, who became Controller of Music in the same year.

descend like a benediction, and some music patron will engage the Queen's Hall for a series of soundless Sunday afternoons. Be that as it may, in ten years from now, when the BBC celebrates its second birthday in its new monumental building stretching all the way down Portland Place to the new Grand Opera House, it can and certainly will look back on its first with pride and congratulate those who made it possible.

———

A LONELY FIGURE IN MUSIC

A tribute to Holst, who had died on 25 May 1934.
Radio Times, 15 June 1934, p. 819.

The untimely death of Gustav Holst removes an outstanding figure to whom English music owes a greater debt that can be alluded to in these few words. His total output, though not large, is extremely varied, ranging over many fields of interest, and including operas, ballets, orchestral and church works, songs and piano pieces. Much of it is relatively unfamiliar to concert-goers, and the BBC has done well, in paying homage to his memory, to select works that will widen admiration for the composer, known as he is to the world chiefly as the author of *The Planets* and the *Hymn of Jesus*.

Holst was a very lonely figure in music, pursuing paths of his own, an explorer like his great contemporary, Vaughan Williams, and it was his fate to die before his last discoveries were charted. A mystic by nature, he had that mixture of profound vision and childlike candour which made him difficult of approach except for those who were his intimate friends.

There is a quality in Holst's music that is very personal to him. It is difficult to define, as it is not expressed in any particular technical mannerism, but rather in a characteristic mood underlying frequent stretches of his music. I became aware of it the very first time I ever listened to a work of Holst, the ode for chorus and orchestra called *The Cloud Messenger*. I found myself in thought transported quite easily and without volition to a region of great remoteness. I experienced a sensation akin to that which overwhelms one in mountains or on high plateau country. It is not a sense of grandeur, of strength or size, so much as a peculiar sensation of extreme distance from the centre of activities, as though the very air one breathed was noticeably rarified. I feel this strongly in certain movements of *The Planets*, in passages in *Savitri* and the *Hymn of Jesus*, and, indeed, most of his last works seem very near the snow line.

This remoteness, this unworldliness was very characteristic of Holst the man. Absolutely selfless where his own interests were concerned, unaware of the advantages and disadvantages of fame, he seemed only to be conscious of the actual world when in the presence of music. He seemed then suddenly to awaken and begin to feel and live intensely. Hence his inspiring gifts as a teacher, and the enthusiasm that his pupils have for his name. Into this channel he poured all the vitality that he had, and everyone was vividly aware of its value. He was not a virtuoso either in life or in music. He preferred an ideal of extreme simplicity and clarity. Anything savouring of fussy overstatement or clever subterfuge was quite alien to his personality.

In his attitude to music there was a strength and purity that braced one like a mountain torrent, an absolute integrity before which dilettantism and half-heartedness shrank away. In this thought of him, it makes one ashamed that one did not give more practical proof of one's admiration for his music during his life, a feeling by no means mitigated by tributes glibly offered after his death.

There is in the best of Holst's music so lofty an aim, expressed with such skill of experience, that he can assuredly rest happy in the knowledge that his will remain a name of honour in English music for many years to come.

———

BBC SYMPHONY CONCERTS

A talk broadcast on BBC Radio, 15 October 1934.
BBC Written Archives.

Tomorrow week the BBC broadcasts the first of its Symphony Concerts, details of which are announced on page 90 of the current *Radio Times*. You will see that a dozen of these special concerts form a series which, starting on Wednesday, October 24th, continue at intervals throughout the winter and early spring. I say 'special' concerts, because it is into these public Symphony Concerts that the BBC concentrates every musical resource it has—full orchestra of 119 picked players, large chorus of selected voices, famous conductors, and soloists brought from all countries, whose names alone are often sufficient to fill a large hall.

Special intensive rehearsals take place before each concert, such as are impossible outside this particular series. The players are in fact trained as athletes might be for some special occasion and only appear in public when in the pink of condition. The highest possible standard of playing is therefore made possible. What can be achieved in this direction we shall hear on these Wednesday evenings—and for a mere song too. An orchestral concert of these dimensions costs several hundreds of pounds. We listen to it for a mere fraction of our ten shillings.[11] Something in us all forbids us to lose the chance of getting so big a something for so practically a nothing.

And what will they play, this trained band of 120 players? They will give us first and foremost a liberal proportion of those masterpieces that Time itself has picked out as the best, and which we can hear and re-hear without any lessening sense of wonder. Bach, Handel, Haydn, Mozart, Beethoven, Brahms, Liszt, Wagner, Berlioz—these masters are all represented and will claim the widest audience.

Secondly these concerts will satisfy that natural curiosity in all of us to know what is going on in music in our own times. What is the living Englishman, Italian, Austrian, Russian creating in music? Will the music of Vaughan Williams, Malipiero, Alban Berg, Stravinsky, representatives of each of these four countries, be judged later as worthy of a place among the great works of the past? We have at any rate the opportunity of listening and forming our own private judgment. If music of today is one of the touchstones for finding out what our times are really like, let us listen in, and see our era as others see it.

I laid emphasis on the word 'special' in connection with these concerts, and there are some special features planned in this coming series. This year three English musicians died whose names will go down in musical history. Each of them is paid a worthy tribute in this season's concerts. At the opening concert Sir Thomas Beecham will pay honour to Delius, at the second Dr Boult will commemorate Holst, and at the last of the series Elgar's greatest orchestral work[12] will be played alongside a new symphony by Vaughan Williams,[13] the acknowledged living leader of English music. It is impossible to think of four names in any other one country more illustrious during the last twenty-five years than these.

Another composer closely associated with England will be similarly honoured—Handel, who was born 250 years ago. This anniversary in February is specially celebrated, and a glorious evening of sound it will be.

The entire series of these Symphony Concerts represents in performance some 24 hours, one whole day during the year—not a very big proportion of the time for such an effort, idealistic and gigantic. Into this small space of time are packed the following names—I mention only a few: Heifetz, Sir Henry Wood, Casals, Sir Hamilton Harty, Schnabel, Sir

[11] The current broadcasting licence fee.
[12] Symphony No. 2.
[13] Symphony No. 4 in F minor.

Thomas Beecham, Hubermann, Weingartner, Myra Hess, Adrian Boult, Stravinsky, Albert Coates—they read like a list of stars drawn up for some benefit performance under royal patronage.

Besides the many thousands who will listen in at a distance, there will be the more fortunate few who have the time, the money, and who live in London. They can go to the Queen's Hall, and see for themselves what is taking place. Everyone likes to see a fine craftsman at work, to watch a solo player or conductor at the top of his form. There is a clear-cut difference between listening in to a great player and seeing him play—all the difference between, say, having a photograph of a friend on your table beside you, and actually shaking him by the hand.

Let all who can, go to these special Symphony Concerts; let the others make a special note to listen in. They will otherwise miss a fine thing finely done.

Aspects of Contemporary Music
(1934)

Let me here sum up my creed.

I believe that the foundation of all music is emotion, and that without the capacity for deep and subtle emotion a composer only employs half the resources of his medium. I believe that this emotion should be called into being by the sudden awareness of actual beauty seen, or by the vision of beauty vividly apprehended. I believe that the emotion resulting from apprehended beauty should be solidified and fixed by presenting it in a form absolutely fitting to it, and to it alone. If I were to define my musical goal, it would be to try for an emotion truly and clearly felt, and caught for ever in a formal perfection. (*See p. 100 below*)

INTRODUCTION

IN the spring of 1934 Bliss was invited to deliver a series of three lectures to the Royal Institution on the subject of contemporary music. It was an audience that he later recalled as 'bristl[ing] with ear trumpets and bath chairs . . . a fearsome-looking audience'.[1] An unexpected result of lecturing was meeting H. G. Wells, who subsequently invited Bliss to write the music for the Alexander Korda film, *Things to Come*, one of the most ambitious undertakings in British cinematic history. His score, completed in 1935, was the first by a major British composer to be an integral part of the production, and it remains his most memorable contribution to the genre.

Bliss's lectures came in the same year as Constant Lambert's classic study, *Music Ho! A Study of Music in Decline*. Despite differences in temperament and emphasis, both composers often survey similar territory with an eye to the social background and functions of music, though generally they arrive at very different conclusions. On the dilemma of the modern composer—whether to please others or just himself—Lambert

---

[1] In an interview by Michael Chanan for Granada Television Historical Record archive recorded in 1974.

prescribes a splendid Sibelian isolation. Bliss, however, is convinced that communication with an audience is essential; and this conviction leads him, in his final lecture, to an explicit statement of his aims as an artist.

The three lectures were given on 8, 15, and 22 March 1934, and contained musical illustrations played by Bliss himself and others and on records, not all of which are specified in the text. The typescript, in the Bliss Archive, Cambridge University Library, is entitled 'Lectures to the Royal Institution'; extracts were published as 'Aspects of Contemporary Music' in the *Musical Times*, May 1934, pp. 401–5. Bliss often turned to these lectures for material for talks in later years; the theme of musical audiences in Lecture II proved particularly fertile.

I

In speaking about contemporary music I am using the word 'contemporary' in a very wide sense. I do not profess to know, nor do I very much care, what is the latest thing in the world of music, or what the best people, for instance, should listen to in 1934. Music is not a fashion like women's hats or complexions which have to be changed every year in order to be *à la mode*. Nor is it the plaything of a small and possibly vanishing social order who have to be given an amusing toy every few months to keep them from yawning their heads off. It is, on the other hand, a great and permanent enrichment of mankind which every fifty years or so receives such an additional impetus that the centre of gravity in music is slightly shifted.

Everyone at twenty should be Athenian-minded. He should think that the new is all-important. He should believe that it *must* be new to be good, and if it *is* new, it *is* good. But at forty, one should not be so shuttle-minded; one should have sifted much of the new into two distinct groups—that which is a mere fashion which dies with next year's models, and that very small, scarce, and seemingly permanent fraction which enriches one's own art. And so in speaking of music, I shall be discussing a span of some twenty or twenty-five years—just the length of time, in fact, to show up the false alloy and reveal the gold.

The search for this gold in music is an absorbing experience. It may come next from a new Russia or a new America, it may more probably come from a slowly evolving new England; but the test for gold differs little from one age to another. If you can pick out the great Schubert song from the lesser ones, if you know when you are listening to an inspired page of Beethoven, and when you are hearing merely a composed one, you can

feel perfectly certain of discussing the last work of Herr Dingsda or
Monsieur un Tel.

To a musician no music is quite unintelligible, any more than a new
theory of physics would be to a mathematician. And what do I mean by a
musician? I mean a man with a sensitive ear, an imaginative mind, and an
intellectual grasp of the subject of his art.

There is no single dominating figure in the world of music today as
Wagner, for instance, dominated music fifty years ago. There is unquestionably no single personality whom every musician would acknowledge,
whether his music were personally sympathetic to him or not. The new
methods of expression tried out since Wagner's death are not as yet
summed up in any one individual, though they are partially expressed by
many. There have been several marked personalities, small in relation to
Wagner, who by exercising to the full a limited personal technique have
impressed that manner of working on a decade—men such as Debussy,
Stravinsky, and Schoenberg. There have been others of greater stature
than these, whose outlook is not so severely confined, whose utterance is
more eclectic than theirs, but whose influence in *shaping* this generation
of music-making is hardly felt at all—of them one might name Strauss,
Delius, Elgar, and Sibelius. They sum up an old epoch rather than
inaugurate a new one.

There is no sign as yet of the one man who is both of sufficient character
and sufficient inventive genius to alter the stream of music today definitely
and conclusively. This is perhaps only to be expected; nature is not in the
habit of throwing up a Titan every 50 years or so, and even if she did, it is
doubtful in the modern world, with its complexity and variety of thought
and ideal, whether one man could stand as the representative of all.
Instead of that we have the spectacle of a dozen or more composers, each of
whom in his best work can be regarded as touched by genius, and many
others living among us, to whom the more insipid title of 'talent' can be
applied, without any feeling of generosity in so doing.

I am going to try in my first two lectures to throw light on some of them,
and by calling attention to their several characteristics to suggest that the
study of their personalities is an ample substitute for the absence of any
one towering genius who would certainly drain his contemporaries of most
of their significance.

In attempting this I am well aware that a composer is that last person to
judge the work of his contemporaries. He is perforce a prejudiced and
narrow critic, to whom a strictly impersonal view is difficult. There are
large tracts of music to which he is entirely unsympathetic, and in listening
to which he feels an irritating discomfort akin to the sensation undergone
in a theatre when a scene that moves most of the audience to tears leaves

him rigidly cold. A composer can, and indeed must, only feel sympathy with those others whose music reflects ideals akin to his. Enthusiasm for them engenders indifference to others. Every 'Long live so and so' involves a 'Down with so and so!'

I have however approached the subject as free from such prejudice as I can, leaving my third lecture to be of a more personal character, with the narrower and more bigoted outlook implied.

There is not great music today in the sense that Bach or Beethoven are great—but there is most certainly music that is good, good that is in the aesthetic sense, good art. Professor Alexander says 'an artist is a good artist in so far as he is a creator of beauty'[2]—but it must be remembered that besides being a creator of beauty, he is bound to show in his work the qualities personal to him as a man, and it is upon the power and breadth of these human qualities that his claim to greatness will ultimately rest.

All good art is not great, but on the other hand there is no great art that is not good. The ingredient of greatness depends on the stature of the man, and that, though sensed perhaps, is not fully shown to a contemporary. Of the past we can say, for example, that a quartet of Haydn is greater than a quartet of Dittersdorf, because the amount of human experience 'felt into and fixed creatively' in the Haydn is greater than in the other. Haydn covers all the ground of Dittersdorf and something more. In simple words, given that the artistry in the two works is of the same excellence, taken man for man, Haydn expresses the bigger all-round human personality.

Our own contemporaries it is more difficult to assess in terms of relative importance, so let us be content to say that we are rich in music of aesthetic worth—good music—and leave the question of greatness to our descendants, who will be able to view the first thirty years of this century from the proper perspective of time.

In discussing the merits and importance of music today, one is aware that one's hearers suspect that some great and fundamental change has taken place in music, rendering their normal standards of judgment useless—that by some iconoclastic force the ideals of the old world have been destroyed or at least condemned, and a complete new set of values set up, strange and foreign to their experience. They feel, so they believe, the same inadequacy to deal with these new manifestations as they would if confronted with a totally new language, whose syntax was unknown to them, or a new calligraphy where the letters were so many hieroglyphics. Faced with music, painting, or poetry that is truly of today, they feel bewildered and angry at having to grapple with the inexplicable.

They can be sure that this attitude of angry doubt is by no means

---

[2] Samuel Alexander, *Beauty and Other Forms of Value* (London, 1933).

confined to their own time. It has been manifested at every turning-point of a generation, when the younger artists and composers revolt, often from a sense of self-preservation, from the standards held in their fathers' times. This revolt only changes the angle of approach, but it is quite enough to upset normal clear thinking. Listen to some of the comments of our grandfathers:

The Times on Tennyson's *In Memoriam*: 'Another fault is not peculiar to *In Memoriam*—it runs all through Mr Tennyson's poetry. We allude to his *Obscurity*.'

The *Athenaeum* in 1850 on Wagner: 'All who refuse to surrender themselves to the insanities of the hour must agree that the scanty and spare and stale melodic phrases which *Das Rheingold* contains are foisted on the public by feeble and inflated efforts at orchestral intricacy.'

The *Spectator* on contemporary poetry, 1854: 'Idiocy is rampant and loose upon our streets.'

At the back of this unwillingness to experience the new is not so much fear of the unknown, as simple inertia. It may be true, as Frazer says, that 'everything new is apt to excite the awe and dread of the savage',[3] but in more sophisticated environments there is unfortunately nothing excited, nothing roused by the unfamiliar. There remains a complete indifference, an inert mass that is very difficult to stir. The music, the painting, the poetry of our time leaves the ordinary public completely uninterested. The reason may lie in what has been termed the time-lag. With but few exceptions we are all children not of our own age, but of the age of our fathers, even our grandfathers. We are all born as it were a generation too late, for it seems that we have just enough vitality to enjoy NOW what was novel thirty years ago, but not sufficient to use to the full what is new NOW. This is of course much truer in rational and imaginative experiences than in physical.

A man will quite readily take an aeroplane to fulfil a business engagement, who would refuse to live in a house designed by an architect on modern lines. A man will grasp any advantage that science gives him to communicate with a friend three thousand miles away, but would be completely indifferent to the stimulus that much of the art of today provides. The pleasure in the house, music, poetry of 1934 will be absorbing the attention of his son or grandson when what is now new has then become an accepted classic. As Jean Cocteau says, 'when a work of art appears to be in advance of its period, it is really the period that has lagged behind the work of art.'

[3] J. G. Frazer, *The Golden Bough*, an influential study, in 11 volumes (London, 1890–1915), of primitive myths and customs.

Anything new—and every work of art that merits attention is new —demands a concentration that a tired brain or a restricted sensibility will not give. When a new symphony, for instance, is played, it unrolls like a map of entirely new country. Into this the composer has put the concentrated thought of months. The listener has to grasp, as it proceeds, the main lines of its form, the shapes and contours of its themes, the subtleties of its lights and shades, often expressed in a manner relatively new to him. When a contemporary painter gives an exhibition, you will find paintings where the human figure is distorted, objects in the landscape altered to fit in with the painter's conception of a formal design, very often abstract designs like engineers' blueprints, which give the spectator the whole responsibility of judging their meaning. They do not meet the spectator half way by placing in front of him recognizable objects. A living poet will issue his considered poems to you in a new syntax, often a new spelling, in which the sense is so obscure as to defy immediate elucidation.

Most people in meeting difficulties of this kind go back to their own age for artistic enjoyment—that is, as I have said, their father's or their grandfather's. The present time is too difficult for them, too new, too complex. They give it up.

That this is a wrong attitude to the arts, I have no doubt whatsoever. Living in the past is vaguely unsatisfying. In some way we feel that living musicians, painters, poets can give us what no dead artist can, the sense of being involved in the same problems of life together, the satisfaction of seeing what is still in the air clothed in forms, of hearing what is but vaguely heard clearly articulated. Every generation has its own peculiar aspirations and difficulties, and it is only their contemporary artists who can authentically define their shadowy problems. It is just the finer intuition and sensibility that differentiates the mechanism of an artist, that enables him to sight a little ahead of the mass of men the emotional and aesthetic current of his age and to depict them in recognizable clarity.

A real artist is a real child of his age; he is the only contemporary figure in the strictest sense. He is the mirror in which we see the tendencies of our time, and in the sense that he explains to us our life today he cannot be disregarded. More than that, I firmly believe that a secondary work of art of our own epoch—be it music, painting, or poetry—is, or should be, of greater value to us *now* than a masterpiece of the last century. *It is us*, in fact.

All art is adventure, and its newness must be first sensed and explored: as soon as we have surveyed and mapped it out, the original thrill of the adventure fades, and the work of art becomes a settled experience. Most of the music of the past which continues still to move us is full of this quality of adventure, of an unexpected slant from the recognized convention, of a strangeness—call it what you will. It is *that* which gives it life today.

Suppose we are listening to a symphony of the classical Viennese school, for example, a movement by Haydn or Mozart. The idiom they use is perfectly familiar to us; you recognize the language that was the cultural expression of the eighteenth century. However beautiful it may be, our attention may begin to wander, simply because we can almost anticipate what Haydn or Mozart are going to say next. Suddenly, however, an unexpected moment arrives when Haydn or Mozart make a gesture that is personal and therefore unique. A train of adventure is set up—we are immediately alert again, stimulated and aesthetically moved.

These moments of adventure should be more frequent in contemporary music than in the music of the past, simply because the conventions and clichés of our art have not yet been formulated. It is still largely in a state of flux, where almost every work of importance contains the adventure of the unfamiliar gesture. It is only after time that the adventurous becomes the accepted, and instead of the thrill of the unknown, you get what may be called a state of established beauty—but of the two possibilities, the earlier thrill of the unknown, or the later calm of established beauty, it is the former that is more valuable.

Gertrude Stein in her essay on 'Composition as Explanation'[4] under-lines this point. It is conveyed to us in her curiously sophisticated childlike technique, but it is not quite so simple and childlike as it first appears. She writes:

Those who are creating the modern composition authentically are naturally only of importance when they are dead because by that time the modern composition having become past is classified, and the description of it is classical. That is the reason why the creator of the new composition in the arts is an outlaw until he is a classic, there is hardly a moment in between and it is really too bad very much too bad naturally for the creator but also very much too bad for the enjoyer, they all really would enjoy the created so much better just after it has been made than when it is already a classic . . .

For a very long time everybody refuses then almost without a pause almost everybody accepts . . . When the acceptance comes, by that acceptance the thing created becomes a classic. It is a natural phenomena a rather extraordinary natural phenomena that a thing accepted becomes a classic. And what is the characteristic quality of a classic. The characteristic quality of a classic is that it is beautiful . . . Of course it is wonderfully beautiful, only when it is still a thing irritating annoying stimulating then all quality of beauty is denied to it . . .

If every one were not so indolent they would realize that beauty is beauty even when it is irritating and stimulating not only when it is accepted and classic.

---

[4] A lecture delivered at Oxford and Cambridge in 1926 and published in the same year.

This quality in contemporary music of stimulating and irritating is what is new. Newness can be of two very distinct kinds. It can be a nihilistic one, so basically different, so iconoclastic that there is no touchstone of the past by which to judge it. This kind of newness is invariably unimportant in the history of music, and needs hardly any mention.

One of the most amazing experiments in newness was made in Baku on November 7th, 1922, when a symphony for factory whistles was performed. 'The basic idea of this new and original form'—I quote from *The Mind and Face of Bolshevism* by Fülop-Miller[5]—'which was used later at many great Communistic festivals, was that proletarian music should no longer be confined to one narrow room, but that its audience should be the population of a whole district. The factory whistle was thought best adapted to be the new and predominant orchestral instrument, for its tone could be heard by whole quarters, and remind the proletariat of its real home, the factory. In the first performance on a large scale at Baku, the foghorns of the whole Caspian Fleet, all the factory sirens, two batteries of artillery, several infantry regiments, a machine-gun section, real hydroplanes, and finally choirs in which all the spectators joined, took part in this performance.' The music was heard far beyond the works of the town of Baku. The disadvantages were reported to be:

(1) the restricted range of modulation in the instruments used;
(2) the lack of uniform performance, in spite of many conductors posted on high towers, who by waving flags gave the numerous leads to the various sirens and steam whistles.

This is of course an extreme example with an obvious political background, but there have been many instances on a smaller scale of groups getting into a balloon made up of their own theories and then detaching themselves from the ground of past experience. Paris is always full of such balloons, that either burst in mid air or come sailing uneventfully down to earth again.

A historic occasion of nihilism in music occurred in the palace of one Count Bardi in Florence in the seventeenth century.[6] It was to usher in a revolutionary art form, with numerous aristocratic dilletanti in attendance. The usual written manifesto to trumpet forth the amazing newness of the idea was written by a composer called Caccini, in the course of which he stated that 'neither in ancient nor in modern times, so far as I know, has music of such transcendent beauty ever existed as that which I hear

[5] René Fülop-Miller, *The Mind and Face of Bolshevism: An Examination of Cultural Life in Soviet Russia* (London, 1927).
[6] Opera is said to have originated *c*.1600 in performances in the house of the Florentine nobleman, Count Giovanni Bardi. Giulio Caccini (1546–1618), one of the early pioneers, provided a manifesto in the preface to his book of songs, *Nuove Musiche* (1602). See p. 15 above.

resounding in my own soul!' The artist reads such statements with considerable scepticism, for he knows very well that life is too short, very much too short, to rid himself of the ties that bind his imagination to the greatness of the past, even if he wished to sever them.

Newness of a consciously conceived kind generally interests no one but the participants in it, and almost without exception proceeds from personalities possessing little or no originality. A living composer once boasted that he had written a piano sonata in C major in which the chord of C major is never sounded. That kind of newness is entirely spurious. The absolutely new work is an absolutely bad work, because it would tend to be so subjective as to have no relation with the world at large.

The real authentic originality, what Gertrude Stein means by the beauty that is stimulating, irritating, and annoying at the first hearing, is of a very different colour. It consists in development. Originality is development: it is, in simple language, doing the next thing—not the last thing, nor the now thing—but the next thing.[7] This may be so inevitable that it does not impinge on the ear as so new as the spurious article. If I employ aeroplane propellers, or a gramophone, or a typewriter in an orchestra, as certain composers have today, that may sound at the moment a piece of startlingly new technique, because it is sensational, as news value. But the real artist does nothing of this kind; by a flash of intuition he broadens, amplifies, twists a piece of technique so that suddenly, without his knowing it perhaps, newness has arrived—a development has taken place.

A friend of Picasso tells how when talking to the painter he saw Picasso idly take up one of his son's toys, a yellow cotton chicken. He watched him, still talking, give the toy a twist, and set it down again on the table. The toy had become a chicken by Hokusai.[8]

To merit attention a composer must have first of all this creative ability for development, which I define as the real originality. He must create something real and actual, and then this creation must impress the hearer with both order and significance.

First, order. He must bring something significant under recognizable control. He must stand as a master of order, and it is just when the elements that he subdues to control are of the wildest and most turbulent that you get the genius of the stature of a Beethoven or a Wagner. The Fifth Symphony of Beethoven is an example of a dynamic fury just kept within the bounds by the most iron will, and it is because order rules chaos that you feel the immensity of the creation. The opera of *Tristan* again is

[7] Suggested by [T. S.] Eliot's remarks on Ezra Pound. [AB]
[8] A gap is left in the typescript for unspecified musical examples.

the outcome of a prolonged effort of will-power. To impose order on a composition so vast as the Second Act needed, as Richard Strauss truly said, a brain as cold as marble.

The technique of composing can be compared perhaps to the bending of an intractable and springy piece of steel into the exact shape which you intend it to have.[9] It will invariably tend to spring back into its normal comfortable traditional shape, and it would be easier and safer to let it so stay. Composition is compelling it by the grip of the fingers and the weight of the body to take up against its will the exact position and shape demanded.

Order in music implies the planning of the work, as an architect plans a house, a plan that will only fit that particular work or house. It is the very reverse of improvization. It rests on a structure, simple or complex, from which all the unessential padding has been taken out.

I feel that a good deal of the recent enthusiasm for Bach can be traced to the fundamental love of logic and order that is innate in everyone, and that the applause that greets even his less important instrumental works is evoked by the consciousness of listening to a texture which, while admitting the finest development, is based on the most logical and orderly growth. In a world of disorder, we do not want the artist who displays his own disorderly imagination, but rather one who puts before us the controlled products of order, the absolute logic of emotions.

Order, however necessary a foundation it may be, is clearly not enough without significance. A composer must not only know how to express himself, but he must have something of his own to say. He must not only have craftsmanship, but he must have personality, and the capacity to express it in that craftsmanship.

He must be significant as well as orderly. What he says must have a real authentic personal ring about it. This authenticity of personality is very marked in all real composers, be they on a large or a small scale. A mazurka of Chopin, a harmonic progression of Grieg, a song of Moussorgsky, a rhythm of Chabrier are just as important in this sense as the great personal touches of a Beethoven or a Mozart. They bring a quality into music which is significant, and without which music would be the poorer. This personal quality is one that an audience will appreciate long before it assimilates the power and beauty of order.

A new personality in music enters the musical world with the same sudden shock with which a new vegetable would enter the culinary world. One cannot imagine what the next one will be like, but when one is familiar with it, one cannot imagine the world without it.

---

[9] The analogy is from T. E. Hulme, *Speculations* (London, 1924).

A simple standard for judging significance is obtained by seeing what composers of various periods do when confronted with a definite problem in music which remains constant whatever style is projected. I have therefore taken the treatment of the cadence, or finishing of a phrase or movement, so that by playing several examples to you we can obtain an idea of what significance and personality means in music. [10]

I have not mentioned the question of beauty or ugliness as a criterion by which to judge music, because those terms do not have any meaning to me apart from order and significance. What is orderly and significant is beautiful; what is disorderly and insignificant is ugly. When a listener tells me that a piece of music is ugly to listen to, I do not accept that as a valid criticism in itself. If it is a question simply of the ear, we know full well that what was considered harsh yesterday becomes pleasing tomorrow— dissonance becomes consonance in a very brief space of time. Consider how difficult to the ear the Prelude to *Tristan*, *Till Eulenspiegel* of Strauss, *L'Après-midi d'un faune* of Debussy must have been at first hearing. Familiarity with new sounds as such is achieved by the repetition of the work, as anyone with a gramophone will testify. If the work still remains ugly long after the actual web of sound has been reduced to a known musical experience, then the cause lies with the personality behind the music, the composer being either insignificant or muddle-headed.

It is certain that music is becoming more complex and therefore more difficult to apprehend except after repeated hearings. This is a natural corollary to the complexities governing the situations in the moral and social worlds of today. The difficulty of much modern music is a problem that must be faced. We do not mind the obscurity, in fact we welcome it, if we feel that the mind behind the expression is a subtle and complicated one, and yet speaking with clarity. What we do object to is the mind that in reality is simple and naive, and which seeks to disguise it by overloading its structure to the point of obscurity.

Composers can be roughly divided into two classes—those who simplify their scores as they revise, and those who ornament them further. It is the latter who so often provide the difficulty of the wrong sort.

In the examples I have played of modern cadences it is clear that a great variety of outlook exists as to the way of dealing with this one problem, a wide difference in method, such as did not trouble composers of the classical period. In the time of Mozart a cadence did not differ very much in the works of a dozen of his contemporaries—it was only a subtle personal distinction that made Mozart's live and the others die, not an entirely new approach. But this age is characterized largely by the more or

[10] The examples are not specified.

less hazardous pursuit of the personal solution. Everything is in a state of flux; there is no convention or ideal to which all would give allegiance; each one falls back on a personal creed. We lack a general sensibility with which our personal sensibilities can keep in touch. This lack of widespread conviction to which all might subscribe is of course apparent in other spheres besides the arts. If you stopped every third man in the street and asked him what he believed in, you would get most illuminating reactions. In many cases there would be dead silence, as if the very idea of a positive belief in something was becoming a strange thought. He would be very ready to declare his disbeliefs, but that is a negative occupation.

An artist is a much more definite personality than the man in the street, and must have a defined goal in which he believes, but it is today a personal one, and you find the utmost disagreement between artists as to the very basis of their art.

This variety of outlook is in one way an advantage to audiences, for if no one can be found to like all music of today, everyone can find something that is of significant beauty to him. There is one class of listeners, for instance, who derive their main pleasure from the purely physical beauty of sound. It is the fabric of musical sound itself that appeals to them, the actual sensuous beauty of tone which arouses their emotion. The sound of unaccompanied choral singing, the surge and swell of a full orchestra, the pure tone quality of a solo flute can put the hearer into a state of almost mystic contemplation, in which analytical powers remain dormant. They perceive beauty without making any intellectual reservations. They form no mental conceptions of the composition; they are not concerned with the adventures of the themes. They sit quiescent, bathed in music, a human column through which sound vibrates.

This attitude is by no means uncommon, is not restricted to the mere amateur and younger audiences, and can be indicative of any point on the human scale of sensibility from a raw emotionalism to an almost mystic state of contemplation. It is in many ways an experience to be envied—the wonder of the child before a new vision of beauty—and has been felt by everyone. Even hardened professional musicians can feel an echo of it at the moment when a full orchestra tunes to the oboe A, string players exercise their fingers, woodwind players test their reeds, and the drummer quietly practises a rhythm. The predominating intellectual outlook of the musician is forced to be in abeyance; there is nothing formal to analyse. The mystery of sound itself is felt, and the moment is to be appreciated to the full.

With the present flooding of the world with music, the art tends to become a mere commodity. We turn it on like water from a tap, and we are losing the sense of it as a strange and precious experience. A month of silence every year will soon be a necessity, if music is not through sheer staleness to lose its beauty and youth.

This simple class of listener is likely also to be stirred to enthusiasm by the use of rhythmic devices. Rhythm is the most primitive and sure way of stimulating an audience. Anyone who heard, for instance, the insistent beating of the tom-tom in Eugene O'Neill's play *Emperor Jones*[11] will remember the effect of its timing with the blood beat of the pulse, and the tightening of tension as both pulse and tom-tom accelerated towards the culmination of that drama of fear. Modern music owes any popular success that it has had to its concentration of a rather crude rhythmic vitality. The power of grasping a melodic line needs some aesthetic training, rhythm hardly any.[12]

A second category of listeners, and a very large one, do not take up such a passive attitude to music. They wish to play an active part, and to do this they relate the sound that they hear to some external experience. They summon some other activity of life or thought to enrich what they are hearing. Some feel that the music embodies a story, others a picture, still others some historical age. They associate music with literature, pictorial art, or drama, and are most pleased when the composer himself gives them the clue to set their imagination in the right direction. This is a perfectly legitimate value to set on music.

Much the greater part of music already written actively invites, indeed demands, an association with some extramusical idea. Every opera, every setting of the Mass, every ballet, every song even, presumes that music is no pure element moving only in its own sphere of action, but that, on the contrary, it is related to many other forms of experience—poetry, landscape, drama, philosophy and even metaphysics. It should, and can in the hands of genius, express anything or everything within human experience, so that the listener, in so actively coupling what he hears with what he has 'read, seen, visualized or conceived in a philosophic concept', is only complying with the almost boundless exactions of music itself. Sometimes the composer himself gives a definite clue to the source of his musical expression, as for example Berlioz; sometimes he even gives a detailed synopsis of it, as in the case of Strauss; at other times the extramusical association is not so clearly defined, but underlies the work in

---

11 A tragedy (1920) about the rise and fall of the native 'emperor' of a West Indian island.

12 Examples of music that makes its appeal through its sheer sound: (1) [*Le*] *Sacre* [*du printemps*]. Raw emotionalism—primitive, almost atavistic force, as though addressed to human beings prior to the order of homo sapiens. (2) [*The Walk to the*] *Paradise Garden*. Sheer beauty of sound—brings an almost mystic sense of contemplation such as a dying sunset brings. Delius the most beautiful dreamer living in music—even on the mechanical and sexless gramophone it can be felt. (3) *Bolero*. Rhythm alone—once heard, of no further interest except (1) how is the crescendo maintained? (2) how will he end so as to give freshness at the last moment? [AB]

the form of a basic mood, which each listener can interpret more fully for himself. [13]

The faculty of descriptive power that music possesses can be abused, and there is little to be said for the many realistic passages that can be found in music. When Beethoven in his *Pastoral* Symphony makes a bird loudly sing cuckoo, impelled perhaps by the knowledge that the recently-perfected clarinet can do it better than any instrument hitherto made, we smile at the naivety of the conception, as we do when Haydn in the *Creation* makes his sinuous worm uncoil its length in the bass. And when Strauss makes his sheep bleat so realistically with his muted brass, and Kodály sneezes with the whole orchestra in his *Háry János*, [14] we feel that the joke belongs to a world apart from music altogether.

Passing from this large category of persons who value music mostly as a peg whereon to hang associations, we arrive at a third group, whose pleasure is of a more intellectual type. There has always been a body of thinkers who maintain that music expresses itself and nothing else, and that being a logical and reasonable language, it should be governed only by its own particular laws. Just as a story or moral has nothing to do with the value of a picture as a work of art, so music should be remote from all other arts, graphic or literary. These listeners would agree with Jean Cocteau's axiom that 'emotion resulting from a work of art is only of value when it is not obtained by sentimental blackmail'. This is the point of view put forward by Hanslick and based on the music of what we loosely call the classics.

Can we find in music a regulated cosmos free from the passions and difficulties of our own? Can we seek in music the pure beauty and elegance that mathematicians find in their science and masters of chess in theirs? Is there beauty to be found in the formal structure of sound 'removed from the necessity of accommodating itself to any other experience'?

The answer, of course, is yes, there is. When we hear a Bach fugue our imagination is presented with 'an object of great aesthetic charm', intelligible only as music, and subject only to the laws of its own texture. It is music in the abstract—just music. The pleasure it gives is in some way analogous to that given by a master game of chess where a controlled strategy brings an inevitable conclusion. Naturally you must have knowledge for this, and it is mainly the trained musician's attitude towards his art, and it brings undoubtedly the most lasting satisfaction.

[13] Purely descriptive music well done: Ravel [*L'Heure espagnole*]. Clockmaker's shop in Spain—hot sleepy afternoon. You hear the pendulum going, chimes, bells, cuckoo clocks. V[aughan] W[illiams] *The Lark Ascending*. [AB]

[14] The orchestral 'sneeze' at the beginning of this work is said to be an old Hungarian custom of introducing a true story.

I

Music finely felt and finely formed—an end in itself—appeals to certain aesthetic tastes in the human personality that can be gratified in no other way. Divorced from romantic association, it moves in a world of its own.

It is in Germany, the home of so much abstract thought, that the idea of music as a predominatingly intellectual force is maintained. To a German musician music is a literal thinking in sounds. He is apt to look on the music of other musicians as a mere light entertainment in comparison. Italy for him is likely to be the land of the mandoline, France of the exquisite miniature, England of a pretty sweetness, Russia of a mere barbaric force. They in turn brand his music as mathematics.

The followers of a Reger or a Schoenberg are not concerned with pleasing the ear, or stirring the emotions, so much as placing before the hearer relations of abstract sound in grasping which the intellect is stirred to pleasurable activity. They aim at—and succeed in—presenting music that requires hard thinking for its enjoyment. They demand not merely a receptive attitude on the part of an audience, but one of active and close attention. I shall give you an example of Schoenberg's music next week, so that you can hear the work of a man who has exerted one of the most powerful influences on the music of the present age.

I have divided the main mass of listeners into three categories—those who feel mostly its physical sensuous beauty, those who react emotionally to it, and those whose pleasure in it is mainly intellectual—but it must be understood that this is but a rough method of cataloguing, as the divisions cannot be so easily separated, each one overlapping the other two.

An amusing description of a concert at the Queen's Hall is given by E. M. Forster in his novel, *Howards End*, in which a heterogeneous collection of his characters have come together to listen to a performance of Beethoven's Fifth Symphony. He writes:

It will be generally admitted that Beethoven's Fifth Symphony is the most sublime noise that has ever penetrated into the ear of man. All sorts and conditions are satisfied by it. Whether you are like Mrs Munt, and tap surreptitiously when the tunes come—of course, not so as to disturb the others—or like Helen, who can see heroes and shipwrecks in the music's flood; or like Margaret, who can only see the music; or like Tibby, who is profoundly versed in counterpoint, and holds the full score open on his knee; or like their cousin, Fräulein Mosebach, who remembers all the time that Beethoven is 'echt Deutsch'; or like Fräulein Mosebach's young man, who can remember nothing but Fräulein Mosebach: in any case, the passion of your life becomes more vivid, and you are bound to admit that such a noise is cheap at two shillings.

But if every faculty in these hearers had been awake simultaneously, would it have not been even cheaper? If a man listens with but one part of his nature, it is a poor tribute to the music that he is hearing. Music is written to move every side of the man, physical, emotional, and mental; and the greatest music invariably does. When hearing any of the great masterpieces, be it the B minor Mass, the *Choral* Symphony, or *Götterdämmerung*, not only is the whole man engaged at high tension, but at moments he should be lifted up to the same heights of inspiration as was the creator of the masterpiece. One becomes a masterpiece *oneself* by its influence, as Nietzsche says—the vital difference being that at those moments one is inarticulate, whereas the creative artist by lightning strokes of genius emphatically declares his condition of thought and emotion.

Now can we say that any music written today so appeals to the whole nature of man that he is similarly utterly absorbed and lit with a like incandescence? If the answer is a strong No, it may be due not so much to the small personalities of composers today as to their avoidance of certain qualities in their music, the deliberate absence of which may prevent this easy surrender on our part. These qualities I shall discuss next week.

II

I stated at the end of my first lecture that a reason for the unpopularity of modern music might be found in the lack of certain qualities which were apparent in nineteenth-century composers, and which listeners had come to demand as an essential factor in music. The last century might well be summed up as characterized by moral fervour. Moral fervour, the ethical passion, is emphasized by the philosophy, the science, the literature, the art and social life of the time. It is the dominating passion in music from the time of Beethoven on.[15]

Professor Dent writes that the spirit of the French Revolution transformed the musician from a lackey to a prophet, and we might add a prophet not only of new realms of music, but of a new world and a new type altogether. We see a vision of it in *The Magic Flute*, though Mozart died too young to record it fully, and it was left to Beethoven to proclaim the emancipation from the old and the entrance into the new in his *Choral* Symphony, *Missa Solemnis* and the last quartets. Beethoven inaugurated a revolution in music that spread ever wider throughout the whole nineteenth century. The artist broke away from an almost feudal servitude, and demanded the privilege of the aristocrat.

---

[15] A summary of the argument in Edward Dent, *Terpander, Or Music and the Future* (London, 1926). Bliss's historical framework in this lecture derives largely from Dent.

It was not only the composer that became a prophet, but also the performer. The virtuoso's reign began; great players like Paganini and Liszt ruled over great dominions, preached to thousands. The descriptions of their tours read like the travel of our present-day film stars. When Liszt left Berlin for Russia in 1842, we are told in very sober language 'that the University to assist his departure suspended its sittings for the day. Liszt was received as if he were a crowned head. He set out in a carriage drawn by six white horses, with beside him the President of the Students' Corps in full uniform. Thirty carriages drawn by four horses [the distinction is worthy of note—AB] followed, and a cavalcade of mounted students wearing their special colour acted as escort. After this, as it were, official convoy, there came a hundred private carriages decorated for the occasion. Even the Court came to town to take part in the ceremony, and the business was made a public event.'[16]

The position as a great prophet that Wagner insisted on in the world is very well known, and he indeed received it, as he did everything upon which he insisted. Neumann's first-hand narration of what he saw with his own eyes in 1879 is evidence of this: 'And now I must tell of the first great performance of the "Nibelungen Ring" in Berlin—days of excitement such as can hardly be appreciated in these later times. Even the drive to the theatre was a spectacle in itself. The whole length of Unter den Linden from the Imperial Palace onwards down was lined with people closely packed . . . The windows were black with heads watching the parade, and even the trees were filled with curious observers . . . the tumult reached its height when Wagner appeared driving up the line . . .'[17]

We are very far removed from the lackey days of Mozart. A great change, both in the status of the musician and in music itself, had taken place from Beethoven's birth to Wagner's death. Music was no longer an exquisite entertainment for aristocratic patrons, and no longer a beautiful but humble handmaid for the service of the church. It had become a proud religion itself, and its large public already revered it as a form of free religious worship, 'experiencing and stimulating mystical experiences for temperaments, which could no longer be satisfied by dogmatic theology.'[18]

Now the danger of this attitude to music is that although in the work of a genius it is defensible, in the case of lesser men it is not. It must be always remembered that the mass of music written in any age is deplorably bad, written either by neurasthenics with feelings but no talent, or by

[16] William Wallace, *Liszt, Wagner and the Princess* (London, 1927).
[17] Angelo Neumann, *Personal Recollection of Wagner*, trans. Edith Livermore (London, 1909).
[18] Dent, *Terpander*.

conceited pigmies who intend to be heard, though they have nothing to say; or by that large mass of innocuous and laborious mediocrities who believe that unless they have something to show at the end of each day, they have not justified their short existences.

Now the bad music of the nineteenth century—that is, ninety per cent of what was in circulation—was of a particularly aggressive kind. Very many artists were stimulated by a sort of megalomania to attempt works of a needlessly colossal scale. A mental elephantiasis seized them. We can understand a genius like Berlioz writing in a letter, April 1835: 'I have begun a gigantic piece of work for seven hundred musicians, to the memory of the great men of France'—but we do not want to sit through similar productions by all the lesser men. It is very difficult when you set out to express religious exaltation not to fall into rhetorical pretentiousness; ethical fervour soon becomes reverent pomposity, and it is too evident that very much music of the nineteenth century, from its consciousness of its new high aims and newly found importance, gives the impression only of impressive platitude.[19]

A debunking process had to set in, and the last thirty years or so have seen that go full circle. 'Nothing is so enervating as to lie and soak for a long time in a warm bath. Enough of music in which one lies and soaks.' So says Jean Cocteau, one of the many typical little spokesmen of his generation. Now one sure method of putting an end to this lying and soaking in a warm bath is to hit the recumbent figure hard on the head with a thick stick. This is the method employed by Stravinsky in dealing with his audience.

Stravinsky is a man of wayward genius, an immensely concentrated determined hard personality. His utterances are dynamic, raw, and brutal. He is the leading living representative of the Russian school, whose collective work, containing as it did the music of Borodin, Moussorgsky, Balakirev, and Rimsky-Korsakov, was the most important contribution to the end of the nineteenth century.

He brings into music a primitive and uncouth force that is new in Western music. One has only to compare his delineation of spring—a series of rites such as Frazer describes in *The Golden Bough*, suggestive both of the teeming fertility and indifferent cruelty of the earth—with the thought that the season of spring called up in the minds of his immediate predecessors. The whole of the *Sacre du printemps* is a ruthless declaration of aims, and in so far the bludgeoning of an audience counts, is his most successful work. The Parisian atmosphere in which he has composed for many years has changed his aesthetic outlook since then, but his voice is undoubtedly the same, challenging and hard.

---

[19] Suggested by Dent's *Terpander*. [AB]

Alongside this bludgeoning, for which Russia is largely responsible, we may put as a contrast the rapier-like wit that entered music naturally via France. I do not mean anything consciously funny or laughter-provoking, so much as a spirit of *esprit*—an art of doing just the right thing at the right moment with the minimum of gesture or disturbance of equilibrium —something rather Chaplinesque—the adroit movement of the foot that at the right psychological second trips the bully up. But let me call to my aid a writer of the eighteenth century, who should know what *wit* is. He writes:

It is in short a manner of speaking out of the plain and simple way, which by a pretty surprising conceit or expression doth affect and amuse the fancy. It raiseth admiration, as signifying a nimble sagacity of apprehension, a special fidelity of expression, a vivacity of spirit. It seemeth to argue a rare quickness of parts, that he can fetch in remote conceits applicable, a notable skill that he can dexterously accommodate them to a purpose before him, together with a lively briskness of humour, not apt to damp those sportful flashes of imagination—whence in Aristotle such persons are termed ἐπιδεξιοι, dexterous men, and εὔτροποι, men of facile or versatile manner, who can easily turn themselves to all things, or turn all things to themselves.

Ravel is a good example of these virtues—he is eminently ἐπιδεξιοι and εὔτροποι. To watch members of the Parisian school juggling their glittering balls in the air, or traversing the trapeze with faultless poise, is to see that their weapon is not the sword of Siegfried, but the stick of Chaplin.[20]

Now for the machine. The conception of the machine as a thing of beauty was bound to influence music some time or other. It has been for a long time apparent in plastic and pictorial art, where we find artists scattering fragments of machines plentifully through their canvasses, and sculptors especially pleased to reproduce forms that resemble engineering models. Many machines which we see on every side of us undoubtedly possess in their lines and volumes a perfection that can well be called beauty, and this is all the more striking when these machines are related to some notion like speed, precision, power. It is perfectly natural that creative artists should try to transfer the qualities of perfection that are expressed in the machine into their own work. The texture of their work can be made more functional—every line in it can fitly play its part—there should be economy of space and material—it should generate power, race with speed, be capable of unerring and effortless precision.

It is so easy to talk like this, but the result of taking the machine as a model for artistic expression is usually rather different from the intention. It may result in a romantic attitude reminiscent of a schoolboy's love of

[20] The example is the Waltz from Walton's *Façade*.

mechanical toys, his wish to be an engine driver or motor mechanic
—anything in fact that keeps him in the presence of his god, the
machine.[21] When the poet Stephen Spender writes his dithyramb to the
express, and Honegger his symphonic movement *Pacific 231*, we are
listening to a new Romanticism, a sentiment evoked by the power of
man-made inhuman mechanical perfection, but a sentiment just as extra-
vagantly romantic as that of the nineteenth century founded on human
individualism and human liberty. It is just as genuine and one-sided, but it
seems to me less mature—the realization of a schoolboy's dream.

Let us have the skilled poem of Stephen Spender first.

THE EXPRESS

After the first powerful plain manifesto,
The black statement of pistons, without more fuss
But gliding like a queen she leaves the station.
Without bowing and with restrained unconcern
She passes the houses which humbly crowd outside,
The gasworks, and at last the heavy page
Of Death, printed by gravestones in the cemetery.
Beyond the town there lies the open country
Where, gathering speed, she acquires mystery,
The luminous self-possession of ships on ocean.
It is now she begins to sing—at first quite low
Then loud, and at last with a jazzy madness—
The song of her whistle screaming at corners,
Of deafening tunnels, brakes, innumerable bolts.
And always light, aeriel underneath,
Goes the elate metre of her wheels.
Streaming through metal landscape on her lines
She plunges new eras of wild happiness
Where speed throws up strange shapes; broad curves
And parallels clean like the steel of guns.
At last, further than Edinburgh or Rome,
Beyond the crest of the world, she reaches night
Where only the low stream-line brightness
Of Phosphorus on the tossing hills is white.
Ah, like a comet through flame, she moves entranced
Wrapped in her music no bird song, no, nor bough
Breaking with honey bud, shall ever equal.

---

[21] Suggested by Aldous Huxley, but I am not sure that it is the whole truth. Cf. my daughter
aged two who never looks up to the sky when aeroplanes pass. See *knows* that's what the sky is for!
[AB]

Those who do not rhapsodize over the machine, but get a sense of perfection from its fine lines and formal designs, which they feel are analogous to what they are wanting to express—those, missing a sense of romanticism, fall into an inhuman, cold manner of composing. Human warmth is damped down, and a chilly impersonal manner takes its place. Their music tends to sound very much the same, just a series of cogs revolving, pistons working, wheels turning. Composers have become aesthetic engineers, but so far the compositions they have designed are on the whole monotonous.

It is difficult to put any defined personality into this class of mechanical writing. The composer seems to have parodied Le Corbusier's phrase that 'a house is a machine for living in'; he writes a score that is a machine for playing in. A kind of rhythmic standardized sound results, as if written by robots for panatropes. The adjective that such a composer likes best to have applied to his work is 'steely'.

It is a curious thing that the steely perfection of the machine should have attracted composers and artists generally at a time when the freedom of the individual seems likely to be crushed by the ideal of the standardized, collective, mechanical man—for it is on the firm preservation of that individuality that the very existence of the artist depends. Honegger, after writing his *Pacific 231*, follows it with a work called *Crise du Monde*, which ends with a human being shouting 'Set me free'—that is, free from the noise and clamour of collective humanity—and Honegger undoubtedly is here on safer ground. To be set free to accomplish one's own work is the dream of every artist. Art at the mercy of a soulless mechanical materialism ceases to exist just as surely as when basely used as propaganda for political or social causes. Today it is more important than ever for a composer's growth that he shall be able to express complete indifference to what opposes his own sincerity. Newspapers, cinemas, broadcasting all tend in the same direction, to make everybody think in the same stock phrases, see the same stock types, react to the same stock emotions.

The ordinary person may no longer be capable of registering an individual emotion. The artist is aware of his, and tries desperately to fix and solidify it. Anything standardized, anything stock, anything relating to mechanical massed production should be anathema to him. Hence I am surprised at the machine complex in music. Here is one example of it. [22]

The point to consider here is the position the composer holds in the life of today. When during the nineteenth century he ceased to be a lackey and was proclaimed a prophet, what he gained in freedom he lost in other

---

[22] Prokofiev [Symphony No.] 3. Not typical of Prokofiev, whose lyric passages are some of the most beautiful written today. [AB]

ways. A prophet may be left to starve, whereas a lackey is sure of protection in return for his services. The liberty that the musician has gained is apparently now so limitless that he is in danger of playing no recognizable part in the social life around him.

With one or two exceptions he is no longer a practical musician such as Bach was, holding a post, playing and composing under the terms of that post. I do not know today of any appointment vacant in the world of music comparable to that offered Bach at Weimar, March 2nd, 1714, the post of Konzertmeister with the obligation to compose monthly a new work for the Court Chapel. Hence proceeded the stream of cantatas, which, drudgery though it may often have been, must have convinced him of his own importance in the cultured life of his town. Nor does the modern composer live in a world of patronage as Haydn or Mozart did, with their own orchestra or quartet, continually writing music for the many special occasions on which that orchestra or quartet performed for the pleasure of their aristocratic patrons.

How many composers would not like to have today the opportunities given to Haydn under the mangificent protection of the Esterházy family? We read that the Castle of Esterház 'had no place but Versailles to compare to it for magnificence. . . . The dense wood behind the castle was turned into a delightful grove, containing a deer-park, flower-gardens and hot-houses, elaborately furnished summer-houses, grottoes, hermitages, and temples. Near the castle stood an elegant theatre . . . brilliantly ornamented, and furnished with large artistic marionettes, excellent scenery and appliances. The orchestra of the opera was formed of members of the chapel, under Haydn's direction; the singers were Italian for the most part, engaged for one, two, or more years, and the books of the words were printed. Numerous strolling companies were engaged for shorter terms; travelling virtuosi often played with the members of the band; special days and hours were fixed for chamber-music and for orchestral works; and in the intervals the singers, musicians, and actors met at the café, and formed so to speak one family.'[23]

In this atmosphere Haydn composed nearly all his operas, most of his arias and songs, the music for the marionette theatre—of which he was particularly fond—and the greater part of his orchestral and chamber works. In Haydn's own words: 'My Prince was always satisfied with my works; I not only had the encouragement of constant approval, but as conductor of an orchestra I could make experiments, observe what produced an effect and what weakened it, and was thus in a position to

[23] *Grove's Dictionary of Music and Musicians*, ed. J. A. Fuller Maitland (5 vols., London, 1906), ii. 353.

improve, alter, make additions or omissions, and be as bold as I pleased; I was cut off from the world, there was no one to confuse or torment me, and I was forced to become *original*.'[24]

The composer of today has no such advantage. There are no musical posts that are not mainly administrative, and there are no great patrons who can support the musician with the practical atmosphere for the perfecting of his art. Instead we find composers living in the most unfruitful surroundings. Shut up in his ivory tower each writes for himself alone. Having little or no function to fulfil in the social world of his time, he has lost touch altogether with an audience, and retreats into seclusion, where introspection sets in, and often a distorted individualism results.

This does not apply only to music: it is the condition of all the arts. They are often completely divorced from practical and general use. Sculptors are no longer commissioned to beautify public squares; painters are no longer invited to decorate churches or public buildings. The result of an unsatisfactory social position, which is mainly due to economic factors, is to force the artist back on himself. He becomes in consequence aggressively individual, often eccentric, so that he appears to be writing for himself alone. He does not attempt to establish any dependable relation with his audience, and the result is that, outside a small clique, who know and admire that composer for his personal integrity, his music has literally no meaning—it is too crabbedly introspective.

Very often the modern music emanating from the ivory-tower seclusion is not a free natural aesthetic expression, but music written to illustrate and defend a personal theory, a new tonality, a system of quarter tones, a new way of using voice or instrument, whatever it may be. It is what might be called music of the laboratory, experimental work which might just as well be summed up in a treatise and printed in a technical quarterly review for musical pedagogues.

Every technical experiment fertilizes the stream of music and helps the genius when he comes along and can use such discoveries for his own purpose; but the worst is that these theoretical essays in new manners are treated as works of art, instead of being regarded as the mere blackboard demonstrations that they are. As a compendium of how to use the new system of atonality, Schoenberg's scores are undoubtedly masterly, but as communication of experience of emotion from one human being to another they are, to me at least, vaguely[25] unsatisfying. Is the state of mind of the composer a psychological one, to which only an intimate circle have

---

[24] Ibid.
[25] [The word 'intensely' has been crossed out.] 'Intensely' is too strong and implies a definite reaction. [AB]

the key, or is the composer definitely refusing certain factors by which contact with listeners in general can be established?

Now this wish to communicate with others is one of the strongest of human desires. It is especially so in the artist. Moussorgsky, writing to a friend, says: 'Music is a means of communication between men and not an end in itself.' It is true that no one can communicate fully, but everyone, I believe, can, if he so wills it, transcend the condition of personal isolation, and make others aware of his own peculiar and vivid perceptions. 'There is no such thing as a private work of art. All art is public property.'[26]

Does the school of composers of which Schoenberg is the master successfully achieve a practical measure of communication? You shall judge in a few minutes for yourselves, when Miss Irene Kohler plays you two Schoenberg pieces, but first a word about musical theory.

How wise was the seductive advice of Mephistopheles to the student in the *Urfaust*:

> All theory, my dear young friend, is grey;
> And green the golden tree of life.

There is far too much grey, and far too little green in modern music. Great emphasis is laid on -isms and -alities, as though such things were the essential part of music. Writers on music are largely to blame for this. Seizing on the one part of music that is graspable, the technical skeleton, they peer and pry, examine and dissect, until the general impression gained is that it is the way the vertebrae are joined together that is important, not the flesh and blood of music which constitutes the living work.

The searchlight of criticism is flashed on the manner of a work, while the matter of it is left in darkness. Hence the innumerable discussions in musical circles of such problems as polytonality, atonality, modality, quarter tones, linear counterpoint, and such like. We hear again the voice of Mephistopheles guying such pedantries:

> Comes the philosopher, and he
> Points you out that so it must be:
> 'The First was thus, and the Second thus,
> And so the Third and Fourth are thus;
> And without the Second and First, you see,
> The Third and Fourth could never be!'
> The students listen and believe,
> But none the better do they weave.

---

[26] Lascelles Abercrombie, *An Essay Towards a Theory of Art* (London, 1922).

II

Schoenberg says that '*das Einfalle*, the inspiration that comes without theorising, is the sole criterion of musical truth.' Well, in the following piano pieces,[27] is Schoenberg an inspired composer or is he only a masterly theorist—does he communicate something living, or is it only a black-board demonstration?

That a great number of composers see the danger of this laboratory school of music is clear. So far from withdrawing into an ivory tower with a few disciples, they shout their wares in the middle of the market-place. They want directly to entertain the public—and with this aim, they compete with other forms of entertainment. They borrow dance rhythms; they exalt the circus; they often adopt the methods of the cinema, where quick and sudden contrasts stimulate the interest; they bring the atmosphere of the *café chantant* into the concert hall. They furnish a high-brow popular music, for which there is a constant demand—a sophisticated jazz, a well-bred vulgarity. Instead of the smell of midnight oil in the study, one gets the heat and scent of a dance hall. Their success is gauged by their knowledge of what is demanded at the moment, and by their skill in presenting it. The necessary aptitude for this is defined in a sentence of Erik Satie. He wrote: 'I want to write a play for dogs, and I have got my scenery. The curtain goes up on a bone.'

These more obvious surface influences that I have touched on, which are to be found in contemporary music, are, I believe, of a mere temporary nature. I except the school of Schoenberg, which commands the utmost respect from musicians because of its highly organized intellectual achievement, though as I have said, it leaves me personally rather devitalized. But the back-to-the-primitive-jungle movement, the let-us-be-bright-and-witty episode, the mechanistic formula, the circus and dance-hall atmosphere have all been destroyed by the vulgarity of their many followers. A man of talent starts a movement, and soon tens, then hundreds, then thousands are rushing in the same direction, watering the original intention down and diluting it, or exaggerating it to vulgarity. 'It is vulgar', says Aldous Huxley, 'to make a display of emotions which you do not naturally have, but think you ought to have, because all the best people do have them.'

Well now, I have been giving you examples of what the best people in their own particular lines feel. Perhaps it would be better to let you imagine how the lesser good people have vulgarized them. Let us turn to more permanent achievement.

One of the distinctive features of nineteenth-century music as distinct from eighteenth-century is the growth of musical nationalism. Haydn,

---

[27] The examples are not specified.

Mozart, or Beethoven addressed themselves to all mankind, and all mankind could, if they would, listen to this universal tongue, but with the turn of the century, composers began to speak primarily to their own compatriots. Their music began to take its qualities mainly from the cultural traditions of their own countries, and be bound up with the temperament and psychological outlook of their own race. Instead of being a world music, it became definitely German music, French music, Russian music, so that very often the music of one country became difficult of appreciation in another, owing to the foreigner missing some association or allusion to which only the native was sensitive.

For example, it is difficult to transplant the music of Bruckner or Mahler. In their own country they produce a powerful appeal that is very largely lacking elsewhere. I feel, again, that the Italian can have very little use for Schumann, or the German for Debussy; Schumann is too German, Debussy too French. One could no doubt multiply instances where the expression of a national outlook in music has localized, at first at any rate, the composer's influence.

This limitation of speaking to one's own people, so far from being a disadvantage, seems to me to provide a great inspiration to a composer, and has certainly been the cause of the best music of today. With the last fifty years of the nineteenth century it was Russia that found her nationality in music. In the first thirty years of this century it has been England, Spain, Hungary, and Finland—and by finding its nationality I do not mean constructing an art based on superficialities, such as might be exploited as local colour, but one founded on a deep inborn feeling for racial emotion and those qualities that contact with the very soil of the country has matured for generations.

The only international music nowadays is jazz, and that's a subject for the pathologist rather than the musician. The best of modern music largely lies in those works expressing most vividly the national genius of the composer's country. You have only to call to mind such typical works as Stravinsky's *Petrouchka*, *Tapiola* by Sibelius, the *Three-Cornered Hat* ballet of de Falla, the *Pastoral Symphony* of Vaughan Williams, Bartók's one-act opera *Bluebeard's Castle* to see what I mean.

It is true that the progress of all these artists has been one from nationalism to a wider individualism, but the initial strength of their music is unquestionably buried in the roots of their own folk music. Some like Bartók and Vaughan Williams have collected and enshrined many actual folk tunes in their works, like jewels in a breastplate; others like Sibelius and de Falla, as far as I know, seldom use an actual folk melody, but convey the unmistakable spirit of their countries in line, rhythm, and colour. Stravinsky's main strength too lies in his Russian heritage, and he seems strangely inhibited in melodic invention when not handling the poignant tunes of his own country. Without them he falls back almost entirely on an excitement of texture or rhythmic urge.

I want to give you two examples of this characteristically national school of composing—the first from Spain, and then as the greatest possible contrast, the second from Finland. The first is the Finale to *The Three-Cornered Hat*—vivacious, restless, clear in design, and permeated with the sun.

The next illustration is at the very opposite pole of emotion.[28] With Sibelius, the north, as Mr Cecil Gray says in his book on the composer, 'becomes fully articulate for the first time in the history of music.'[29] In much of his music is apparent the northern winters burying the country for months under snow, and the northern summers with their white nights and protracted days. We have here a new and powerful utterance, the mystery of the north.

Between the extremes of north and south lies England, and indeed it seems in every way situated in a middle position, a clearly-defined no man's land facing on either side opposing forces. As in the political world, we tend violently neither to the right nor to the left, but extract what is needful to us from opposing principles, welding them together, so do English composers adopt a novel kind of equipoise. They have not the academic thoroughness of the German to pursue a train of thought to its logical and often tedious conclusion, nor have they the volatile spirit of the Latin which makes their best music run on so swift and vivacious a course. They are not dramatic like the Italians, nor dancers like the Spanish. What have they then which gives so distinctive a flavour to their music?

I believe that the chief characteristic of English music is its essentially poetical character. It seems to go hand in hand with our poetry in extracting a peculiarly sweet and sensuous essence from the contemplation of nature. Its inspiration seems to rest on a communion with nature akin to the expressive attitude of, say, the Wordsworthian school of poetry.

English music does not naturally explore psychological states of mind, or seek abstract perfections in its own medium, so much as seek to mould its expression on the ideal of the English tradition of poetry, the art in which as a nation we are supreme. It is lyrical rather than dramatic, contemplative rather than passionate, Apollonian rather than Dionysiac. The best of it has sweetness without sentimentality. It seems a mirror in which we can see the English landscape more subtly than in a Constable or

---

[28] The example, not specified in the text, is possibly *Tapiola*, which Bliss has mentioned previously.

[29] *Sibelius* (London, 1931).

in a Crome painting. It springs from an immense satisfaction in the aesthetic beauty of the land. While new ideals have arisen in other countries, and in other arts, English music in bulk has retained an earlier ideal of beauty, not one envisaged in the formal perfection of the machine, nor one based on a purely intellectual integrity, nor on the exciting dynamic possibilities of contemporary life, but an entirely different ideal —a lyric beauty springing from the inspiration of nature. It implies a poetical imagination, and can be defined generally as Wordsworthian.

It is helped in its expression by possessing a technique based on vocal rather than instrumental line. English music is predominantly vocal in style, with freedom of rhythmic flow. Continental music is mainly instrumental in style, with definite fixed stresses. English music has an emotional basis, European an intellectual.

Its *strength* lies in its absolute genuineness of emotion, its *weakness* in its willingness to abide by that alone. Established in a definite tradition, it is mainly unwilling to experiment. Experiment may not be the most important factor in a composition, but it is an absolutely necessary ingredient in it, if the music is not to become static, or a mere sterile repetition. Experiment provides music with a relation to the present, without which it is apt to prolong its life parasitically. Ezra Pound remarks about literature: 'Willingness to experiment is not enough, and unwillingness to experiment is death.' The same remarks apply to music.

The strength of English music lies in its courage to express emotions which can casually be termed obvious. By obvious I mean those that are significant in human nature, common to mankind of all periods. To hear many composers abroad express their anxiety to write music that has no relation to obvious human emotion is to think at first that some immense change must have taken place in man's nature recently. Can it be that the emotions of mankind, their reactions to life, death, and love have suddenly, as it were, frozen up? Is the human animal never again to feel love, tenderness, gaiety, melancholy? Are we to feel in the future nothing except what the crowd, the machine, and muscular athleticism bring?

The truth, of course, is that there has been no change in man's emotions—that man feels just as he always did, and that the avoidance of what I have called obvious emotions and significant truths on the part of the artist is largely due to the fear of failing when such subjects are essayed.

Holman Hunt, the painter, is alleged to have said once: 'I feel really frightened when I sit down to paint a flower.' It seems that many composers also feel really frightened when they sit down to express an emotion. It may be that there is a natural repugnance on the part of an artist to deal with what has been so vulgarized, but as the large part of existence is made up of the obvious, the artist is compelled to confine his activities to a very small fraction of it, if he wishes to avoid obvious subject-matter.

And it is not only the subject-matter of the obvious that he avoids, it is the obvious way of expressing himself. He makes the greatest effort both in his matter and in his manner to produce something which no one else has done. Hence the cold and self-conscious efforts of such music, ending in a small *cul-de-sac* of frustration.

Now England has always been the last to go to an extreme in any direction—I am stating this as a fact and not as a necessary compliment —and its music is a signal example of this national habit of mind. It is not nihilistic, it takes the obvious emotions for granted, and it trusts to character and personality to prevent the expression of them from becoming either vulgar or timid. Sometimes it succeeds, sometimes it fails, but it seldom avoids the difficulty through fear.

I do not believe that it is the purely English quality of our music which prevents the spread of interest in it abroad. Much more likely is the unwillingness of governments and officials to depart from the rule not to use English art for propaganda purposes. They do not realize that in English music and in English poetry they have two of the finest ambassadors in the country, and that with one of our great orchestras touring with English music, and one of our picked companies touring with English drama, they can spread an understanding of English thought and character that no conference, even if it sat continuously for years, can do. One day perhaps a government will use the names of Byrd, Purcell, Elgar, Delius, Vaughan Williams as ambassadors, coupled with our dramatists from Shakespeare to Shaw, to form effective ties of friendship with foreign countries, after more outworn methods fail.[30]

This ends my first two lectures with their very cursory survey of other men's music. At my next lecture I propose to analyse myself.

III

In my first two lectures I spoke at some length on various trends in contemporary music, and time prevented any but short musical examples from being heard. In this final lecture I propose to reverse the process—to speak but briefly, and let the music be more eloquent on my behalf.

[30] Bliss would appear to be anticipating the formation of the British Council in the following year (1935).

No composer can really claim to judge the work of his contemporaries. . . .[31] I am glad therefore to be speaking personally now and not generally, and in doing so I am conscious of the benefit that I am myself deriving. It is good to clarify one's thoughts by fixing them in so impersonal a medium as a typed script.

A composer's aesthetic should be a simple one. He is there to create something, and not to psychologize; his function is composition, and not the formation of an elaborate system of musical theories. If he binds himself with too-closely formulated laws, he cannot keep himself free to feel.

I judge music to be of two kinds—music that is alive, and music that is dead. Music that is dead is all music that has no personality of its own, but has borrowed the personality of someone else, which is then watered down, diluted, and distributed wholesale. Dead music is music that is not inevitable, but which meanders along uncertain which way to go, like sheep in a lane. Dead music is all music that proceeds primarily from a cold unemotional act of conscious will or duty.

Living music is the reverse. It is the product of a distinctly rounded and definite personality, goes straight to its mark without deviating on the way, and is actuated by a spontaneous emotion.

'The desires which impel a poet to write are two,' says Mr Auden, 'the desire for creation and the desire for company.' I agree with that. A composer wishes to make something and to communicate that something made.

What is the initial stage? The impulse to creation is an emotional one, and can be defined as a state of vivid awareness. Let me try and explain what I mean. Artists of my generation had an unparalleled experience —they were suddenly flung into war, and though it undoubtedly destroyed the artist in many, it may have aroused it in others. One cannot for long as a young man face the immediacy of death without becoming filled with excitement for the values of life. The smallest evidences of a positive vitality as opposed to a destructive force became of immense significance. A butterfly in a trench, the swoop and note of a bird, a line of poetry, the shape of Orion became as it were more vividly perceived and actually felt than ever before imagined possible. They were clung to desperately, as it were, because of their intimate contact with the saving power of beauty. One developed a sense of awareness more acute than at any other time in one's life—one saw objects for the first time, simply because, I imagine, it might also conceivably have been for the last.

---

[31] Bliss here repeats an earlier passage ('He is perforce a prejudiced and narrow critic' etc., p. 71 above).

III

This knife-like edge of awareness spread to all the senses. One's sense of touch, latent in most Europeans, developed, so that a subtle texture or a fine substance met with again after a long period, was truly experienced by the fingers. It was in a way as though the shades of the prison-house in Wordsworth's melancholy poem[32] had been removed, and one discovered again freshly and vividly as the child, only with the adult's appreciation of the fact.

I have emphasized this personal experience because it is absolutely akin to that of the artist gestating a work. He is filled with this vivid awareness. While at other times he sees an object or grasps a thought with the intensity *two*, at the moments of creation he sees and grasps them with the intensity *four*.[33] This generates a sense of power in him, which impels him to communicate that intensity to others.

Great artists, I believe, must experience this higher voltage over considerable periods of time, enabling them to create sustained and powerful works. They must often be astonished on returning to normal vitality that they were capable of such prolonged effort. Lesser artists feel this vividness only at fleeting, brief intervals, and they have to eke these out with all the technique at their command.

But whether it is momentary or prolonged, it is the essential power from which creation springs. It has been wrapped up in words like inspiration and divine afflatus, it has been termed a kind of madness by those who are only too sane; but whatever the label attached to it, it manifests itself as a definitely higher voltage of living, in which the values of beauty are the more clearly envisaged and its many forms found to be of an absolute necessity for the continuance of existence.

Without this awareness, life crawls greyly. Everyone is born to the realization of it, nearly everyone experiences it, but few can communicate it articulately. That is the function of the artist. How does he set about expressing this intensity of *four*? How does he satisfy his desire for company?

The musician begins by tentatively throwing out hints to himself, scraps of melodies, rhythms, cadences—vague premonitions of something still rather hazily apprehended. The mind remains like some surcharged chemical solution only awaiting a definite moment to crystallize. It seethes with a sort of restless uncertainty. Suddenly one of these hints—a rhythm, a turn of melody—takes a twist, and is instinctively known to be exactly what has been awaited. One seizes it, pins it down; it begins to proliferate; one has started.

---

[32] *Ode: Intimations of Immortality.*
[33] Suggested by T. E. Hulme. [AB]

An excitement caused by the actual musical subject-matter now grips the composer. As it grows, more and more possibilities occur to him. These possibilities are important. If I taught composition, I would make my pupils write endless variations on the most unpromising beginnings. It teaches the possibilities of growth. That is why the *Diabelli Variations* of Beethoven are a course in composition themselves. With them on the piano, the pupil requires no other master.

I mentioned in my first lecture that this stage of composition can be compared to the bending of an intractable and springy piece of steel into the exact shape which you intend it to have. It will invariably tend to spring back into its normal comfortable traditional shape, and it would be easier and safer to let it so stay. Composition is compelling it by the grip of the fingers and the weight of the body to take up against its will the exact position and shape demanded.

It can also be compared to building, where piece fits into piece, section grows out of section, material that is tautologous or unfit is thrown away, and audacity is shown in the new and fitting relation of parts. It is both a hammering into shape and a building up of the raw material, until that raw material, emotion, is expressed in logical blocks and lines of sound.

Let me here sum up my creed.

I believe that the foundation of all music is emotion, and that without the capacity for deep and subtle emotion a composer only employs half the resources of his medium. I believe that this emotion should be called into being by the sudden awareness of actual beauty seen, or by the vision of beauty vividly apprehended. I believe that the emotion resulting from apprehended beauty should be solidified and fixed by presenting it in a form absolutely fitting to it, and to it alone. If I were to define my musical goal, it would be to try for an emotion truly and clearly felt, and caught for ever in a formal perfection.

How easy to formulate, and how impossible of achievement, except for the very few! To feel an emotion deeply is difficult enough, but to separate it clearly from its surroundings and associations so that it can be handled and presented is very hard. This difficulty is discussed in a poem by Mr Tessimond, one of the contributors to that book of contemporary poetry, *New Signatures*:[34]

---

[34] *New Signatures* (1932), edited by Michael Roberts, was an influential selection of the work of younger British poets, among them W. H. Auden, William Empson, Cecil Day Lewis, Stephen Spender, and A. S. J. Tessimond.

III

ONE ALMOST MIGHT

wouldn't you say
wouldn't you say one day
with a little more time or a little more patience one might
disentangle for separate, deliberate, slow delight
one of the moment's hundred strands, unfray
beginnings from endings, this from that, survey
say a square inch of the ground one stands on, touch
part of oneself or a leaf or a sound (not clutch
or cuff or bruise but touch with fingertip, ear-
tip, eyetip, creeping near yet not too near);
might take up life and lay it on one's palm
and encircling it in closeness, warmth and calm,
let it lie still, then stir smooth-softly, and
tendril by tendril unfold (there on one's hand)
one might examine eternity's cross-section
for a second, with slightly more patience, more time for reflection?

'The ordinary life of ordinary cultivated people', says Mr T. S. Eliot, 'is a mush of literature and life.' To perceive something accurately in this mush, like a diamond glittering in a mudbank, is the first task of the composer. He has then to enshrine it in its setting.

In some artists the content is more interesting than the form. In others the form is more satisfying than the content. But somehow or other the two must be made to coalesce, must be equally interesting, 'and not interesting as two separate entities, but as one'. I am absolutely well aware how far I am from such ideals, but the actual slow progress towards them gives me the keenest joy and excitement.

I know that in every work there is a piece of my own personality combined with a piece of other personalities, too shadowy perhaps to be analysed, but still there. One hopes to work oneself gradually more and more to the front in one's efforts for clearly defined utterance, so that the other personalities recede, and finally one is speaking for oneself.

After you have the ideas that are emotional enough to prompt musical expression, the object to aim at is the attainment of unity; when complete, the musical work must display an internal unity. Paul Valéry, talking about poetry, remarks that a poem is like a heavy weight which the poet has carried to the roof bit by bit; the reader is the passer-by upon whom the weight is dropped all at once. I do not want my music to give the impression of a desultory shower of unaimed bricks, but rather of a compact weight thrown all at once.

There are two main traditional ways of producing this effect of unity on a listener. One follows the universal idea of growth, allowing a single idea to expand and spread as a tree might from a single seed, so that in spite of the resulting shape and subdivisions of the trunk, the intricacy of the branches, and the decoration of the leaves, one is aware that it proceeds from a single source. This is the form employed in many of the fugues of Bach, for example.

The other method is unity in diversity, the employment not of one idea that spreads, but of two or more antagonistic ideas that are gradually compelled to harmonize and form one complete whole. This implies drama and struggle, and is the formal idea lying behind the first movement of a Beethoven sonata, for instance. The first develops from a single thematic idea, the second is based on the interaction of several contrasted ones.

I have used both these devices in my Quintet for clarinet and strings that you are going to hear this afternoon. I had prepared a detailed analysis of my Viola Sonata[35] in order to demonstrate to you practically on the piano how growth could take place almost from bar to bar, and by playing the various themes to you to demonstrate what change and modifications these themes could undergo during a movement.

Time has prevented me from submitting this Clarinet Quintet to a like dissection. In one way perhaps it is an advantage. To begin with, it is a much easier work to grasp at a first hearing than the other, and then the mere fact that it will impinge on your hearing freshly and for the first time may induce an alertness that something known and anticipated does not.

It is perfectly possible to enjoy a piece of music without an intimate knowledge of its formal details, just as it is possible to enjoy a tree without a knowledge of botany, or a dish without being a cook. So, with such a justification, I will give you a general view only of the work.

It is written in four contrasted movements, each a separate entity in itself. These four movements gain by their juxtaposition, owing to the difference in mood. The whole work has a certain happy contentment and optimism about it, due directly to the clarity and brightness of the clarinet tone, in contrast to the Viola Sonata which is tinged with a romantic melancholy, a perfectly natural mood for so Byronic an instrument.

Being chamber music, that is, music written to be especially suitable for performance in a private room, it has certain general characteristics. It avoids theatrical or dramatic elements such as are suitable in an opera house, and refrains from literary or pictorial associations such as are possible on a full orchestra. It does not describe to you any story or paint

---

[35] See Appendix B, below. The reason for replacing the Viola Sonata is uncertain; possibly the players were unavailable. This handwritten analysis of the Clarinet Quintet is separate from the volume containing the lectures.

any scene. It seeks to please an audience by conversing musically to them.

It is in truth the conversation of five different persons, each of whom is equally important, and each of whom should only open his mouth when what he is going to say is directly to the point.

In the first movement, for instance, you hear the clarinet start off with a theme alone; it is soon joined by the viola, then by the cello, and finally by the two violins, each discussing the same subject. A little dry the opening, you may say—wait till you see where the discussion may lead. I am pleased myself with this first movement, because from an idea which apparently promises little I believe I have extracted some beauty—it sounds to the ear very simple, but it is not so simple to do.

This first movement, which flows easily and gently—an invention, as it were, on a single theme—is followed by one of spirit and vivacity. It bounds along on a staccato rhythm, throwing out on its course very distinct and easily apprehended tunes. The shape of this second movement is built on the simplest of all patterns, the symmetrical. Its energetic opening section is balanced by an equally vital closing section; in between comes a middle contrasting joint well secured in, and at the end a coda or tail piece which grows naturally from what precedes it. To me the merit of this movement lies in its joinery. It is like a table of large size in which the carpentry work is almost, if not quite, invisible.

The third movement is a romantic one, slow and lyrical. Long lines of melody follow one another, and there is one dramatic climax in the middle to which all these lines tend.

The last movement is gay and light-hearted. It is a conversation of *esprit*, in which the table talk of these five personalities is tossed about like a ball on the top of a fountain spray. Except for one moment of gravity near the end, the subject matter is devoid of any brooding seriousness.

To sum up the work in non-technical terms I should describe the first movement as calm and easily flowing, the second as energetic and spirited, the third as lyrical and romantic, and the fourth as gay and sparkling. These adjectives almost sum up the personality of the clarinet itself, one of the most lovely sounds we have in all music, and invented at the end of the seventeenth century. Just as Mozart exalted the role of the viola, an instrument which he played himself, so did he exploit to the full the possibilities of the new clarinet, writing many solo and ensemble works for it. Since that time it has been the most important woodwind instrument in the orchestra.

It has a curiously varied manner of expression, being capable of sounding almost like three different instruments. In its high register it is brilliant and piercing, with an almost pinched trumpet sound; in its middle octave it is beautifully pure and expressive, with a clear even tone; in its lowest register it is reedy in sound, with a dark, mournful and rather hollow quality. It is an immensely agile instrument, capable of extreme speed and dexterity, both legato and staccato. It has great dynamic range, extending from a powerful forte to the softest pianissimo than we have on any orchestral instrument.

All these qualities you will find expressed in the hands of a master player like Mr Thurston.[36] I am indeed grateful that I have been enabled to get not only the finest clarinettist in England, but so notable a string quartet as the Griller to play this work now to you, as quite apart from the music itself you will have half an hour's experience of very fine playing.

[36] Frederick Thurston and the Kutcher Quartet gave the first performance of the Quintet on 19 Dec. 1932.

A Musical Pilgrimage of Britain
(1935)

INTRODUCTION

BLISS often admitted to a need to turn to 'pure' music after a dramatic project, and *Things to Come* was followed in 1935 by *Music for Strings*, which took him to Salzburg for its first performance in August. In September there were press reports that he had been asked to succeed Adrian Boult as Director of Music at the BBC. Although he had shown an increasing interest in the role of broadcasting, he did not in fact join the BBC until several years later. He was, however, commissioned at this time to write a series of articles for *The Listener* giving his impressions of musical activity throughout the country, with special attention to the effects of broadcasting.

The Depression gave rise to many social surveys, both personal and professional. In 1934 J. B. Priestley published his *English Journey*, 'being a rambling but truthful account of what one man saw and heard and felt and thought during a journey through England during the autumn of the year 1933'. Later in the decade the Mass Observation movement went into the streets in an attempt to find out what ordinary men and women were thinking and doing. Bliss's pilgrimage, undertaken during the autumn of 1935, is a product of this curiosity. However, unlike Priestley and the Mass Observers, who treat their acquaintances and informants as typical and therefore anonymous figures, Bliss records the names of those he met out of a powerful conviction that 'it is these isolated personalities . . . who act and keep music going—not vague bodies, groups or committees' (p. 131 below).

It may well be that Bliss modelled his journey on that of Priestley, a friend since the late 1920s.[1] Both accounts are in twelve parts and cover similar ground, beginning in the south west, then moving north, and

[1] See J. B. Priestley, 'My Friend Bliss', *Musical Times*, Aug. 1971, pp. 740–1.

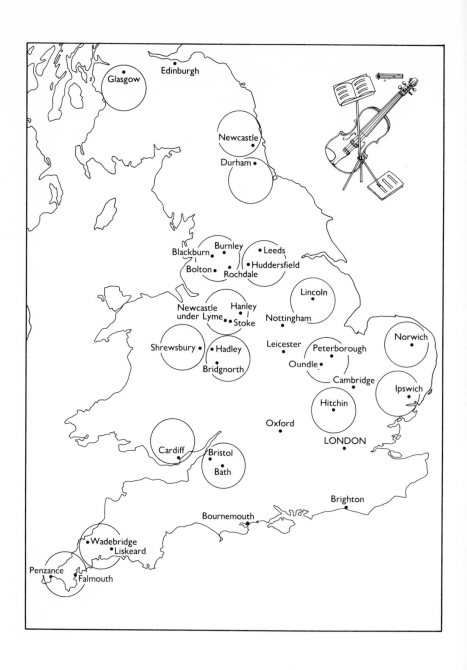

returning along the east coast, though Bliss extended his coverage to include Wales and Scotland. In all he travelled some 2,500 miles, in a pilgrimage which took him through extremes of living conditions and landscapes: from barns to cathedrals, and from lonely fishing villages to black industrial towns. It is a valuable social document, and for Bliss it provided many new experiences and impressions that were to influence his music.

———

I. WESTWARDS: BATH AND BRISTOL

The Listener, 2 October 1935, pp. 585–6.

I have started this week on a musical exploration of England—exploration defines my purpose exactly, for it is to discover the lesser-known activities in English musical life that I have set forth, and not primarily to visit those that are already famous.

Every musician has first-hand knowledge of the Hallé Orchestra, or the City of Birmingham Orchestra, for example, or the Bournemouth Municipal Symphony Orchestra, just as he knows the character of the Three Choirs Festivals, the Leeds Festival, the Norwich Festival, or the National Brass Band Contest at the Crystal Palace. They are all as justly famous in their own ways as the *de luxe* symphony concerts in the Queen's Hall, or opera at Covent Garden.

I want to discover something very different. I aim if possible at penetrating that immense activity that underlies the more spectacular high points. I shall be, geologically speaking, excavating at a lower stratum of musical deposit. At present a lot of it is mere hearsay to me. I am told, for instance, that every week throughout England alone over 200,000 men and women meet to rehearse together, that 2,000 choral societies, some big, some small, are actively functioning. I read of 196 brass bands in competition, of amateur orchestras, chamber music clubs, operatic societies, children's concerts, guilds, leagues, associations. What are they all doing, and who are the controlling personalities? It will be very enlightening to find out. Even a cursory investigation, such as this necessarily must be, will perhaps answer a few pertinent questions; for instance, does a city of 200,000 inhabitants offer sufficient facilities for a student of music to stay in his native town, or must he swell the stream of emigrants to London? Has the BBC unwittingly hindered some of these many varied societies, making it difficult for them to continue, or has it given a great stimulus to music-making generally?

On paper at any rate the statistics that have been given me seem to prove conclusively that however unmusically-minded *Officialdom* may be throughout the country, the enterprise and talent of the amateur, stiffened by professional experience, warrant this country being known as one of the very few 'Lands *with* music'.

It is perhaps more as an amateur detective than as an explorer that I shall get the best results. I shall mould my technique on one of those fictional heroes—cross-examination with a strict eye and ear for facts, I think, and no nonsense about psychoanalytical deduction, pseudo-scientific trial and success, or aesthetic intuition.

One must start somewhere, and I have started from Bath. It is musically a historical point of departure, as its Municipal Orchestra is the oldest in the country, having begun its concerts in the Pump Room as long ago as 1704 under the patronage of Beau Nash. There was actually a 'band of musick' some thirty years before that date, which played in what is now the Orange Grove under a large tree. When, therefore, the new orchestral director, Mr Frank Gomez, opens his season on October 5, he will be carrying on a tradition of 264 years. He will have sixteen players under him, and will, among other programmes, give symphony concerts every week for the period of the season of thirty weeks or so.

Here comes in for the first time in these pages the economic factor that will crop up at every turn and corner of my journey. This little orchestra is supported on the rates, quite rightly, as being one of the necessary amenities of the spa. The municipal authorities have no doubt from time to time discussed the possibility of permanently enlarging this body of players in order to make it more adequate to the artistic demands made on it, but have found it too great a financial burden to justify the increase. The result is that last season's programmes, consisting of the whole of the Tchaikovsky symphonies, the *Eroica* and *Pastoral* symphonies, the six *Brandenburg Concertos*, the *Unfinished*, the César Franck symphony, to mention only half the list, were played in this world-famous spa of Bath with its seventy thousand inhabitants and constant stream of visitors by an orchestra that is but half the size that it should be for adequate and compelling musical expression.

I wish the municipal authorities had the means of making an even more dramatic gesture. There is something akin in spirit between towns such as Bath and Salzburg. Both have that definable air of 'style' that only a few towns now possess. Both have great traditions of culture, both are famous for the men who have lived, worked, and created there—but at this point the comparison ends. One has its great yearly festival, the other has still to have it, and has to be content with spasmodic manifestations.

The Spa Director is a man of vision and imagination, as his Festival of

Contemporary Arts held last spring vividly testified. The recent Boughton Festival,[2] with its production of his new opera, *The Ever Young*, is another notable landmark for the city. But what would be of more lasting benefit to it would be the exploitation of the beauty and natural resources of Bath for a musical and dramatic festival on a large scale. There could be serenades and masques in Prior Park, festivals of music in the Abbey and in the Pump Room, opera in the Pavilion, open-air performances and ballet. A dream, perhaps—but one consonant with the environment!

To pass from Bath to Bristol is to transverse several centuries. Bristol seemed even bigger than it is—a bustling, modern, energetic town. To approach it along Victoria Street early in the evening is as slow a progress as driving down Shaftesbury Avenue at theatre time. Most seaports give one the impression that all the vital and enterprising citizens have already sailed away. Here the reverse is the case; there is a distinct up-and-doing tang in the air.

Musically the situation is rather complex. Instead of the activities being centred in one spot, as in Bath, they are here diffused through many channels. There is the Philharmonic Orchestra, for instance, of professional members, reinforced from London for their concerts, which owes its continued life to the public spirit and generosity of its conductor, Mr Arnold Barter. The outlook of the society is progressive, and in its four concerts this year (one is given by an outside organization) there is a large assortment of modern English works. Then there is the newly-formed City of Bristol Orchestra of nearly seventy professional musicians, which has been rehearsing hard under its director, Mr Maurice Alexander, for, I hope, a successful future series. There is, of course, the Bristol Choral Society, which is giving three Saturday evening concerts during the season. These are conducted by Mr S. W. Underwood, and the members of the chorus are rehearsing programmes of the works of Bach, Handel, and Elgar.

Alongside these bigger organizations are the activities at the University of Bristol. Although it is one of the smaller universities, numbering only about a thousand students, it can normally muster with members of the staff an orchestra of thirty and a chorus of two hundred. I expressed my surprise at the large percentage of singers in the university, and it was explained to me by Mr Arthur Warrell, who directs the music here, that the students in the Education Department of the university, who are being trained as teachers, are empressed willy-nilly into the service of

---

[2] Inspired by Wagner, Rutland Boughton (1878–1960) inaugurated the Glastonbury Festival in 1914 for the production of his Celtic music dramas on the Arthurian legend. Plans to build a festival theatre were eventually abandoned, and in later years his operas were produced elsewhere.

music. 'Since singing is so good a thing I would all men would learn to sing', writes Byrd—and in this Department Byrd's wish becomes law. Only the few out of the 180 in this Department who actually dislike music are released, and they find their way into what Mr Warrell termed the 'non-choir', where they learn the rudiments of music and are often converted.

This chorus of two hundred practise weekly and give one concert a year, the programmes being of high musical value, drawn mainly from contemporary English sources. Like all university choruses, the problem of the standard to be maintained is complicated by the fact that every year the veteran quarter of the chorus leaves and has to be replaced by newer recruits. From this chorus a picked body of about fifty voices has been formed into a madrigal society. Listeners may have heard the University of Bristol Madrigal Singers, for once a year they give an open-air concert which is usually broadcast.

Besides this training of amateur singers and instrumentalists, there is opportunity for the students to hear professional players in the Great Hall of the University. A series of chamber concerts is arranged, in which string quartets such as the Brosa, Kutcher, Griller, and different soloists take part. Gramophone discussions are held prior to the concerts and analytical notes on the works to be performed can be obtained well in advance. Groups of young students from outside accompanied by a teacher are encouraged to come on a low rate of subscription, and on a good evening as many as four hundred may attend.

It seems a pity that in a town numbering 400,000 there should not be provision made for incorporating a music course in the Faculty of Arts at the University. If, instead of coming to London, students could get a comprehensive course here, they would remain and enrich the musical life of the town.

There is another and noteworthy madrigal society, the Bristol Madrigal Society. This must surely be one of the oldest of its kind in the country, being within two years of completing its centenary of music-making. An interesting feature is that it employs boys' voices to replace the usual women sopranos. Dr Hubert Hunt, one of whose activities is to conduct this society, gave me some interesting data emphasizing the change in the outlook towards music among music pupils today to which I shall hope to refer in a future article.

Bristol may not have an opera house, but it possesses an opera school founded and directed by Mr Robert Percival. For thirteen years he has trained a school to give performances of such operas as *Ivan the Terrible*,[3]

---

[3] Diaghilev's renaming of Rimsky-Korsakov's *The Maid of Pskov*.

Sir John in Love,[4] *Savitri, King Arthur,*[5] and *The Magic Flute.* Except for a few professional leaders in the orchestra, they are all amateurs, comprising, beside principals, a chorus of forty, an orchestra of twenty-four, and even a *corps de ballet.* They paint their own scenery and design their own costumes. The fact that the hall in which performances are usually given was burnt down last year has in no way discouraged this enterprise which indomitably enters its fourteenth season.

I am well aware that I have not nearly exhausted the musical life of Bristol. I have probably only scratched at the surface. I have had no chance of seeing the work of Mr Douglas Fox at Clifton College and in another sphere I have not heard the City of Bristol Police Band which broadcasts occasionally from the BBC studios. But I have seen and heard enough to be quite certain that with all these independent activities the time will soon be ripe for a concerted effort. Bristol possesses right on the spot most of the necessary artistic elements for self-sufficiency. It even owns its own composers, and it has the advantage of a first-class practical musician on the press—a rare asset. Given a leader in municipal affairs who realizes that music is a normal and integral part of a town's life—the town's soul, in fact, as opposed to its blood, bone, and sinew—a move could be made to organize a week's festival in Bristol, to which all these several societies would contribute, and which would call attention to activities engaging a large number of its citizens.

II. CARDIFF AND THE THREE VALLEYS

The Listener, 9 October 1935, pp. 633–4.

The annual report of the University Council of Music[6] in Wales makes remarkable reading. Here is a council formed in 1919, under the directorship of Sir Walford Davies, which has penetrated in its sixteen years of life into almost every musical activity in the Principality. The fourteen headings under which these activities are ranged give a vivid idea of the varied scope of this vast social and musical organization. A few examples

---

[4] Vaughan Williams (1925–9).

[5] Purcell.

[6] The National Council of Music (1919–61), a university body concerned with musical education in schools, colleges, and adult centres. Its first chairman, Sir Walford Davies (1869–1941), was Professor of Music at Aberystwyth 1919–26 and Master of the King's Musick 1934–41.

only will have to suffice. In each of the Universities of Cardiff, Aberystwyth, and Bangor, by arrangement with the Council, resides a professional trio: a pianist, a violinist, and a cellist. They are engaged as full-time servants of the colleges. They are available for teaching and playing, and train an orchestra in each college of which they are the musical nucleus. Two of these trios make tours of schools to give free lecture-concerts—the Cardiff trio gave 114 of these concerts during the season of 1933–34.

Another side of the Council's activities consists in violin classes. Throughout the elementary and secondary schools, pupils are encouraged to learn the violin and buy their own instruments. They can do this on a weekly instalment system, paying 1s. a week, to own eventually an instrument that is priced by the Council at 35s. Including the adult classes, these violin students of all ages number over twelve hundred, and this aggregate is exclusive of all those learning under schemes independent of the Council's work.

I was taken by Mr Bumford Griffiths, the Assistant Musical Organizer, to see one of these classes. It is to him that I owe my vivid musical experiences of the last few days, and indeed music in this district follows very closely the record of his dreams and achievements. This particular class rehearses in the Rhondda Valley district. I found about thirty boys and girls playing in a string orchestra; they gave a programme of music, starting with a movement from Haydn's *Surprise Symphony* and pieces by Locke, and ending with a difficult solo piece played by their leader, a little girl of, I should say, twelve years—a born musician and player. Every work was played with assurance and feeling. I am going to mention this well-disciplined orchestra by name: it has already broadcast from the Cardiff studios, and when it does so again be sure to hear it, and listen with the full realization of the environment in which such an orchestra has flowered. It is the Blaenclydach Juvenile Orchestra, and it owes its accomplishment to the skill and devotion of Mr John Phillips.

Instruments of all kinds are also lent by the Council where purchase is impossible—there are at the moment about £700 worth of such instruments out on loan: horns, trombones, timpani, every kind of instrument in fact—and this policy of making it easy for a man to start playing has had very fruitful results. A collier, for instance, who under this scheme started to learn the oboe two years ago, won the first prize at the National Eisteddfod[7] this year.

A great deal of attention is paid to the organization for children's choirs; there are fifty such choirs in Cardiff alone. A week before Good Friday a

---

[7] The Welsh gathering of the bards (*eisteddfod* means 'session'). Although much older, since 1817 it has been an annual competitive festival of poetry, song, and music.

festival is held. In the spring of 1934 there were 4 massed choirs, 640 children in each choir, with an orchestra to accompany them of 104, again all children. These are very large numbers, but the same supervision is exercised in the care of very small groups outside the more thickly peopled areas. At Oakley Park, a mere hamlet of a few scattered houses, where the children have to walk perhaps three miles to school, there is a choir of ten formed out of the total attendance at school of thirty. These ten will sing you Elgar's *Snow*, and in three parts too. I went one evening to hear a children's choir near Tonypandy. The hall in which the singing was to be held was occupied by a fighting match. That is very typical of this district; up and down the valley, just two main activities, boxing and singing, singing and boxing. So they switched over to a vestry and sang half-a-dozen pieces to me, mostly in two parts, including Purcell's *Nymphs and Shepherds*. They were a proud little chorus, having just won a competition shield, and they had every confidence in their success, for they too have broadcast. The rhythm was excellent, the diction clear, the tone pure and unforced.

This enthusiasm for singing is universal here. South Wales is choir-mad. Singing is in their blood. The Welshman views music quite differently from the Englishman. It is not so much a relaxation as a justification. Every chapel has its choir, a preacher sings rather than speaks his sermon. He is proud of using a full two-octave range when preaching in Welsh to emphasize and dramatize his meaning. A public figure has been known to come on to the platform at a meeting to say a few words to the audience and has then sung a song to them instead. A Welsh audience listening to the *Hallelujah Chorus* would never think of just standing up dumb— everyone joins in. The thousands who swarm to a football match hours before it starts, pass the time singing. It may be the vowel sounds in the Welsh language that give such a tone quality to the singers round here, or it may be the presence of *hwyl*[8] that so often seizes a Welsh chorus, but the fact remains that there is a special quality in their voices that differentiates them from any others—a warmth and vitality that is very moving.

I went out to Mountain Ash to hear an adult chorus rehearse. This chorus is typical of many in the Three Valleys district. Of the hundred that were at rehearsal ninety-odd were out-of-work colliers and their families, whose employment for the past eight weeks averaged but three days. It must be remembered that Mountain Ash, where once a year in May is held the biggest musical festival in Wales—the Three Valleys Festival—is in

[8] A Welsh word whose many senses include 'gusto, zest', 'characteristic musical intonation or sing-song cadence formerly much in vogue in the perorations of the Welsh pulpit', and 'merry-making, hilarity, jollity' (*Geiriadur Prifysgol Cymru: A Dictionary of the Welsh Language* (Cardiff, 1980)).

the heart of a densely populated colliery district. Long rows of houses run through the valley, follow the contour of hills, forming a great tightly packed wedge of stone—there are no detached cottages found here. Massed dwelling-places cluster round coal mines and steel works that are so many skeletons, dead and decayed. What once were prosperous communities are now poverty-stricken centres, where the men have the appearance of drifting ghosts and the atmosphere is thick but unreal, as though life had passed on elsewhere. In these distressed areas the Council has redoubled its efforts. It braces the choruses, it forms listening clubs and singing meetings, it keeps stringed orchestras going, it organizes yearly and terminal classes in music. This is done at the definite wish of the men, not forced on them. In an atmosphere of such deadening inactivity, a weekly chorus practice assumes a very different psychological aspect. On *that* night, at any rate, men and women feel themselves employed. They can check in on that evening for certain.

The members of this Mountain Ash chorus pay 1*d.* each a week for the rent of the rehearsal room: then there is the question of buying the music. Now the Council advances half the money necessary for copies of the music to be rehearsed, but very often even this is not enough. A family of three in a chorus, all unemployed, have to think twice before handing out 1*s*. 6*d*. each for the privilege of singing the Brahms *Requiem* or the Bach B minor Mass. Here, I think, is a chance for a man or woman who wishes to be a real patron of music. A present of £150 to the University Council of Music would ensure just that extra sum that would allow them to pay three-quarters of the price of the score, and the singer would readily fork out his 9*d*. for the masterpiece that will sustain him through the winter.

The great day towards which all these choruses work and look is the three days' Three Valleys Festival. It is held at the Pavilion in Mountain Ash, a big cold barn of a place just above the valley. This is not an old-established festival; it started only about six years ago. Both Dr Malcolm Sargent, who was the first festival conductor, and Sir Henry Wood, who directed it during his illness, are household names here. They have completely captured the imagination of the singers. To give some idea of the scope of this festival, a few figures in black and white are necessary. At the third concert this year on May 28 there were 4,538 in the audience and 930 in the choir.

I visited a listening group in this region, typical of many—forty or fifty unemployed men in a ramshackle barn that served as a primitive gymnasium. Their group leader was not a Welshman, but a Londoner, an artist, who had come, like others, to live here and try to hold things together by the force of his personality. He showed me the list of wireless talks and musical courses that the men had listened to, and made some trenchant suggestions as to what was wanted in this medium. 'Unemployed Welsh-men associate music with doing a job', he said—'they want to take part'; and he gave me suggestions as to how that could be done. It is quite clear that unless, to these unemployed listening groups, music is to be only a drip-drip accompaniment to the sound of card playing and dominoes, a vivid personality must be at the other end in front of the microphone.

Quite apart from the work instigated by the Council of Music, there remains a good deal of independent music-making in Cardiff itself. There is the Cardiff Musical Society, which starts this season to prepare three choral concerts under its new conductor, Dr J. Morgan Lloyd. Cardiff is not naturally orchestrally-minded. It is hard to make the public in-terested, and the lack of a good hall is not helpful. I believe, however, a scheme is in the air to construct a fine concert hall right in the middle of the city, and things may then improve.

There are several enterprises in the orchestral world going on in Cardiff. Mr Garforth Mortimer, for instance, has done a signal service for un-employed musicians ever since the coming of tinned music in cinemas and theatres has so impoverished living music. He has gathered together fifty of these players, and has kept them in good heart and practice by holding weekly rehearsals. This orchestra has broadcast several times, as has the Cardiff String Orchestra under Mr Herbert Ware. Both this and the Herbert Ware Symphony Orchestra have been running for twelve years. This second orchestra has initiated a very good scheme which might suit other organizations of similar kinds. They sacrifice one rehearsal every week to give a concert in which those symphonic works are played which cannot normally be included in the more popular public concerts. The audience at these semi-private sessions are confined to members of a club, now numbering 250, who pay 2s. 6d. for the privilege of hearing these five rather special programmes.

There are undoubtedly other phases of musical life of which I have not in this first visit been able even to get a hint. But what will remain fixed in my mind—it is indeed unforgettable—and what all who value music as a living force should experience for themselves, is the great chorus of singing that goes up continually from these workless stricken colliery towns of South Wales—a tribute by an indomitable people to their love of life even under conditions so unnatural.

III. SHROPSHIRE

The Listener, 16 October 1935, pp. 683–4.

My journey has led me from Cardiff to Newport, then up the valley of the Usk and Wye, through the cathedral town of Hereford to that loveliest of counties, Shropshire. From mountains and mines to ploughed fields. On the way I passed close to Tenbury, and it was only when it was too late that I learned that I had thereby missed one of the finest musical libraries in England.

St Michael's College, Tenbury, was founded by Sir Frederick Ouseley partly to set and maintain the highest standard of church music, partly to offer a fine education primarily to the sons of clergymen. It possesses a music library that has been fully catalogued by Dr E. H. Fellowes and contains a collection of Tudor MSS. of great value, including the famous *Batten Organ Book*.[9] Thanks to the courtesy of the present Warden I learn that among several thousand books there are to be seen there the MS. score of the *Messiah* which Handel himself used at the first performance in Dublin, with some numbers in his own writing, a Purcell autograph, and a little vellum bound MS. book initialled W.B., which is believed to have been the property of William Byrd; the library is further enriched by the 'Toulouse–Philidor' collection[10] of French operas of the Lully school, and by MSS. of the Purcell period. It is typical of the astounding value of the musical life of England, which I am discovering for the first time, that tucked away in this orchard country there lies so valuable a heritage.

Shropshire itself is essentially an agricultural and sporting county. I had, therefore, expected to find that music played a pretty small part in its life, for generally speaking it appears that the more prosperous the conditions the less the need for music, just as the higher the social scale, the lower the spontaneous artistic impulse. I was certainly not prepared to find flourishing here an educational experiment indigenous to this part of England.

Now the relation of music to the community, especially in reference to schools, has been undergoing momentous changes for many years. It is fifty years, to be precise, since competition festivals were first started, and

[9] A collection of 16th-c. church music by the composer and organist, Adrian Batten (1591–1637).

[10] Now in the Bibliothèque Nationale, Paris.

from Stratford (London) and Kendal they have spread like mushrooms all over the country, and have paved the way for a musical regeneration that has reached the smallest and most elementary school. Anyone who is interested in the complete change in outlook towards music on the part of educational authorities could not do better than read carefully the *Cambridgeshire Report on the Teaching of Music, 1934*. Here is an authoritative guide to the subject compiled by some of the best brains in the country. In its blend of idealism and practicability it is a model for all teachers to adopt. With this book in mind it was stimulating to make the acquaintance of a pioneer who had started a similar scheme on his own initiative.

He is Mr U. C. Brunner of Bridgnorth, and he is the headmaster of a school there that nearly ten years ago served as the starting point for his educational experiments. The objects that he had in mind were these (I quote from his own modest pamphlet):

(a) To promote a love of good music in schools.
(b) To give encouragement and assistance to the teachers of music in schools.
(c) To create such a love of singing that boys and girls will, in later life, desire to participate in the musical life of the places in which they live.
(d) To hold annual non-competitive festivals at which schools shall sing both individually and massed, and at which both children and teachers of music may receive from the Director helpful hints and criticism.

This scheme was originally drawn up for his particular area of some 22 schools—some with as many as 150 pupils, some with only 20—but whether big or small, music was to be an integral part of the daily life. All music is ultimately based on singing; so singing was to be the keystone of the whole scheme. There were naturally schools where teachers had no musical knowledge whatever, schools where there were not even pianos, but these facts did not discourage him. Every school can sing a unison national song or folk song, he declared, and once started both teachers and pupils will get assurance and improve. They can go on to simple rounds, catches, canons, and two-part singing. The luckier schools where some musical experience was available would attempt more advanced work: sight reading, formation of percussion and pipe bands, musical dictation, etc.

To co-ordinate the scheme, he instigated the annual festival, 'The Day', for which all the schools worked. It was to be a strictly non-competitive affair; it did not matter how good they were, or how bad they were, teachers and children came together to enjoy the thrill of massed singing, and learn from the professional musician who was invited to come and direct the festival and give critical aid.

The idea spread rapidly; from the district of Bridgnorth it spread over the county of Shropshire, and then into eleven other counties. At the annual festivals held last year in Shropshire at eight different centres, 168 schools entered with 297 different entries; 5,759 children performed in the festival activities, of which 3,511 took part in massed concerts.

A typical school music festival under this scheme will start about 10 o'clock in the morning and continue all day. First may come classes for percussion bands, handbell ringing, and pipe bands; then violin classes from the grammar schools, followed possibly by an orchestra. All the time the Director is writing comments which are later given out privately to each class teacher. There will be infants' classes with singing and dancing games, country schools singing hymns with descants, junior classes up to ten years of age, and senior classes up to fourteen, each with its own songs. After each item there is a general discussion, and at 'Tea' the Director holds an informal conference of teachers, and gives them a talk on some musical technical problem that is pertinent to the year's work; it may be on tone production, phrasing, rhythm, interpretation, etc. Most of these conductors have to learn their job while actually taking their classes, so this is the time to ask questions and benefit. Finally the choirs are all assembled for a rehearsal of the massed concert, and the big event of the day arrives.

The lack of the competition element, at least with children, seems to offer great advantages. There is no marking of the results; the smallest village school or the largest town school is encouraged to send *all* its children, not merely a selected school choir. Again it affects favourably the question of repertoire. The number of different songs prepared in the aggregate is very large; instead of two set fixed pieces sung by every choir, each one can choose what it likes for its individual singing. At one festival I was told that 152 different songs were prepared. Teachers, too, greatly benefit from the removal of the responsibility of being judged competitively. They can come with a definite wish to learn and meet others, and are not under the restraint of possible defeat.

I have the programme of the last June festival for the Bridgnorth and District Schools, to which Dr Geoffrey Shaw, Chief Inspector of Music, came. It shows a much higher standard of repertoire sung and played than could have been ever imagined a decade ago here. Mr Brunner is a signal example of the right man coming at the right psychological moment.

This same spirit of non-competition, aiming at communal effort, is shown by the Shropshire Association of Musical Societies. This consists of 24 choral societies dotted up and down the county. A characteristic of these choruses in a county such as this is their varied composition. They consist of people of all ages and types, the different social groups mingling freely. You may in the very nature of things find anyone there from the Lord Lieutenant of the County downwards. These choral communities, therefore, serve a wider purpose than a mere musical one; each member in pursuit of music learns a sympathy and understanding with his fellow members that other conditions make more difficult of realization.

Most of these choruses, which are found throughout the whole of England, consist of men and women who have been at work all day prior to gathering together and being gingered up by a conductor in the evening. According to the district they may be school teachers or shop assistants or miners, mill hands, farmers, engineers, ironworkers; they may belong to every sort of trade in fact. These expert choruses, professional in achievement, are all amateur in point of standing. Music is just the added relish to a hard day's work, and in speaking of their character this fact must be kept in mind.

The Shropshire Association holds an annual two days' festival at Shrewsbury under its conductor, Mr Arthur Fagge. As many of the choruses consist of women's voices only, the first day is devoted to them; they sing first in individual classes, and finally as many as possible take part in the massed concert; the chosen work this year is the choruses from Pergolesi's *Stabat Mater*. On the second day it is the turn of the mixed choirs, who will finally combine in a performance of a Bach cantata and Stanford's *Songs of the Fleet*. The standard of music chosen by individual choirs is uniformly high, and rubbish has been eliminated. It is good to see a young and contemporary-minded musician like Mr Leighton Lucas working in this festival: it is an assurance that the outlook of the younger generation will be represented.

Shrewsbury possesses its symphony orchestra. Founded in 1888, the Shrewsbury Orchestral Society is now the nodal point of all amateur and unemployed professional musicians in the neighbourhood. The conductor, Mr F. C. Morris, gives two symphony concerts a year with soloists, and holds weekly rehearsals which are enthusiastically attended. I am coming across many organizations of this kind, a first-class musician at the top holding the talent of the district together. The keenness on the part of individuals is striking. I hear of a player who sold his motor bike to buy the instrument he wanted. That meant a long journey into town and back from rehearsal by road and train as best he might. He generally reached home at midnight, and being a farmer he begins his day earlier than most. I have even learnt of an enthusiastic player who had the misfortune to fix his wedding day on an important rehearsal date. Nothing daunted, he married his bride, and bore her off to the orchestral practice.

I was sorry not to be able to see the good work that Mr J. B. Johnson is planning at Shrewsbury School, but the Christmas term had not yet begun, so I took my way east along Watling Street towards the industrial district of Wellington, where nearby, at Hadley, is a well-known male voice choir.

The Hadley and District Orpheus Male Voice Choir has been in existence for thirty years and has at present 56 members, most of them ironworkers. It seems to have collected a very large proportion of the prizes that are going, and has some forty first and second wins at festivals to its credit. Mr Ray Lewis has conducted them since 1919. I traced him to the iron works where he is employed and got a few minutes' talk with him. I asked him what kind of songs his choir likes best to sing. He replied 'fighting songs', so when next they broadcast a performance, listen to this full-throated choir of ironworkers.

———

IV. MUSIC IN THE FIVE TOWNS

The Listener, 23 October 1935, pp. 731–2.

This district of the Potteries contains one of the most famous choruses in England. The North Staffordshire District Choral Society has made a considerable amount of musical history since its birth in 1901. A member of the committee proudly told me that the society had made Elgar, Delius, and Sir Thomas Beecham, and although this remark may be considered only the natural boast of a master potter when handling the finest clay, it certainly has facts to substantiate it. Elgar had been a name to conjure with ever since 1896 when he produced his cantata *King Olaf* in Hanley, so it was only fitting that this society should later be invited to give the first performance of *Gerontius* in London. The work had previously been given in Birmingham and Sheffield, but Londoners had not as yet had the opportunity of judging its greatness. The performance took place on June 6, 1903, in Westminster Cathedral, under the composer's direction, and in that vast and incomplete building, with the chorus keyed to high tension, it must have been an impressive one. Elgar himself, at any rate, was pleased, as his subsequent letter of gratitude to the chorus eloquently shows. After that he frequently visited the Five Towns to conduct his own music, and performances of most of his major works figure in the programmes.

The name of Delius first appears in 1908, when a performance of *Appalachia* was given. He seems to have conducted this himself—a rare role for him to play. This led to a deepening interest in Delius, for at the beginning of the next season, Beecham's name appears as conducting *Sea Drift*, the composer coming especially over from Paris to hear it. To show the enterprising vigour of this society it is worth mentioning that the same concert opened with a performance of Granville Bantock's *Omar Kháyyám* (Part II) and included the first performance of *Hero and Leander*, a tone-poem by Havergal Brian. Beecham must have been satisfied with the capabilities of the chorus, for in the next year, 1909, we find them at the Queen's Hall taking part under him in the first performance in this country of *A Mass of Life*.

That the same spirit of adventure animates the chorus today was vividly brought home to me at a rehearsal that I attended. The first concert of their season opens on October 24, and they were rehearsing Walton's *Belshazzar's Feast* for its repeat performance on that date. Under Mr John James, their conductor, the chorus made light of the difficulties of this work. The whole evening was indeed an object lesson in choral rehearsing. The elements of success were here—no time wasted, a complete understanding on the part of the conductor of what was to be done, and clear definite guidance for the different voices as to how best to do it. The chorus seemed to me to be very quick in taking up points. They have the same dexterity and nimbleness that I had seen displayed by the workers in the potteries that afternoon—throwers, decorators, painters, etc.—the maximum result achieved by the minimum exertion. They rehearsed later the choral section of the Ninth Symphony. High notes were taken as easily by basses as by sopranos. There is an absence of strain about this chorus of two hundred that is very restful. They take difficulties easily, and without worry, as indeed their expert training should enable them to do. Their first concert will be a series of mighty hammer blows that should set the season ringing.

This is the largest organization in this district of 270,000 people, but there are many other musical activities here from which I can only select a few. Those, for instance, who want something more operatic can attend the coming concert of the Stoke-on-Trent Choral Society which is giving a concert performance of *Carmen*, or they can join the Newcastle Clef Club which in past seasons has included amateur productions of Mozart operas in its syllabus.

Those who enjoy unaccompanied singing can hear the Potteries Choral Society which has been conducted by its founder, Mr Carl Oliver, for twenty-six years, or the Newcastle Male Voice Glee Union, which has a record of thirty-five years under Mr S. E. Lovatt. This latter is a choir of 70 voices and gives two concerts during its season. It is good to see in their programmes several works by their conductor; for from the scores he showed me he is an experienced writer in this medium. That there is a public demand for such organizations is shown not only by their vigorous length of life, but also by the fact that new ones are continually springing up. The Etruscan Choral Society started with a flourish last year under Mr Harry Vincent. A new chamber orchestra starts off this season conducted by Mr H. L. Jones, and is rehearsing good programmes of Vivaldi, Bach, Mozart, Boyce, Parry, and Warlock.

As in South Wales, the public here seems as yet to prefer choral concerts, but all the same a full symphony orchestra is consolidating its position. Mr John Cope is the conductor, and this North Staffordshire Symphony Orchestra has had its share in building up the reputation for musical enterprise that the district retains. I am told that it gave the second performance of the Elgar Violin Concerto in the same week as its first London performance, and that if it did not actually have the notoriety of playing *Finlandia* for the first time, it only missed this by a day.

Here again the enthusiasm of the players is for music, not for reward. This orchestra, like so many others, has had bad times, but even during the seasons of slump, when not sufficient money was forthcoming to launch public concerts, the members still continued to meet weekly for rehearsals, and at the present time there is a waiting list of performers who cannot be accommodated.

Some strong centralized policy will, I hope, be put forward to enable these orchestras to get on to a firmer financial basis. A few pounds this way or that makes all the difference to the coming season, and the majority of them have to live precariously, as it were, from concert to concert. It is not perhaps generally known how many of their conductors give generously of their time and experience for no financial compensation. These orchestras, of which there may be hundreds in the United Kingdom, fulfil as important a function in the musical life of the district as that of the choral societies. The problem of their maintenance must be grappled with.

It was surprising to me to learn of an orchestra assembled from the staff of attendants at a mental hospital—but close by Stoke there is a notably efficient one. Music is, I believe, an acknowledged part of the treatment in these institutions, and it will be remembered that Elgar, when a young man, held a five years' appointment as conductor in such a one. The Superintendent here is a keen musician and conductor, and perhaps new applicants for posts on the staff are not viewed unfavourably if they happen to pass musical as well as general tests.

Shrewsbury was unlucky in having inadequate accommodation for its concerts; the Potteries, on the other hand, have in the Victoria Hall, Hanley, an almost ideal place acoustically. Every conductor since Richter seems to have enjoyed conducting in it, there being good resonance without echo, and no dispersal of sound. I went to have a look at it, and from personal experience can say it has a certain drawback.

If there is one policy in which cinemas have shown the way, it is in the matter of comfort; there is hardly one of these cosy palaces where you cannot drop off for a few minutes' sleep quite comfortably. Even the cheapest seat will give you something reasonably soft to sit on, something reasonably soft to lean against. To go from these Babylonian pleasure-houses to the average concert hall such as the Victoria Hall is to exchange luxurious ease for a penitential rigour. If at the end of a day's work you have to choose between the armchair or the wooden plank, which calls you?

V. FOUR LANCASHIRE TOWNS

The Listener, 30 October 1935, pp. 779–80.

A heavy grey wet blanket rested on Manchester when I arrived there. It was impossible to distinguish details, everything was so sootily blurred. I was glad that the Hallé concerts were too famous to need further mentioning, and that the constricted scope of these articles precluded discussion of the many other musical organizations there. That dark obscurity did not invite investigation. So after spending an enjoyable evening listening to Mr R. J. Forbes and Mr Henry Holst play a new and finely wrought sonata by Procter-Gregg, I left for an unplanned tour of central Lancashire. I took four towns at random, each with a population of some 100,000 or over, and proceeded to unearth the condition of music in each one of them. The first place I chose was Rochdale, the birthplace of Gracie Fields, Norman Allin, and probably many other famous people.

It is a town of cotton spinning, iron founding, machine-making, blanket and calico production. It would seem that whatever improvement has been shown in other industrial districts during the last few years, these parts of Lancashire have still a long way to go to reach satisfactory conditions. There is ample evidence to prove that things are statically dull rather than progressively good. What money there is must therefore be spent on more basically important needs than music. It is left to private enterprise to provide for a town like Rochdale an escape from these prevailing monotonous conditions. I was glad to meet Mr F. Leach who conducts the Rochdale Philharmonic Orchestral and Choral Society. This is an old-established organization, and has during its life compiled a very varied list of important works given in Champness Hall. It can muster a full orchestra of fifty players, all local people, and possesses an excellent musical library of orchestral music.

One small but fairly sure test of a town's financial condition is whether their choral organizations are rehearsing new works or not.

Can the members afford to pay the prices which publishers ask for large-scale new choral scores, or must they fall back once again on performances of *Elijah* and the *Messiah*? I feel fairly certain that when you see the continual reappearance of these two veteran favourites year after year in provincial programmes the cause can be laid to economic considerations rather than to lack of enterprise. Mr Leach has another orchestra some fifteen miles off, in Todmorden, and combined these two forces some years ago in a notable performance of *Gerontius*.

I was interested to learn from him that he uses the orchestra to illustrate public lectures; and that he intends in November to analyse Sibelius's Fourth Symphony in this way. I have the impression in towns close to Manchester that the uphill fight of local musical societies is made harder by the fact that rich lovers of music in the neighbourhood support the Hallé Orchestra and not the musical enterprise at home. This may be inevitable, but it is none the less disheartening. It was therefore good to find in Rochdale a man like Mr Norman Scott who by his writings in the press, and by the musical atmosphere in his own house, is a source of encouragement to musicians generally here.

Another musician I called on was Mr George Whitaker. Born in Rochdale, he has remained working there. He obviously draws from the underlying vitality of the environment an impulse to creation, and it is all to the good of the town that it should be so. I saw a string quartet movement of his that was original and striking, and some songs in which the vocal line was modern and eloquent. Mr Whitaker also gives lectures here, and he has formed a chorus to which anyone can come, whether he or she possesses a good, bad or indifferent voice—a truly democratic body!

I learnt of two other musical societies in the town, the Rochdale Ladies' Choir conducted by Mrs Turner, and the Rochdale Festival Choir. This latter is a competition body, and is conducted by Mr Oscar Clifton. I went to see him at a rather inconvenient time, for his tobacco shop was besieged with customers, but he kindly told me that the chorus had only been started a few years, and had already several successes in competitions to its credit. It had been one of the small choruses represented at the Royal Command Concert at the Albert Hall.

My next stop was at Burnley. I had heard of the Municipal Concerts there, and was interested to see how they were run. Saturday afternoon was a bad time to see the Town Clerk, but I learnt enough to know that Burnley is well served musically. It has all the ingredients required: a public-spirited man who has bequeathed money sufficient to perpetuate concerts for the townspeople, a Municipal Council which manages the scheme practically, and a musician on the spot capable of taking artistic control.

With the annual funds available six concerts are given: three are orchestral, and are conducted by Mr T. H. Morrison, who comes from Manchester for these occasions; and three are choral and orchestral, and are conducted by Mr George Altham, who lives in Burnley. The prices of the seats are unusual. They range from 1*s*. 6*d*. to 3*d*. The concerts are enthusiastically attended—and no wonder! These prices are the prices of the future. No one is any longer going to pay 10*s*. (the payment of a year's listening to wireless music) for a single seat at a single concert. He will even jib at 7*s*. 6*d*., except for a very special occasion, and will consider 5*s*. the reasonable top price. There are evidences of this everywhere. I listened a few days ago to a splendidly diversified programme given by Mr Leslie Heward and the City of Birmingham Orchestra. There was obvious cordial enjoyment of each work. The cheaper seats were crowded, the expensive ones thinly held. I believe this matter of a few shillings' difference in price would have filled the hall, for Birmingham by this time must surely be aware of the quality they get in their symphony concerts. A new adjustment of prices for concerts to meet modern conditions is due. At Rochdale, for instance, the Philharmonic Society is giving an experimental Celebrity Concert—that is, an orchestral concert plus visiting soloists with box-office appeal. The price of every seat in the hall will be 1*s*. regardless of position, and anyone who wants to reserve his seat beforehand can do so for an extra 3*d*. I believe this experiment will be successful.

But to return to the Municipal Concerts of Burnley. Mr George Altham, who has only recently taken over these three choral concerts, is a young man who knows what he wants to do and is both enthusiastic and gifted. He has a good many of the musical strings in Burnley in his hands. He has his duties at the parish church, he conducts a male voice choir, and rehearses a brass band as well. Here is an example of a practical musician serving the town with his art and knowing that he is fulfilling a useful function in the town's life.

I descended into Blackburn latish one afternoon. The low sun was catching the forest of chimneys rising from the town, which lay in a slight autumnal haze, and from the hills above it had a strange and powerful beauty. I had heard of the performances of the B minor Mass given by Dr Herman Brearley with his picked chorus of thirty voices, and I was anxious to meet him. I was taken by his son, himself an oboe player, to the Cathedral, where Dr Brearley was about to play at a service. There was no chance to talk to him, but he contrived to pay me a most delicate compliment, for, without hint or suggestion, he began in his opening voluntary to build up an improvization of one of my own themes.

Operatic societies seem to thrive in the soil of Blackburn; many of the congregations at churches and chapels form groups that arrange these performances. There is shortly going to be a week of Shakespeare's *Midsummer Night's Dream* with Mendelssohn's incidental music. The orchestra will be conducted by Mr E. Romaine O'Malley, an old member of the Hallé Orchestra. One could stay in this district of central Lancashire a long time without exhausting its musical life, but time was a pressing factor, and I could only visit one more town.

I chose Bolton. I was glad I did so, because there I met Mr Thomas Booth, one of those men, a combination of successful business expert and sensitive artist, who are perhaps more common in America than here, but rare anywhere. He took me up to the top of Rivington Pyke where the view from this last spur of the Pennine Range is magnificent; I believe on a fine clear day one can see the Isle of Man. On the way he told me some of his musical problems. I hope one day Mr Booth will write a book and, in the simple and dramatic way he told me, describe how, after deciding on a professional musical career, fate in the shape of the new possibilities of steel construction flung him into the whirl of business activity and practical success. But for a coincidence, a heap of musical scores lying in his drawer might have been the evidence of his life's work instead of vast steel sheds that stretch on the horizon. Although a busy man on many committees, he carries the Bolton Choral Union and other musical work in Bolton on his shoulders. With a strong municipal interest he would not have to play so lone a hand.

Nearby, at Westhoughton, is the bandroom of the Wingate's Temperance Band, and the colliery from which the majority of the players are drawn. This band bears one of the most famous names in the country. You may hear it playing during the summer at Crewe or at Nottingham, in Yorkshire or in Wales, or for a week in uniforms of green, black, and gold trimmings its players may be drawing crowds on fine evenings to Hyde Park. These bands are a very distinctive feature in English musical life. Their members may be employed in some large motor-works, or in a boot and shoe factory, or a colliery, or in fact in any big industrial concern. The players are all amateurs in the sense that they have their own skilled work to do outside music, and only take engagements by courtesy of the factory or colliery management. But so great a hold have they on public esteem, and so valuable are they becoming as a good advertisement, that they are given every facility to perfect themselves. Their rules are nearly as rigid as those of football teams; they have to guard against the luring away of their best players by competing organizations, they are ever on the alert for new promising virtuosi, and the competitions culminating in the annual Crystal Palace festival are severe tests of training and discipline.

Mr Harold Moss, the conductor at Westhoughton, is a popular and excellent musician. He has been a member of the band, first as a trombone player and then as conductor, for 26 years, and has arranged many pieces for them. He described to me the difficulties of transcribing the *Oberon* Overture or a Mozart overture for brass band.

My last glimpse of Lancashire (and I was sorry to leave this friendly and forthright part of England) was the inside of a huge cotton mill, a miracle of inventive genius. Let anyone who thinks that a Honegger or a Mossolov[11] knows anything of mechanical noise visit a doubling room, covering over three acres in extent, where hundreds of bobbins and spindles gyrate, or a weaving shed, where great teams of automatic looms clack and roar. The rhythmic percussive effect is deafening. In this atmosphere of shrill thunder hundreds of human beings work eight-and-a-half hours a day, seemingly impervious to it all.

VI. SOME WEST RIDING CHORUSES

The Listener, 6 November 1935, pp. 835–6.

There are many surprises for anyone who does not know this part of England, and who visits it for the first time. One can, for instance, take a five-minute tram ride from City Square, Leeds, and suddenly come on a majestic twelfth-century Cistercian abbey. Hemmed in by railway and tram lines, blackened by smoke from neighbouring factories, stand the remains of Kirkstall Abbey; to get any comparison of its grandeur, one must compare it with Fountains.

Or to take a musical example, a few miles' journey from Huddersfield will land you in the Holme Valley, which possesses probably the finest male chorus in England—at least, I have never heard a finer myself. This Holme Valley Male Voice Choir of sixty or seventy tenors and basses —there are no male altos—is about to celebrate its silver jubilee. Twenty-five years ago it was founded by Mr Irving Silverwood, who has conducted it ever since, and has put the lasting impress of his personality on it. I heard them rehearse for an hour and a half works by Vaughan Williams,

---

[11] A reference to Artur Honegger's musical evocation of a locomotive, *Pacific 231* (1924), and Alexander Mossolov's constructivist *Iron Foundry* (1927).

Armstrong Gibbs, Sibelius and a particularly fine setting by Rutland Boughton of a poem called, if I remember rightly, 'The Blacksmith'. There are two distinct features of this choir. The first is the tone quality of the voices, especially the basses. They have an unforced power and resonance that are unknown in the South. The basses are like superb diapasons and their range is remarkable; they held in the Sibelius work a pedal note on low B-flat with powerful effect. I did not know that any but Russian basses could so easily take these very low notes, and I should be surprised if singers in any other part of England could get near them.

The second obvious characteristic about this chorus is the impression it gives of feeling what it is singing. Most choruses suffer from a pitiful self-consciousness in this respect; they are afraid to let themselves go. Whether they are singing about love or hate, war or peace, celebrating the most sacred parts of the Mass or a drinking bout, their faces and their voices remain serenely the same. They express a truly benevolent neutrality towards every emotion. The Holme Valley choir has too much character for this pale aloofness to music. Without undue dramatic emphasis or effects of a stunt-like nature, they give an eloquence to their vocal lines that is most moving. One can imagine what a stirring thing a perfect emotional blend of words and music could be in the singing of a large chorus. This choir has not reached perfection in this, but it is well ahead of all others I have heard. Each piece was sung in the appropriate style, from the delicate fanciful work of Armstrong Gibbs to the hard-hitting realism of Rutland Boughton's setting.

I understand that whatever money the choir makes on its engagements goes to swell a fund for the commissioning of new English works, and for the performance of more expensive works such as Strauss's and Holst's male voice settings which require orchestral accompaniment.

Composers are not, I believe, fully aware of the possibilities of such male voice choirs, or they would have provided them with a larger repertoire. I should like to see Mr Irving Silverwood inundated, during the year of his choir's jubilee, with works by leading English composers.

Two other organizations in Huddersfield celebrate anniversaries this season. The Glee and Madrigal Society, now conducted by Mr Roy Henderson, is on the eve of its diamond jubilee, while the Huddersfield Choral Society, which Dr Malcolm Sargent conducts, celebrates its centenary. This last is a large chorus of over three hundred voices. They were rehearsing under their chorus master, Mr Herbert Bardgett, the C minor Mass of Mozart and Elgar's *Music Makers*, for their opening concert. Here again one is impressed by the sustained power of the basses. There must be something in the air here that, besides being good for steel and wool, is good for voices too. All sections of the chorus are fine, the large number of contraltos, for instance, having the real deep character-istic tone. It would be a stimulating experience to have this chorus singing some time in the Queen's Hall.

Huddersfield is exceptional in its appreciation of music. It can be compared with South Wales, in that music is in the air. Concerts of this society are events of importance; they are social occasions with all the paraphernalia of cars, policemen, and crowds at the doors. Then there are the informal 'sings' of which I have been told—gatherings that take place during the summer and in the open, if it is fine. Different places in the neighbourhood of Huddersfield are chosen, a leader appointed, and anyone who likes can bring along a copy of the *Messiah*, *Elijah*, or *Creation*, and spend a Sunday afternoon singing.

Leeds is four times as big as Huddersfield, and its musical life is correspondingly more dispersed. There are two main large choruses, which contribute together with the Huddersfield to the famous Leeds Festival Choir. The older of these, and indeed the parent body, is the Leeds Philharmonic Society. It is now in its sixty-sixth season, and has a fine record of musical achievement. Since its foundation in 1870 it has sung under most of the famous conductors of the world, including, besides representative English conductors, Mottl, Nikisch, Richter, and Wein-gartner. Sir Charles Stanford was one of its permanent conductors, and was the first to take the society to Paris for concerts in 1906. Its conductor since the war has been Sir Edward Bairstow, and the chorus has greatly benefited from the fact that he takes every weekly rehearsal himself, coming over from York for that purpose. This constant discipline under a distinguished musician has been a great asset to the society. It is good to see the *Sea Symphony* of Vaughan Williams down in their programmes this season. This early and inspiring work was first produced at Leeds.

The other large chorus is the Leeds Choral Union. I heard them rehearsing the Verdi *Requiem* and the Third Act of *The Mastersingers* in the Philosophical Hall of the Museum. Their conductor is Mr Norman Strafford, who never wasted a minute, and never passed a fault—a stimulating rehearsal.

All these Yorkshire singers are great workers. They do not mind how often they repeat a phrase, as long as they get it right. It has been very invigorating to hear them at rehearsal, where without the special stimulus of an audience and in the early stage of preparation, they still manage to administer a current of higher voltage than most.

Both these societies have the advantage of the collaboration of the Northern Philharmonic Orchestra. I am hoping to return to Leeds once more to hear this orchestra give one of its symphony concerts under its permanent conductor, Mr John Barbirolli.

This article set out to deal exclusively with choruses (and in this connection it is disappointing not to have been able to include the famous choruses of Bradford and Sheffield), but there is one further experience I should like to record. England is traditionally a great country for organs and organists. I had heard much of the 'Armley' organ at Leeds, and wanted to hear it. Mr Herbert Bardgett (who has, by the way, his own chorus of a hundred, the New Choral Society) is the organist of St Bartholomew's Church and he kindly took me to see it. This organ has had rather a restless career. Built about 1870 by Schulze of Paulinzelle, Germany, for a private enthusiast in Leeds, it was later sold to a church at Harrogate, whence in 1879 it was once more removed to its present permanent home. Mr Bardgett played for me a Handel concerto and the *Third Organ Rhapsody* of Herbert Howells. The instrument has a particularly beautiful tone. Without being exceptional in reed quality, its choir flutes and clarinets are strikingly lovely and even in colour right up to the extreme notes, and the 8-foot diapason is mellow and satisfying.

It was interesting to compare it aurally with the fine organ in Durham Cathedral, which I heard as I passed through on my way to Newcastle. This has recently been completely renovated by Harrison (the 'Armley' organ has never been revoiced), and is a magnificent example of English work. Mr J. Dykes Bower has been the organist here for two years, and the cathedral is one of the numerous centres in England where, day in, day out, fine music is to be found. Whether there be five, fifty, or five hundred listeners, the music of Purcell, Byrd, Handel can be continually heard here beautifully sung. The intonation of the boys' voices could hardly be improved.

Once a year in the summer comes 'Miners' Day', and around these gigantic columns sit thousands of miners, who pour in from the neighbouring districts. They bring their own brass bands, and the sound must be impressive. The setting too seems exactly right—this superb towering Norman mass, looking half cathedral, half castle.

VII. NEWCASTLE

The Listener, 13 November 1935, pp. 891–2.

I am told that there are over forty different dialects in and around Newcastle. I can well believe it, for they go in for diversity up here, even in music. Indeed the variety and number of societies is bewildering. There is, to start with, the Felling Male Voice Choir, one of the most famous in the country, followed closely in competition by the Prudhoe Gleemen, the Wallsend, and the Bebside and District choirs. There are to be found here great names in the brass band world, notably those of St Hilda and the Harton Colliery; Newcastle maintains, in the performances of the Gateshead Operatic Society, a high standard in Gilbert and Sullivan operas, and it also possesses one of the most successfully run chamber music clubs in the North of England. This Newcastle Chamber Music Society has its fifty-first birthday this season, and a glance at the programmes shows that most of the great names in Europe have played at one time or another in the beautiful eighteenth-century Old Assembly Rooms.

Besides these more specialized societies there is a plethora of other choral and orchestral activities. It is plainly impossible to do justice to anything like the majority of them, and I shall therefore confine myself to a few, particularly those which revolve round one or other of the responsible musicians in the town. And if I seem in these articles to be mentioning too many individuals by name, the justification lies in the fact that it is these isolated personalities, each a dictator in his own sphere, who act and keep music going—not vague bodies, groups or committees. Committees are generally dominated by caution verging on fear—Ought we to? . . . Dare we *this* year? . . . What will the others say? . . . Is it in our tradition? . . . Must we? . . . Can we? . . . Isn't there a risk? Such phrases are constantly trembling on the lips of committees throughout the country, at least in music. Where things are happening, you can be sure that the initiative lies with one man, and if he is backed by a committee willing to shoulder and carry through his policy in its original strength, so much the better. This well-known fact of the decaying fungoid-like properties of the committee system is only introduced here to explain the use of the personal name associated with the activity described. Not to do so would be as misleading as to give a series of talks on the zoo without reference to the lion house.

The first personality I went to see in Newcastle was Mr George Dodds. He has three societies to direct, the Newcastle and Gateshead Choral Union, the Jarrow Philharmonic Society, and the Newcastle Symphony Orchestra. The first consists of a large chorus of over 250 voices. They sing fine music, and are preparing for this season the Mass in B minor and *The Apostles*. [12] They are accompanied by the Symphony Orchestra, an organization of some twenty year's growth, the members of which are amateurs. With professional leads, this orchestra also gives two orchestral concerts in the fine new City Hall, at one of which some distinguished guest conductor is invited to direct them.

---

[12] Oratorio (1903) by Elgar.

Mr Dodds took me down to a rehearsal of the smaller group, the Jarrow Philharmonic Society. Jarrow is, of course, one of the most notoriously hard-hit centres in the country. At one time I believe eighty-five per cent of its total population were out of work. But this little chorus of seventy has pluckily continued its fight for good music through the bad years. The two-hour rehearsal of *Acis and Galatea*[13] was a signal example of a man giving his whole skill and energy to bring about a positive achievement, and meeting in consequence with an instant wholehearted response.

My next visit was to Armstrong College. This originally small member of Durham University has by now grown to a community of 1,100 students. The music here is under the direction of Mr Sidney Newman, who conducts the Choral and Orchestral Society, the Madrigal Society, gives lectures and teaches. He is both a scholar and a practical musician. Among several experiments that he has introduced to make music a living force here is the institution of informal recitals that take place in the music room every Friday in the late afternoon—a very good time for listening. I heard an excellent violin recital given there in much the same surroundings as one finds in an Oxford or Cambridge musical club. Mr Newman also has taken over the conductorship of the Bach Choir Society founded by Dr Whittaker, and gives regular concerts with it in the King's Hall of Armstrong College. Although this small chorus naturally specialises in the singing of Bach—a four-day festival was given last April to commemorate the 250th anniversary of his birth—its programmes are full of the loveliest music of all periods. The choice and juxtaposition of works are dictated by a fine critical taste, which is again evident in the notes that enrich the programmes.

It is unfortunate that Newcastle is another of those big towns where there is not enough regular work to induce professional instrumentalists to stay. If they want to continue a professional career, they must go elsewhere; if they want to remain in Newcastle they must regard music as a side-line, and take to other work as a means of earning their livelihood. I learn here, for instance, of an excellent first horn player who has given up music and opened a bicycle shop. This kind of expedient, disheartening for local and successful music-making, is common throughout the country. It is to keep the remaining players together as a nucleus for the future, that so many of these local professional orchestras are started. Here there is the Newcastle Philharmonic Orchestra, which Dr Leslie Russell conducts. He is a comparative newcomer to the North, and followed Dr Bainton as head of the Conservatoire of Music. Four good programmes are announced by this orchestra, including performances of Vaughan Williams' *Job* and the

[13] Oratorio by Handel.

Rio Grande by Constant Lambert. This orchestra has started giving concerts up and down the Tyne, the members taking nothing but expense fees: this generosity enables them to give music in the poorest districts. In addition they gave last year two Children's Concerts under the scheme inaugurated by Mr Robert Mayer[14] throughout many parts of England. On these days 2,250 children packed the City Hall and enjoyed themselves.

Talking of large numbers, the biggest chorus in Newcastle is the YMCA Choral Society and numbers over 400. This combines with the YMCA Orchestral Society to give concerts under Dr J. E. Hutchinson. Profits on the concerts go to charity—and this is no mere matter of unsubstantial words either.

My last morning in Newcastle was perhaps the most interesting to me, because it provided a new angle on musical organization. Newcastle possesses one of the oldest schools in the country, the Royal Grammar School, with some 800 pupils in it. The directing spirit in music is Mr A. F. Milner, who with a staff of six or seven teachers has created real enthusiasm for music among the boys. He has been lucky in having a headmaster who believed that music could serve a wide educational and social purpose, and encouraged every effort towards its realization. He took up the cello himself so that he could tell from experience the difficulties besetting a young musician. The school possesses a set of good orchestral instruments and a comprehensive library of miniature scores and gramophone records, and lithographs its own orchestral parts. Out of the 800 boys in the school ranging from the age of 8 to 19, there are 230 learning music in some form or other. Of these 60 are wind players. There are three orchestras, graded according to technical proficiency, which combine to give an annual concert. There is a conducting class for the older boys, who can try their skill on the orchestra. The school can muster a string quartet, a piano trio, and a string trio, and the sixth form are at present analysing the Seventh Symphony of Sibelius with miniature scores and gramophone records.

I went to see the school on Saturday morning, which theoretically is leisure time, but in reality is devoted to music. One might have been in some Junior Conservatoire of Music. In one room a young oboist was practising, in another a budding trumpeter; an orchestral rehearsal was about to take place, and each string player was passing a tuning test before entering the hall. It reminded me irresistibly of the players' march past before each Promenade Concert with Sir Henry Wood at the saluting base. Finally, when they were all assembled, some thirty to thirty-five players, they attacked Handel's *Fireworks Music*. The orchestra is rich in

---

[14] In 1923.

clarinet tone, five instruments in all, including a bass and alto clarinet. As each player must have something interesting to play, this necessitates Mr Milner re-scoring works for each concert. One of the problems with these young players is to know what to do with them musically after they leave school. This difficulty is in part solved in Newcastle by encouraging the best of them to join the Northumberland Orchestral Society. In this way boys who have taken up instrumental playing for several years need not drop it just when they are becoming proficient.

Newcastle runs the biggest competitive musical festival in England, the North of England Musical Tournament. This took place this year during the later part of May and filled the whole of ten days. Almost every variety of music-making was represented in the 240 classes of competition, from Children's Singing Games (qualification under seven years) to Amateur Operatic Societies. Most characteristic of these northern tournaments are the classes for Sword Dancing the playing of the Northumbrian pipes. I have seen these small pipes, but never heard them. I am told an expert player can produce a real staccato, and can manage rapid runs with the ease and speed of a clarinettist.

―――

VIII. GLASGOW

The Listener, 20 November 1935, pp. 939–40.

A few miles from the mysterious beauty of Loch Lomond lies the second largest and grimmest city in the British Isles. But black and depressing as it can be in the late autumn rains, it holds for anyone who wants to explore, artistic treasures of priceless value. Who would expect to find, for instance, so many magnificent examples of painting as are collected in the Art Gallery here, or what musician would not be enthusiastic over the four great libraries of the city, culminating in the Mozart treasures of the University? These, by the way, have a rather interesting history. One of the early conductors of the Glasgow Amateur Orchestral Society was Commendatore Ladislao Zavertal, and on his return to Italy he gave to Glasgow University the Mozart relics which his father had received from Mozart's own son.[15] They consist of the last letter Mozart ever wrote to his

[15] Zavertal (1849–1942) came from Italy in 1872 to conduct the orchestra, later moving to London. He became a British subject in 1896, and in 1906 returned to Italy, whose king bestowed on him the title 'Cavaliere della Corona d'Italia'. His father, the Czech conductor Vaclav Hugo Zavrtal (1821–99), had received the relics from Mozart's son, Carl, in the 1850s.

wife Constance referring to performances of *The Magic Flute*, a sheet of MS. music, a portrait in oils of Constance, and a petition of Mozart's father on behalf of his son to the Emperor of Austria.

Of Mozart's music I heard not a note during my short stay, but of Bach's and Handel's a good deal. My first day was made memorable by hearing a rehearsal of the Bach Cantata Club under Dr Whittaker. In a top room of the spacious Scottish National Academy of Music, a group of students and staff were rehearsing for the opening recital of the series of six which they give each year. This choir was founded five years ago by Dr Whittaker when he came to Glasgow to be both Principal of the Academy and Professor of Music at the University.[16] It specializes in performances of the cantatas, and has already given one hundred and six of them in public. From the programme of the coming season I see that twenty-two of these masterpieces will be given at intervals between October and March. You can hear them all for five shillings, or if you are a student, for half a crown.

Is there any better value to be obtained elsewhere for such a sum?

The rehearsal was a joyous affair, not only because of the music, but also because of the spirit in which it was sung. The Scottish National Academy of Music is a splendidly roomy block of buildings, once the premises of a big club. It is equipped with large halls admirably adapted for choral, orchestral, and chamber music rehearsals. One is envious of the sound-proof teaching-rooms; I have never heard so quiet an academy. Adjoining is the Athenaeum Theatre used for the annual production of opera with past and present students as principals.

The next opera week will see staged three short works, Dibdin's *The Ephesian Matron*, a new ballet by Whittaker, *The Boy Who Didn't Like Fairies*, and Vaughan Williams' *The Shepherds of the Delectable Mountains*. This last work is to be introduced by a special prelude to music by Dowland, showing Bunyan, violin in hand, dreaming of the scene from the *Pilgrim's Progress* to be enacted.

A lot of modern English music finds it way into programmes here, for the Senior Choral Society makes a point of studying contemporary music. During the coming season Bax's *The Morning Watch*, Hadley's *La Belle dame sans merci*, and Moeran's *Nocturne* are all fixed for performance. I also saw on the notice-board in the hall an announcement by Dr Erik Chisholm of four concerts, intriguingly called 'Music of Exceptional Interest'. One of them is to be devoted to a study of Busoni's operas, and another to the music of Shostakovich.

The Glasgow Amateur Orchestra, to which I have already referred, has

[16] W. G. Whittaker (1876–1944) was principal, Scottish National Academy of Music (now Royal Scottish Academy of Music and Drama), 1929–41, and Professor of Music, University of Glasgow, 1929–41.

passed its diamond jubilee, and is one of the few societies that can muster a full amateur orchestra with all brass and woodwind. The conductor is Mr J. Peebles Conn, Professor of Violin at the Academy here, and one of the band of distinguished musicians who were interned at Ruhleben Camp during the war. I learnt from him that the players have formed chamber music groups amongst themselves, and enjoy playing chamber works for unusual combinations of instruments. Their invitation concerts contain many rarely heard works ranging from Beethoven's *Three Equali* for four trombones to modern wind and string chamber groups. Even the percussion section makes an appearance in *Two Military Marches and Polonaise* by Beethoven for piano (4 hands), bass drum, cymbals, side drum, and triangle.

Of choral societies there are many. The most famous, undoubtedly, is the Orpheus Choir[17] directed by Sir Hugh Roberton, but there are many others, Gaelic choirs, industrial choirs, socialist choirs. The competition festivals have brought many such choirs into being, the extra spur of rivalry urging on the formation of societies in factories and industrial concerns. These festivals have perhaps brought something of an alien character into music. It is as though no one would dive into the sea except to compete with other bathers. The advantages of becoming a strong and regular swimmer must be weighed against a possible indifference to water for its own sake.

The two choirs about which I have had an opportunity of learning at first hand were the Glasgow Orion Choir and the Glasgow Choral Union. The first was formed in 1926 by Mr William Robertson to sing madrigals. Their first object was to enjoy themselves and the next to induce people to come and enjoy their programmes with them. In both these aims they can be said to have succeeded. They give two concerts of their own on successive days in March, and also keep in practice with festival work and outside concerts. The programmes are full of fine Elizabethan and contemporary work, and embody a type of music not perhaps touched by other societies in the neighbourhood.

The Glasgow Choral Union is a much larger chorus, which combines with the Scottish Orchestra in three of their Symphony Concerts. I heard a rehearsal of this chorus under its conductor, Mr Wilfrid Senior. It is a body of finely disciplined voices, excellent in rhythm and attack. In few choruses can one find basses that are so powerful and yet quick in their leads. There was no tendency to drag here. Two Handel works gave them good opportunities to show their prowess, and as a complete contrast

---

[17] The Glasgow Orpheus Choir (1901–51).

Debussy's *La Damoiselle élue* was also included in the programme. The women sang this last beautifully.

I should add that the remainder of the concerts of the Choral and Orchestral Union of Glasgow are allotted to the Scottish Orchestra, one of the finest in Great Britain. This orchestra, in which there are many young players, gives thirteen Tuesday-night and sixteen Saturday-night concerts during their three months' season in the city, all under the conductorship of Mr John Barbirolli.[18]

Every musician has heard of the performance of *The Trojans* given in full last March by the Glasgow Grand Opera Society, surely one of the most ambitious gestures every made by amateurs. This society has grown from quite modest beginnings. It started in 1905 unostentatiously to provide a chorus that could support the Moody–Manners Opera Company[19] when it visited the town. As confidence grew the singers began to wonder why they did not give performances of their own, hence the early productions of *Carmen* and *Faust*. From 1916 onwards every year the society staged a week's opera, though it did not stray very far from the well-worn track. Lately a much more progressive spirit has been shown, and with the arrival of Dr Erik Chisholm as conductor, it was decided to put into rehearsal operas that have rarely, if ever, been presented in Great Britain. This gives to the society a personality very different from other amateur operatic organizations. It automatically avoids wounding comparisons with professional opera companies, and also enables the members to feel that they are contributing a real service to music. Hence we find given in 1934 the first performance in Great Britain of *Idomeneo*, and in 1935 that of *The Trojans*, the two parts being given on successive nights during the week. The President, Mr Meighan, himself one of the original members, made very clear to me the immense difficulties that underlie the simple announcement that a week of opera will be given.

Let me emphasize again that all the members are amateurs, that they have their own work to do all day, and that they are only available in the evenings or at the week-end; this applies to principals, chorus, painters, designers, costume makers, and the majority of the orchestra. The following is something like the schedule of rehearsal possible under amateur conditions, supposing the opera week to be fixed some time in March. The chorus and principals, mainly by weekly rehearsals, are supposed to know their notes by heart before Christmas. In the new year

[18] The Scottish (now Scottish National) Orchestra was founded in 1891. Barbirolli was its conductor 1933–6.

[19] A touring company (1898–1916) formed by the Irish bass and impresario, Charles Manners (1857–1955), and his wife, the soprano, Fanny Moody (1866–1945).

the producer takes them and 'puts them on the floor'. A suitable hall is hired, and chalk marks indicate scenery, entrances and exits, etc. During this time the students of the School of Art are busy with the scenery, and as many people as possible are rounded up to make and fit costumes. The week preceding the actual performance reveals a considerable tightening up of rehearsals; there is one every night, still held, of course, in the substituted hall, as the theatre is busy with touring companies until the last minute. On Saturday the opera is run through from beginning to end supported by a nucleus of an orchestra. On Sunday the theatre is entered for the first time, and now takes place the only proper producer's rehearsal on the actual stage. The conductor does not get a chance to direct a full orchestral rehearsal until Monday morning, the morning of the first performance. The chorus are not there, because naturally they are at their daily work elsewhere, but with luck the principals will have managed to be free. I feel sure that this rehearsal takes place in the nerve-racking atmosphere of last-minute adjustments on the stage amongst all the inevitable hammering and general confusion. When the curtain rises in the evening, the chorus, full orchestra, and principals really meet together for the first time.

Compare this nightmarish triumph over practical difficulties with the almost error-proof time-table of a subsidized opera house on the Continent, and you will get the measure of Dr Chisholm's and his committee's audacity and enterprise. Last year with *The Trojans*, difficult though it must have been, they had the advantage of continuity of scenery and costumes. This year they are staging two entirely different operas by Berlioz, *Benvenuto Cellini* and *Beatrice and Benedict*. Each of them naturally demands a totally different cast in a totally different setting. The first obstacles are already overcome. The music has been obtained—no slight difficulty this—and translations written in. It is good to see Professor Dent's name announced as having undertaken the English version of *Cellini*. Not only is it an encouragement that he is helping, but it ensures that the translation will have distinction and dramatic value. Mr Guy McCrone is doing a similar service in the second opera.

Dr Chisholm showed me the full scores of the operas. There are many musical problems to solve; hidden brass bands, a guitar orchestra, and an important ophicleide[20] solo are some of them. I expect he knows that an example of this obsolete instrument lies in the Museum of the Scottish National Academy of Music. The producer of these operas will be Mr William McLean, whose students are busy on the décor. These works of Berlioz are planned for production in March. I hope contingents from

---

[20] A keyed brass instrument once used in military bands and later superseded by the bass tuba.

different centres of England will make journeys to see them. It should be known that every penny the society makes is handed over to charity. Up to 1931 over £3,000 had been thus distributed, and even on the expensive production of *The Trojans* £70 was raised. Each year, in fact, the society starts financially from near zero and may incur as much as £1,200 in expenses for the forthcoming week of opera. It relies entirely on public recognition of its boldness, and I hope many, both in Glasgow and outside, will remember this. I shall certainly be at the performance myself.

IX. SOUTHWARD

The Listener, 27 November 1935, pp. 987–8.

Before coming south I paid one more visit to Leeds to hear the Northern Philharmonic Orchestra give a concert in the Town Hall. It was my only chance of getting an impression of this orchestra of seventy local professional players. Adolf Busch had come to play the Beethoven violin concerto, and the orchestral items were the *Oberon* Overture and the Second Symphony of Elgar. At this concert, for which Mr John Barbirolli had taken two sectional rehearsals and one full orchestral rehearsal, there was a very large audience; in fact every seat both in front and behind the orchestra seemed to be taken. Great enthusiasm prevailed, and one came away feeling that Mr Barbirolli has created an orchestra here of which the city may well be proud.

From Leeds I took the road to York and then turned south to Lincoln. I had never been in Lincoln before, and my first view of it was unforgettable. Alongside the road ran a canal, and the spreading coloured canvas on the barges emphasized the peculiar beauty of this fen country. In the distance the towers of the gigantic cathedral pierced the evening mists. How difficult to associate the invention of military tanks with so peaceful a place.[21]

A cathedral city has one great advantage in music. The position of the organist gives the holder a natural leadership in its musical life. The appointment implies an influence stretching well beyond the precincts of the cathedral, and when it is held by a musician of considerable gifts, this influence can be very widespreading indeed. Dr Gordon Slater's personality in music, for instance, is felt throughout the whole of Lincolnshire. He

---

[21] 'Little Willie', a prototype of the tank later used by the British army in France, was completed at the workshops of Foster's of Lincoln in Sept. 1915.

is a man of unwearying energy and optimism; he travels all over the county, teaching, lecturing, organizing, giving practical help and counsel. As is to be expected, he conducts the local chorus and amateur orchestra, without which no town of over 50,000 inhabitants can be regarded nowadays as civilized. The voices in the fen country are not generally judged to be very good—it is surprising how the quality differs with the locality—but the Lincoln Musical Society seems exceptional in this respect, possessing fine contralto and bass sections. Perhaps this is due to the influence of Yorkshire voices, which helps to give a brilliant quality to the singing. Besides two concerts each season in the Corn Exchange, the chorus gives annual performances of the *Matthew Passion* and the *Christmas Oratorio* in the cathedral. I heard a rehearsal of the Lincoln Orchestral Society during my visit. Dr Slater worked hard that evening, for besides taking the orchestra through an arduous programme, he rehearsed the Bach D minor Piano Concerto, in which he is playing the solo part.

One of the ways in which the organist of the cathedral can influence the music of the diocese is exemplified in the twenty-eighth report of the Church Music Society. This society was inaugurated in 1906, to help in the choice and performance of music best suitable for all ecclesiastical occasions and to make available by publication the music recommended. The society supplies information and advice to its members, issues publications, organizes lectures and summer schools, and generally stimulates interest in the masterpieces of church music. It embraces in its scope every choir from that of the largest cathedral to that of the humblest village church. In Lincolnshire, for instance, the results are very striking. Through Dr Slater and his assistant at the cathedral, Dr Willis Grant, sixty or seventy village, town, or country churches are influenced. Every three years a festival is held in the cathedral to which all these choirs come to sing. Over a thousand singers on this occasion meet together and take part in fine music. Six weeks before this day sectional rehearsals are taken in the various villages, some of them over forty-five miles apart. The smallest church choir has the opportunity of benefiting from this musical experience. Besides these triennial meetings smaller festivals take place in village churches, so that the feeling of unity is not allowed to be lost.

In connection with the Church Music Society, I heard a lecture given in the Chapter House of the cathedral by Dr Ernest Bullock, organist of Westminster Abbey. He made some wise and practical suggestions as to the musical ties that should knit congregation, choir, organist, and parson together. Coming from such an authority, the penetrating and helpful criticisms should go far to raise the standard of music in any place where performance and choice of music are still poor.

Another organization that touches the humbler aspect of music is the Lindsey Rural Community Council. This was started three years ago by inviting four neighbouring villages to form choral societies under a visiting professional tutor. It was not known whether their villages had any musical talent or even wanted to spend their leisure hours in this way. The suggestion, however, proved very popular, and in a short time the four societies had a total membership of a hundred. In each society an amateur conductor was found to take three out of every four rehearsals, the professional musician taking the remaining one in rotation. Later in the same year four more villages formed a second group on the same plan, and some villages were combining in twos and threes to give informal concerts. This logically led to the whole eight societies meeting together in Lincoln for a combined effort.

To show how rapidly a movement like this can spread, it should be noted that this last spring, in a microphone impression of the Lincolnshire countryside, over 500 voices drawn from these village societies sang groups of madrigals. During the last singing festival held on April 29 in Lincoln, music by Morley, Dowland, Gibbons, and Handel was sung by these groups of singers, the large majority of whom could not have read a note of music a few years ago. This group system has obvious advantages. Combined rehearsals overcome the difficulty of the balance of vocal parts, local conductors learn their technique by watching visiting professionals, and looked at from a social point of view the barriers that often exist between villages are swept aside in pursuit of a common pleasure.

My last impression of Lincoln was hearing evensong in the cathedral, where the choir sang the Second Service of William Byrd. The Magnificat and Nunc Dimittis contain solos for treble, alto, and tenor voices and a quartet for the unusual combination of two trebles and two altos. There is also an independent organ accompaniment, a feature not met with again in any service until more than 200 years later. Byrd himself was organist of Lincoln Cathedral, and his music is constantly played and sung here to the joy of all who come.

I arrived in Peterborough during the final rehearsals for the Festival of the Friends of the Cathedral. This was to consist of two plays staged in the cathedral, a lecture on its architecture and history, and a Festival Service. In this last the Master of the Music, Dr Henry Coleman, was to conduct a choir of a thousand voices, orchestra, and organ. He very kindly took me into the cathedral late one evening and let me hear the fine organ and the beautiful acoustics of this giant building. Looking up, one could just distinguish the curiously painted wooden ceiling of the nave, with its pictures of musicians as a fourteenth-century artist conceived them.

A few miles from Peterborough lies Oundle School. One realizes on going over it how greatly the attitude of educational authorities towards music has changed. Music is no longer regarded as an oddity to be squeezed ungraciously into a boy's play hours; and boys who want to study music are no longer looked upon as inherently peculiar. Music is now a regular part of the curriculum, and in progressive schools bears an important part in the social life. Oundle School has 600 boys on its roll, and when music is given every boy takes some part in the performance. The school has a regular chorus of about 250, and an orchestra of 40. These numbers include the staff, and are made up of masters and boys who can sing or play an instrument and have a natural aptitude for music. That leaves over 300 who, because they have no ear, or because their voices are breaking, are regarded as outside the musical section of the school. They form the non-choir. They attend practice, bringing copies of the music to be sung, and join in unison singing at special passages which are marked for them. These are short easy phrases, generally in the treble or bass parts, which are learnt by heart. For instance, if the school is singing sections of the B minor Mass, which it has done on six different occasions, the non-choir probably sings the first few bars of the opening Kyrie, or the start of the Sanctus, taking the bass octaves. In each chorus there will be something for them to do which will keep their interest awake, and gradually train their artistic sense. The conductor, Mr C. M. Spurling, or Mr J. A. Tatam, faces the body of the hall, which is completely filled with the boys of the school, the chorus in front, the non-choir behind. On the platform behind him sit the members of the orchestra. The effects at moments is of the whole audience taking part.

In the Festival of the Friends of Peterborough Cathedral the boys of Oundle School performed the seventeenth-century mystery play by Calderón, *The Great World Theatre*. Here again the same plan was put into practice. Some twenty-five boys played the acting roles. The rest of the school went to the cathedral to take part in the incidental music, sitting in the choir for that purpose.

In the same spirit in which the Lindsey Rural Community Council introduced singing into small villages, the Hertfordshire Rural Music School has revived instrumental playing. This artistic enterprise in Hertfordshire began in 1929 and is the work of Miss Mary Ibberson, its founder and director. The natural love of music differs very considerably from county to county. In many parts of England it is comparatively easy to set enthusiasm alight, in others it is almost impossible to strike a spark. I feel that the struggle in Hertfordshire to make country districts aware of the pleasure of playing music may have been no easy one, and Miss Ibberson's achievement compels all the more admiration on this account. It began six years ago as a query—'Can village communities be persuaded to start playing instrumental music together?' To answer this question, a music room was hired, a staff of local teachers assembled, and the countryside invited to learn string instruments. Weekly classes of adults and children were formed, and a small sum was asked for professional lessons. With a little encouragement the idea took root and grew. At the present time there are 70 classes with over 750 students. It should be stated (I quote from the issued pamphlet) that 'the school is by constitution a charity, its main object being to bring competent instruction in music within the means of village people, and funds have to be raised to supplement class fees'. In other words here is arduous and possibly unnoticed work in pursuit of a high unselfish aim. Throughout England there are many such experiments, bringing into remote districts a practical knowledge and love of music.

X. CORNWALL

The Listener, 4 December 1935, pp. 1035–6.

To a musician Cornwall and Wales seem to possess characteristics in common. Not only do the two languages sound alike, but the voices, especially as you travel further west, take on the same vibrant singing tone. The Cornishman, like the Welshman, has a natural love of music, and wherever you go in the Duchy you are sure to find evidences of this. The large crowds at football matches while away the time singing, the innumerable chapels have their choirs, the clay workers, miners, and fishermen have their brass bands, which meet for annual contests at Bugle each summer, and there is a notable interest in string playing. Cornwall has no great central city; it is a county of small scattered communities, with the larger towns on its more westerly boundaries. I started on the borders of Devon and zigzagged down the peninsula towards Land's End.

My first stop was at Liskeard, where there is a well-established amateur orchestra. Liskeard is only a small place of some 4,700 inhabitants, so that it is all the more to its credit that it can raise an orchestra of 40 and collect 600 people together to listen to orchestral music. The incentive here is provided by Dr C. E. G. Busbridge, who founded the orchestra immediately after the war and has conducted it ever since. He is, by the way, a doctor of medicine, not of music. He gives with his orchestra an annual concert as Liskeard in the spring and several educational concerts in Truro. His programme last February included Beethoven's Fifth

Symphony, Handel's *Water Music*, and Bach's Concerto in C minor for two pianofortes.

I was glad to hear from him that his list of patrons was not a camouflage one. They support the concerts in the most practical way—i.e. by attending them.

At Wadebridge, some twenty miles west of Liskeard, I learnt of a good example of musical co-operation. The associated Musical Societies of Cornwall embrace, besides Wadebridge, the small towns of Helston, Par, Bugle, St Austell, Port Isaac, and Tavistock just over the border. Each of these places has its own choral society and arranges its concerts on a co-operatively planned basis. At the end of March a week's music is organized, each society giving its own programme in its own town.

On Monday, for instance, it will be the Tavistock Chorus, on Tuesday the Par Chorus, on Wednesday the Wadebridge Male Voice Choir, and so on. Soloists from London or from the district are engaged for the whole week to go from town to town and sing the solo parts in whatever works are being given. Each society is responsible for the hospitality and transport of soloists in its own region. By sharing the same singers the expenses of concert-giving are considerably reduced, and as for the soloists, they get a good week's trip in Cornwall, and a different audience every night. Mr Felix George is the Secretary of this society, and I believe his plan has solved the problem of these scattered choral units by enabling them to give good concerts and yet keep solvent.

It is the medical men in Cornwall, seemingly, who have a large share in keeping music going. Dr A. F. Wilson-Gunn conducts the male voice choir in Wadebridge, and Dr C. Rivers in Redruth is responsible for the Cornwall Symphony Orchestra. I went to see Dr Rivers in his surgery where full scores of Elgar jostle books on medical research and the volumes of *Grove's Dictionary* separate treatises on diseases. Dr Rivers, an enthusiastic student of music since his Cambridge days, started the Cornish Symphony Orchestra in 1920 and has generously supported it for these fifteen years. I hope that he will find it possible to carry out his ambition to give a performance of *Gerontius* in Truro Cathedral. It would be a fitting gesture if some group of music lovers could find a means to make this dream a reality.

I motored over one wet day to St Anthony in Roseland, a little village at the end of the Roseland Peninsula, to see the Misses Radford. I wanted to learn about the Falmouth Opera Singers, an organization that has for the last few years done some remarkable work. These two sisters can between them undertake most of the practical work of opera production. If necessary they translate the libretto, they are good players themselves, and in addition one of them conducts and the other stage-manages. They have also a seriousness of purpose that stamps their work with artistic importance. Those who take part in the performances are chiefly local people. The St Mawes Choral Society acts as supporting chorus, and the company is lucky in having Mrs Peters and Mr Tregenna, two local amateurs with fine voices, to sing principal roles.

To celebrate the 250th Handel anniversary, the Opera Singers have just given three dramatic performances of *Athalia* at the Princess Pavilion, Falmouth. This is the first time in England that this oratorio has been presented on the stage. I saw a little model of the set in Miss Radford's studio, on which all the groupings of chorus and principals are worked out. I was also interested to see the full score, which was new to me. It has a beautiful aria for contralto and some fine eight-part choruses. A list of the operas produced may be of interest, as showing what this society has accomplished: *Orpheus* and *Iphigenia in Tauris*, by Gluck; *La Clemenza di Tito* and *Il Seraglio*, by Mozart; *King Arthur*, by Purcell; *Samson* and *Saul*, by Handel; and three modern English operas, *The Travelling Companion*,[22] *The Shepherds of the Delectable Mountains*,[23] and *Prince Ferelon*.[24]

In addition to opera the Misses Radford are influential in promoting the annual Music Competitions Festival held at Truro and are leading members of the Falmouth Music Club. This club gives programmes of chamber music played by members, arranges lectures and visits by professional musicians, and organizes an annual free concert for school children. On this occasion a prize is given to the child who writes the best essay on the concert. I saw excerpts from some of these essays which in candour could give points to music critics generally.

My last stopping-place in Cornwall was Penzance. Near by are the fishing villages of Marazion, Mousehole, and Newlyn: all three possess good male voice choirs. In Penzance itself there is a well-established Orchestral Society, which you may have heard broadcast. It is entering on its thirtieth year, and the amateur members of which it is mainly formed come from all parts of Western Cornwall. Three annual concerts are generally given, and the programmes are good ones. At the next concert, for instance, the symphony is C major by Schubert, and the other orchestral items are the dances from *Prince Igor* and the overture *Fingal's Cave*.

This orchestra, which attracts a large audience to its concerts, has collected a fine library of music and owns its own premises for rehearsals. Mr William Barnes, who conducts the society, has had a strong influence

[22] Stanford (1926).
[23] Vaughan Williams (1921–2).
[24] Nicholas Gatty (1919).

on orchestral playing in the West of Cornwall. Besides directing the Penzance Orchestral Society, he has another orchestra in Falmouth, and leads for Dr Rivers in the Cornwall Symphony Orchestra. From my short meeting with him I should gather that he stands no slipshod playing, either from pupils or from orchestras.

In the list of players in the Penzance Orchestral Society are the names of Mr and Mrs William Lloyd. Their son, Mr George Lloyd, is a composer of promise. His opera *Iernin* attracted attention when he conducted it himself first at Penzance and later in London, and although only twenty-two years of age he is the composer of three symphonies. Another Cornish musician of distinction in Penzance is Mr Donald Behenna. He conducts the Penzance Choral Society, which gives two concerts a year. This coming concert in December has a particularly good programme and includes 'A Cornish Christmas Carol, words by Henry Jenne, late Grand Bard of Cornwall, music by Peter Warlock—to be sung in the Cornish language'.

Cornwall is too scattered to be easily accessible in one visit, and there are many things I have had to miss. I should have liked to see the work that Miss Rowbottom is doing in Camborne with instrumental players, and I am sorry to miss hearing such a fine band as that of St Dennis, but there is plenty of evidence from what I have seen to show that music is well established in this corner of England, and that there is aptness in the motto 'Bedhens Kernow en Kesenyans'.[25]

I want here to say something about the National Federation of Music Societies,[26] an important and newly-formed organization to which belong the large majority of the active musical societies throughout the United Kingdom. Anyone who has read these articles must have realized that it is difficult for the hundreds of smaller choral and orchestral societies to continue on their own responsibility. Their expenses are considerable, and in the poorer districts the members can only afford a small contribution towards the cost of music, rent of hall, printing of programmes, and the fees of soloists. It was obvious that if musical societies in different parts of England could be brought by a central control into closer touch, they would profit by the exchange of ideas, and solve their major artistic and financial problems by some form of co-operation. The Incorporated Society of Musicians[27] has been dealing with this problem for the last few years, and establishing Regional Federations of Music Societies in dif-

[25] 'Let Cornwall be in harmony', the motto traditionally displayed on banners at the Cornwall Music Festival. I am grateful to Mr Barry Smith for this information.

[26] Founded in 1935 to advance 'the art and the practice and the public performance' of music.

[27] An association of professional musicians founded in 1882 and concerned generally with musical education. It was reconstituted in 1928 for 'the promotion of the art of music and the maintenance of the honour and interests of the musical profession'.

ferent parts of England. This has been done on a geographical basis. Cornwall, for instance, is served by the South Western Federation, which also includes Plymouth, Sidmouth, Torquay, and Exeter. It issues calendars of the season's concerts in its area, helps in administrative work, serves as the headquarters for the exchange of information, and generally binds together its various musical bodies.

This division of large geographical districts into organized regional federations has been successful. It was based on a careful and comprehensive statistical survey carried out by the Incorporated Society of Musicians a few years ago. At their London offices can be seen a fully documented record of the musical and financial state of hundreds of these societies —societies in which amateurs and professionals combine together for the love of music. Profit-making is not their aim; their only wish is to meet expenses.

A further plan to unite these societies is now in progress of completion. Last February delegates from the various regional federations met together at York, and the establishment of a national federation was discussed. It will have the support of the Carnegie United Kingdom Trustees, and all these keen struggling societies will have for the first time the generous financial aid that they deserve. More adventurous programmes can then be attempted, better performances given, and in consequence large audiences attracted. An immense amount of spade-work has had to be done to clear obstacles and build up a united executive federation such as this. A particular debt of gratitude is due to Mr Frank Eames, Secretary of the Incorporated Society of Musicians, for guiding this scheme to practical achievement. Amateur societies will soon be realizing what they owe to his hard work and ability. I shall in my last article make suggestions concerning the relationship between this National Federation and the British Broadcasting Corporation.

XI. IPSWICH AND NORWICH

The Listener, 11 December 1935, pp. 1083–4.

A friend told me before I started for Suffolk that Ipswich was 'a sleepy old place' and hinted that there was more than a touch of Dickens about its 'quaint old-world atmosphere'. I was all the more surprised then at seeing from a slight rise on the London road a large modern city spread itself out, a city of ninety thousand people, famous for its engineering works, and striking the observer as a town strictly contemporary in its outlook. Ipswich has grown rapidly in the last few years and appears generally prosperous. It is discouraging therefore to the musician to find music here in rather an uncertain and hazardous position. Just after the war music in Ipswich received a great impetus, but the enthusiasm seems to have somewhat cooled, and a rather disorganized transitional period has set in. There are far too many small musical activities at work, each a self-contained unit unwilling to co-operate with the others. As a result it is impossible at the present time to perform a work like the *Sea Symphony* of Vaughan Williams, because the resources necessary for a big choral work are dissipated.

I heard of nine quite different choral societies operating in this town. The concerts of the Bach Choir take place in St Mary Le Tower Church and are conducted by Mr E. Percy Hallam. Mr Hallam also directs two societies in Bury St Edmunds, the Choral Society and the Bach Choir, and the two Bach choirs combine together in performances of the *St John Passion*. Then there are three choral societies conducted by Mr Jonathan Job, organist of St Mary Le Tower Church—the Ipswich Choral Society, the Male Voice Choir, and the Ladies' Choir. The first of these, a mixed choir, originally had a large membership, reaching at one time after the war the huge figure of 400, but it has dwindled sadly in numbers and only about 80 will take part in this year's performance of Handel's *Alexander's Feast*. The Male Voice Choir on the other hand is having a great success. The choir gives one concert a year, varying the unaccompanied choral works with solo items. The society is enabled by the comparatively small expense attached to *a cappella* singing to engage the finest soloists. Suggia, Szigeti, Elisabeth Schumann, the Lener String Quartet have all recently performed at these concerts. In consequence the hall is packed, and the collaboration of famous players with this fine body of singers gives these concerts a special character. The Male Voice Choir numbers about seventy members with a good percentage of male altos to help the first tenor line. It certainly seems a waste of good material if these fine tenors and basses do not join the Choral Society *en bloc* for an annual perform-ance of some extended choral work. A policy of isolation greatly restricts the choice of possible music. At present the mixed chorus is too small to tackle the difficulties of a big work with confidence. Seventy extra men would just tip the scales.

This plea for collaboration also applies to the Ladies' Choir, although women are as a rule more ready for co-operative effort than men. This choir of 60 has only been lately formed, and provides, as Mr Job said, an opportunity for that large section of women's voices which are neither true sopranos nor true contraltos.

Ipswich and Norwich

The Ipswich Orchestral Society is also suffering a little from local musical conditions. Although there is a large string section of amateurs led by Miss Cubitt, the majority of wind and brass players have to be fetched from London for the concerts. For many years the orchestra has been conducted by Mr Edgar Whitby, who comes from London to rehearse it, but has a long and continuous teaching connection with Ipswich. I cannot help feeling that the future of this orchestra would be much more assured if the municipal authorities showed a lively interest in the music of the town. Among the players I noticed the name of Mr Stanley Wilson, a composer whom I have not seen for some years. He directs the music at the Ipswich Grammar School, and I was glad to have the opportunity of meeting him again and hearing some of his recent work. He played to me on the piano sketches from his Double Concerto for violin, viola, and orchestra, which I shall hope soon to hear in its true instrumentation.

A journey of forty miles through country of spacious horizons brings one to Norwich. Norwich is only half as large again as Ipswich, but it has various advantages that make it one of the most attractive musical towns in the whole of England. It is a cathedral city, and so possesses a natural focal point for its artistic expression. England is very lucky in this respect: there must be forty or fifty cathedral towns dotted throughout the country, each a potential centre for music and musicians. In these you can hear well-trained choirs, fine music, and often superb organ playing. It is clear that the post of cathedral organist is a coveted one, carrying as it does the possibility of considerable musical influence. And yet many talents thus employed are apt to be wasted. On this journey of mine I have been forcibly struck by the indifferent attitude that ecclesiastical authorities generally adopt towards music. Music has always been religion's most serviceable handmaid. If these cathedrals are ever to be thronged again with worshippers, the compelling power of music must be used in all its dramatic strength. The help of music is often discouraged, or but barely recognized. In Catholic countries the cathedral is filled night and day; it belongs to the people and they use it as a home, a refuge, a place where the eye and the ear are soothed by beauty. In England the cathedral is too often a shut or empty tomb, where the lonely footstep echoes alarmingly. I sat last Saturday in the north transept of Norwich Cathedral listening to evensong. A Byrd service was being sung, followed by an anthem of Charles Wood, its scoring for altos, tenors, and basses without treble voices sounding strangely mediaeval. The magnificent massive Norman columns, the majesty of the language, the nobility of Byrd's music formed a harmony of beauty and dignity. About twenty of the 140,000 inhabitants of Norwich were there.

I walked round the cloisters afterwards with Dr Heathcote Statham, organist of the cathedral. From one point there was a superb view of the soaring spire rising without effort from the Norman tower. What a magnificent setting these cloisters would make for a performance of one of Handel's dramatic oratorios! We stood there planning the arrangement of the orchestra buttressed into one corner of the great stone square, the chorus and principal singers on a raised dais along one side, while trumpeters and further singers in the tower would add splendour of sound. There is certainly no artistic obstacle to the realization of this project. Norwich possesses in its own right the musician and the dramatic producer.

As it is, most of the music in Norwich takes place elsewhere. The Norwich Philharmonic Society is one of the oldest and most honourable musical societies in England—it is not far off the celebration of its centenary. With the exception of a few principals among the woodwind, the whole of the orchestra is recruited from local musicians. For the last seven years it has been conducted by Dr Statham, a strong and sensitive musical personality, whose programmes show aristocratic taste and liberal sympathies. The society gives a season of five concerts, including one chamber concert, and a carol service in the cathedral. Both chorus and orchestra are well disciplined and capable of meeting the demands made by contemporary composers. The impression of 'style' is further emphasized by the beauty of the fifteenth-century St Andrew's Hall, in which the concerts are held.

Norfolk is a county particularly rich in native composers. At the present time the three best-known names are those of Moeran, Patrick Hadley, and Benjamin Britten. Works of the first two are included in the Philharmonic programmes this season, and a new work by the last named is announced in the prospectus of the coming Norwich Triennial Festival.[28] The syllabus of this festival next year is a model of its kind. The committee is obviously determined to give a Norwich Festival, and not just a festival in Norwich—there is a distinction here that should be more often observed. New works by its own composers will be given, its own conductor will share with Sir Thomas Beecham the honours of the occasion, and a new work by Vaughan Williams of pronounced Norfolk significance will be sung by the Festival Chorus drawn from Lowestoft, Yarmouth, Bury St Edmunds, and Norwich. This new work by Vaughan Williams should provide some robust entertainment for the singers. It is entitled 'Five Tudor Portraits, a Choral Suite in Five Movements with Soli for Contralto and Baritone and Orchestral Accompaniment, founded on

---

[28] Britten, *Our Hunting Fathers* (1936). Bliss's choral symphony, *Morning Heroes*, was first performed at the Festival in 1930.

poems by John Skelton (Laureate) 1460–1529, sometime Rector of Diss in Norfolk'.

There are a number of other societies in Norwich, but I must be content with naming just three. The Junior Philharmonic Society is conducted by Mr Edmund Weeks, who leads for the older society, and incidentally is playing a concerto at their last concert this season. The town runs Saturday-night Municipal Concerts at cheap prices. These are directed by Mr Maddern Williams, the deputy organist of the cathedral. Lastly there is the Norwich Chamber Orchestra, a very alive and progressive society. Their programmes are full of rarely-heard and interesting music, with a good percentage of English works. I again notice the names of Moeran and Britten. These concerts are given in a poorer quarter of the town, and there is no regular charge for admission. The directing spirit in this enterprise is Mr Cyril Pearce.

XII. CONCLUSION

The Listener, 18 December 1935, pp. 1133–4.

My short tour through musical England is over, and I am fully aware how sketchy is the result on paper. I have travelled twenty-five hundred miles, and seen many activities in various branches of music. But the prevailing impression left with me is of the vast tracts of musical enterprise not yet seen. For instance, there is the world of brass bands. Except for one outstanding example, I have not been able to visit the representative leaders of this active side of music. Let the reader put the number of these bands at 6,000, the number of players at 150,000, estimate a total audience for their music running into millions, and he will realize the gigantic figures with which he must deal in judging the extent of this one musical interest.

Again, the whole twelve articles could have been equally well devoted to the description of organs and organ-playing throughout the country. Different educational schemes, competitive and non-competitive festivals could have monopolized most of the space. I have deliberately left out professional orchestras, such as the Hallé and the Scottish, as being too well known. I have avoided London altogether, a self-contained musical unit in itself. I have not included the specialized centres of Edinburgh, Oxford, or Cambridge, each famous for the personalities living and working in them; the Midland towns of Leicester, Derby, and Nottingham have had to go unmentioned, as have the numerous holiday resorts along the South Coast. I state these omissions to show how great and widespread are the facilities for making and hearing music.

There remain over and above the specially-picked localities marked on the map, literally hundreds of other musical places, information about which would fill a large book.

It is indeed the quantity of music everywhere that has most astonished me. There seems hardly a village which is not touched by some musical organization. In a general way broadcasting has been the most potent cause of this growth. It has awakened the sense of music in vast sections of the population. There is naturally a percentage of this new audience who are lazily content to take the ready-made article as handed to them, but there are other listeners who wish to get into closer touch with music by learning to take part themselves. I believe it can be proved by statistics that many more are learning to play instruments or are keen to join musical societies now than in the pre-broadcasting days. This statement rests on the result of discussions with professional teachers of music in widely separated parts of the country.

One curious fact emerged from some of these talks. Several musicians told me that pupils today are inclined to base their standard of tone production on the mechanical noise transmitted rather than on the actual sound of voice or instrument. Most of them have cheap sets which distort the natural pure sound, and they imitate what they are accustomed to hear. A generation ago no one born with a sensitive ear could have borne the tinny acid whining that comes from out the screen in cinemas any more than the fat wheezy blarings of cheap radio sets. Today our ears, from motives of safety first, have had to capitulate.

There is a danger in this great increase in active musical production. Saturation point is being reached. The supply here as in other industries outweighs the demand. Public concert-giving by these thousands of societies should imply a similar growth in audiences willing to come and hear them. But is this so? In many cases, I fear, amateur societies are hard put to round up supporters even for their one or two annual concerts. There are frankly too many societies. Often in the same town there will be two or three orchestras with very much the same personnel, but directed by a different conductor, and managed by a different committee. They have only one public to draw on, that is the section of the town interested in music, and where sympathies are divided between different competing organizations thin audiences are to be expected.

Then again, probably due to the effect of broadcasting, the public demand superfine performances. Technical proficiency in all the arts has risen so spectacularly since the beginning of the century that what was considered a reasonably good performance thirty years ago is treated now as a disgracefully poor one. The standard of broadcast programmes and the performances of visiting celebrities have set high standards. Accustomed to these, the ordinary concert-goer naturally sees only too quickly the flaws in the playing of his own local orchestra. I do not see any remedy for this.

Undoubtedly when the economic condition of amateur and orchestral societies improves, as it is hoped it will under the administration of the National Federation, the standard of playing will be raised. Later, better instruments can be obtained, more rehearsals held, better professional players engaged. But what would immediately stimulate many of these societies to finer efforts would be some helpful recognition from municipal authorities.

These vague bodies that rule over the destinies of towns are often notoriously indifferent to any form of art. Busy, harassed, and impeded though they may be, it would be more than a polite gesture if they held out helping hands to local musicians. It would be a wise and diplomatic move on their part. They would find the number of music lovers much more numerous than they suspect. In certain go-ahead towns where municipal authorities have encouraged civic music in some practical way, results have been notable. In other places where not a single number of the town council has ever heard of music as a civilizing influence, the struggle to exist is hard and bitter.

One characteristic of English musical life is the close bond between professional and amateur, that is, between the man whose life work it is to play, compose, conduct, or teach, and the man who works at music enthusiastically as at a hobby. All over the country they have joined forces. You will find in the same orchestra amateur string players led by professionals, amateur woodwind players sitting alongside professional brass players; the conductor may belong to one or other category. Choruses are always composed of amateurs, directed by a professional musician.

For the good of music every one of these choral and orchestral societies must somehow survive in spite of the audience problem. They form the backbone of the best music in the country. Practically every professional musician of repute is connected with one or more of these thousands of societies, and the fact that in most cases their own services are given without any expectation of financial reward emphasizes the spirit of altruism which characterizes so much music in England.

I have mentioned that the National Federation of Music Societies will soon be in a position to grant them financial aid. I have suggested that municipal authorities might adopt a more civilized and future-looking attitude. Is there any way in which the Broadcasting Corporation can lend its powerful aid?

It looks at first as though it could do comparatively little through its own special medium. Although it broadcasts a considerable amount of music performed by local societies, it cannot hope to touch more than a small percentage of the whole, and what broadcasting it does must be based on a ruthless system of elimination. Only those societies that reach a sufficiently high level to interest listeners in general can expect to be considered.

Everywhere I went I put the same questions to conductors and musicians generally: 'In what way has broadcasting affected you or your society?' A practically unanimous answer was returned. 'I do not feel that it has affected us one way or the other. Even the finest concert on the radio never prevents the members of my society from coming to rehearsals, or my normal audience from attending the concerts. If one of our own concerts is broadcast, and it happens to be a wet night, a few may stay indoors to listen, but not enough to make this a deciding factor in the financial result.'

That is a fair gist of the usual answer, and I was quite prepared for this reply. Concert-going and 'listening in' are two quite separate functions, fulfilling different needs. Their relationship one to another is analogous to that between the theatre and the cinema. Each inhabits a different plane, and the two planes need not necessarily intersect. The concert hall is a place of drama, where the eye helps the ear. In broadcasting, though science by means of the finest set can give us an almost exact representation of music, it cannot excite us as does the actual presence of music. There is somewhere a dimension missing.

I heard of one musical enthusiast in the north who started to listen to his local choral society broadcasting from the town hall. The performance sounded so fine that he rushed to the hall to hear the second part of the concert under actual conditions. He was obeying a perfectly natural musical impulse.

Although regional broadcasting stations cannot keep on their lists more than a relatively few of the finest societies, they can help all of them in one small but practical way. One or two regional stations have included in their talks a bulletin giving the forthcoming musical events in their regions, with precise information as to date, time, hall, name of soloist, programme, etc. This action has been much appreciated, as one of the difficulties which all musical societies find, is to make the public aware of the work being done. I believe this policy could be justifiably extended. Why should not well-known figures in each county be invited to talk on the musical enterprises of their districts? These talks might be announced under some general title as 'The Musical Life of the County' or 'Music in Daily Life'. This is the kind of helpful step to bring results.

One other suggestion is put forward here. In every regional headquarters a completely documented catalogue of all musical societies suitable for broadcasting purposes is naturally essential. But what in my opinion is equally necessary is a carefully selected list of societies who *with a little help* would reach the standard for broadcasting.

By help I mean the stiffening of chorus or orchestra by contingents of singers, or players from outside the society. This policy of introducing shock troops to aid those less perfectly trained or equipped has already been tried with success. It produces a feeling of confidence, and indeed close co-operation between societies will be a necessity in the future. The National Federation should be able to furnish practical schemes for this 'stiffening' policy.

To estimate the value of music in England, one must travel. When representative foreign critics next come to England, they would do well on this second visit to avoid London. Let them start with a Hallé concert, and let the Hallé committee arrange an adventurous programme. The visiting critics can then be led quietly up to Huddersfield where they will hear the finest choral singing in England, perhaps in Europe. A visit to one or two prize-winning brass bands might interest them as much as it apparently has Casals. If they want danger and excitement let them act as judges at some important competition festival, and if they want to take away a lasting impression of something beautiful and characteristic, let them listen to the singing of our own music in the setting of an English cathedral.

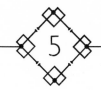

1936–1952

INTRODUCTION

THE middle of Bliss's career saw him involved predominantly in projects for stage and screen. Music for the film *Conquest of the Air* (1937) was followed in the same year by the most successful of his ballet scores, *Checkmate*, which took him to Paris for its first performance. In 1938 he visited Brussels to sit on the jury of the Ysaÿe International Piano Competition, and shortly after he was commissioned to write his Piano Concerto in B flat, a large-scale dramatic work in a romantic idiom, for the New York World's Fair of 1939. In the summer of that year he sailed with his family to New York to attend the first performance of the concerto, in Carnegie Hall on 10 June 1939, with Solomon as soloist and Adrian Boult conducting the New York Philharmonic, and it was there that a friend from his Santa Barbara days, Albert Elkus,[1] invited him to take up a Visiting Professorship in music at the University of California at Berkeley. Three months later Britain and Germany were at war.

Bliss accepted the invitation, and in January 1940 began lecturing on English music and on instrumentation.[2] While in California, he took the opportunity to visit Stravinsky and Schoenberg in Los Angeles, and wrote *Seven American Poems* for voice and piano (1940) and the String Quartet in B flat (1941). Uneasy about remaining abroad while his country was at war, he returned to England alone in June 1941—his wife and daughters were to follow some two years later—to assist in the Overseas Music Department of the BBC. In April 1942 he became Director of Music in succession to Adrian Boult, and held the post for two years before resigning in order to devote himself to composition. The remainder of the decade saw a succession of dramatic works in an often allegorical vein: the ballets *Miracle in the Gorbals* (1944) and *Adam Zero* (1946), the films *Men of Two*

---

[1] Chairman of the Music Department at Berkeley 1937–51.
[2] Some 500 pages of lecture notes are preserved in the University of California Music Library at Berkeley.

Worlds (1945) and *Christopher Columbus* (1949), and, most ambitious of all, a romantic opera, *The Olympians* (1948–9), with a libretto by J. B. Priestley. In the following years Bliss alternated between chamber music and further dramatic projects on a smaller scale: String Quartet No. 2 (1950) was followed by a *scena* for contralto and orchestra, *The Enchantress* (1951), and a Piano Sonata (1952) by music for a film version of *The Beggar's Opera* (1952–3).

From 1944 to 1953 Bliss and his wife kept a flat in London but made Pen Pits in Somerset their permanent home. After the war he resumed his travels abroad for performances of his music—to Budapest in 1947 and Ankara in 1948—and took on various administrative duties, chairing the Music Committee of the British Council (1946–50) and representing the Performing Right Society at an international conference on musical copyright in Madrid in 1950. In the same year he was knighted and became President of the Composers' Guild. The award of an LLD by the University of Glasgow during its quincentenary in 1951 was one of many academic honours for his services to music.

IMPRESSIONS AND THANKS

Bliss had been impressed by the Wingate's Temperance Band
during his 'musical pilgrimage' and wrote his *Kenilworth Suite* as a
test piece for the National Brass Band Festival of 1936. The Crystal
Palace was destroyed by fire later in the same year, and thereafter
the festival was held at the Royal Albert Hall.
British Bandsman, 3 October 1936, p. 3.

To one who has never before attended the National Band Festival, the sight at the Crystal Palace is unforgettable. Stretched outside as far as one can see are rows and rows of parked charabancs, which have brought bands and their supporters from every part of the country. In the grounds there are friendly and smiling crowds everywhere, obviously enjoying themselves—there goes a bandsman clutching in one hand a trombone, in the other a small child!

The concert hall itself is packed to overflowing with a tense and expectant audience; there is not a vacant seat anywhere. One senses drama in the air. First, the nonchalant entrance of each competing band on to the stage, the members outwardly cool, but inwardly nervous, the welcoming cheer, the few awkward moments of waiting, the warning whistle, and then the impact of the opening chords.

It was those first shattering full chords which made me jump. They were definitely exciting, so exact was the precision, so brilliant the tone, so irresistible the rhythm.

There are very few times in a composer's life when the actual performance comes up to the ideal dreamed of, but I can truthfully say that last Saturday was one such occasion. The mastery of technique and the musical understanding were alike superb.

I was greatly interested in the sympathetic enthusiasm of the audience. They almost seemed to be going through the work bar by bar with the players themselves. At one moment, early on in *Kenilworth*, there is a nasty responsibility thrown on the shoulders of the soprano cornet—a wicked high C[3] to take and hold quietly. Probably at rehearsal each competing player managed it quite easily, but in the strain of the concert hall it became a severe test. As this moment approached the audience stiffened a little (I felt myself clenching my hands). Would he or would he not get it?—he *has*! Bravo!—applause breaks out—now all is set for a glorious finish.

In the midst of this rivalry and comradeship sits Mr Iles.[4] He looks both proud and happy, as well he might! To have brought the standard of playing to this pitch of excellence and to have aroused such enthusiasm, is a great and lasting achievement for him and his colleagues.

I would like to extend to all members of the bands in the Championship Section and their conductors my wholehearted thanks for their great performance of *Kenilworth*, and my very best wishes for their good fortune in the coming season.

[3] Soprano A. [AB]
[4] One of the originators of the festival in 1900.

DEATH ON SQUARES

An account of the genesis of the ballet *Checkmate*, first performed by
the Vic–Wells Ballet, conducted by Constant Lambert, at the
Théâtre des Champs-Élysées in Paris on 15 June 1937. Bliss gave
the first performance of a concert suite at the Queen's Hall on
7 April 1938.
Great Thoughts, January 1938, pp. 18–22.

The ideal of composing a ballet on the game of chess first occurred to me
one summer evening about fifteen years ago. I had been dining with
Karsavina[5] and her husband in their house overlooking Regent's Park.
Grace Lovat Fraser[6] was there too, and there may have been others whose
names and faces elude me, perhaps because they did not make any actual
contributions to the subject of this essay.

As may be supposed, the talk was about dancing, and it led us to reflect
upon the many possibilities in the art of the ballet that were still un-
explored. My natural inclination was towards dramatic music, and after
the experiences gained in composing music for productions of *The
Tempest* and *As You Like It* I felt particularly drawn to an art form in
which the composer was freer to control his medium.

The presence of Karsavina on this occasion acted as a stimulus to my
wish. I remember how, when the curtain went up on the first Diaghilev
ballet that I ever saw, it was she who had dominated the stage in the role of
the savage queen Thamar.[7] Her gesture, as she waved her scarf at the
castle window, luring yet another victim to his death, is as clear to me now
as it was then. Perhaps the strong impression that this particular ballet
made upon me determined the trend of our talk on that subsequent
evening, for I remember that the discussion turned on the drama of
games, and the idea of the pitiless queen in chess leapt from someone's

---

[5] Tamara Karsavina (1885–1978), formerly a member of Diaghilev's company from its formation in 1909. Bliss had orchestrated Christian Sinding's *Fire Dance* for her at the London
Coliseum in July 1921.

[6] The soprano Grace Crawford, wife of Claud Lovat Fraser. She had given the first performance, as dedicatee, of *Rout*.

[7] Balakirev's *Thamar*, choreographed by Fokine, performed at the Theatre Royal, Drury
Lane, during the season 25 June–25 July 1913.

brain to become, as it happened, the starting point of the ballet *Checkmate*.

The origin of chess seems lost in unrecorded history, but whether it came from Persia, India, or China, all opinions agree as to its fierce and barbaric associations. Personally I prefer to accept the myth that it was invented by a Persian minister of state to save the kingdom from the sadistic war impulses of its ruler. Let the Shah slay and win with pieces of ivory or jade, or carved wood, rather than with human flesh!

The chief personality in a chess ballet should, of course, be the Queen—the most powerful and ruthless piece on the board. As regards the King, it was, I recall, Grace Lovat Fraser who suggested interpreting him as an enfeebled old man, powerless to protect himself and succumbing at last to the fury of his enemies, and this interpretation is the one that has been adopted at Sadler's Wells today just as it was conceived fifteen years ago, for not only is it good theatre, but it is also true to the tradition of the game itself.

A worthy opponent of the Queen would be, I thought, one of the enemy Knights. This conception of his purpose brought to my mind a vivid memory of much earlier years. At school I had read in a bound volume of *Strand* magazines the story of a man who played chess for his life against some barbaric chieftain. If he could win, he would be set free, but play as he might he was outwitted time and time again by one of the red knights, who seemed almost demoniacally alive and malevolently capable of anticipating every move against him. So with these three chief personalities—the ferocious Queen, the helpless King, and the enigmatic fighter, the Knight, we began to construct a scenario. Fate, however, intervened, by sending me to America, and the project gradually faded from my mind. It seemed another proof that in the theatre world what is exhaustively talked over seldom gets translated into action. Yet in this case things were to turn out differently. Thanks to a lucky combination of circumstances the whole matter, after lying submerged for many years, was brought once more to the surface.

The Sadler's Wells Ballet had been invited to go to Paris to give a display of English dancing, music and stage design. It was thought a compliment to offer the Parisian audience a new ballet, written specially for the occasion. When I was invited to collaborate, I thought immediately of my long-cherished subject of chess. Many composers, I feel, do their best work when they are faced with a definite 'reality', and by reality I mean a decision as to the nature of the work and the place and date of its presentation. In my case the 'reality' facts were June 15th, 1937, Le Théâtre des Champs-Élysées, and a ballet designed to show the Sadler's Wells dancers to the best possible advantage. At once I set about elaborating my scenario, and at this point there stepped in another friend of mine, W. Bridges Adams,[8] a highly imaginative, and at the same time eminently practical, man of the theatre. To the recollections of Karsavina's enthusiasm and Grace Lovat Fraser's brilliant intuition were now added other impressions, those of quick, nervous steps up and down my Hampstead room, of deep bass grunts and fierce clutchings at a pipe, as Bridges Adams threw out suggestion after suggestion. I played sketches of what I had written, he hinted at possible dramatic action, I disagreed, he asserted other possibilities. Gradually the preliminary misty outlines appeared, and then the rounded work of art became visible. Its form, its character, its logic, the disposition of its climaxes—all were fixed.

What I felt compelled to write was a stern and thoughtful prelude, giving the impression of stress between the opposing forces rather than a light-hearted overture. I examined, therefore, more abstract ways of depicting antagonists. They might be any two opposites—night and day, black and white, a circle and a square, Fascism and Communism. The laws of the theatre finally indicated the choice of two armoured figures, one in gold, the other in black, symbolizing Love and Death fighting for the lives of their subjects. They sit on either side of the stage throughout the ballet. The scene is a chessboard, on which the Red pieces are seen assembling —first, the Pawns, light-hearted pages, then the two Red Knights, fierce and powerful fighters. The two Black Knights enter on a reconnoitring visit of chivalry. They are followed by the Black Queen, the most powerful of the pieces. Before her departure she wins the love of the Red Knight and flings him a rose. Captivated by her vitality and beauty, he dances a joyous mazurka. The two Red Bishops enter. Their dignified ceremony is interrupted by the two Red Castles, inhuman and menacing monsters. Finally the Red King and Queen approach. The King, old and feeble, is the weakest piece of all. The parade of the Red pieces is complete.

The game begins. A savage onslaught is started by the spear-heads of the enemy Black pieces, the manœuvre ending with the 'check' of the Red King. His Bishops and his Queen try to defend him, but in vain. The Red Knight, as champion, jumps into the arena. He brings the Black Queen to her knees but, torn between love for her and loyalty to his King, hesitates to kill. She stabs him, and his body is borne off in a funeral cortège. The Black Queen then threatens the powerless King but insultingly disdains to touch him. Left alone on the board, he attempts to flee, only to find his lines of escape blocked by the Black pieces, who enter and force him back

---

[8] William Bridges Adams (1889–1965) was Director of the Stratford-upon-Avon Theatre 1919–32, and from 1935 a member of the Drama Department of the newly-formed British Council.

to his throne. At the point of death he remembers his past youth and power, and once more faces his assailants. They waver, but the Black Queen appears behind him with spear uplifted. She plunges it into his back, and he falls. It is Checkmate.

I worked at the music during the autumn and winter of 1936, and finished the piano score in the early spring of 1937. The more I concen-trated on it, the more fascinated I was by the subject. I visited the Reading Room of the British Museum and, with my wife, pored over books dealing with the history of chess, stimulating my imagination with ancient illustra-tions of Charlemagne playing with Death and of vast games contested in the open air with living pieces. We hunted out Indian and Chinese sets, many with fantastic masks. I kept on my piano a reproduction of a coloured print by Tokoyuni, portraying an actor, whose fierce warrior-like pose and savage intensity of expression served to fix the personality of the Red Knight on my mind. I was guided, too, by a pregnant utterance by my friend, Bridges Adams. 'This must not', he said, 'be so much a divertise-ment on chess, as the game itself. To make an audience grasp that, you must start from reality and *then* venture into fantasy.' Hence my decision to introduce each piece in turn and at one moment show the whole set drawn up, ready for the game to start.

By the time the piano sketches were ready to be shown to the choreo-grapher, the ballet had become a drama.

And now began a really interesting period for me. How would my collaborators, Ninette de Valois and McKnight Kauffer,[9] see this subject of chess from their special angles? I had interpreted it musically. How would the dancer solve its problems, and how the painter?

I had had the pleasure of working with Miss de Valois before in two short ballets.[10] I knew she was perhaps at her finest when dealing with subjects of a bizarre and dramatic nature. I was not prepared, however, for the quickness with which she visualised and composed so difficult a ballet as this. She confessed she knew nothing about the game and could not even distinguish the pieces, let alone their characteristic moves. As I played the music over to her, a large chessboard set on a table near by, she used to sit as if turned to stone, a frozen image of concentration.

With McKnight Kauffer I was equally fortunate. Most contemporary painters are sympathetic to music; some even find it a stimulus to creative effort, when broadcasted. But McKnight Kauffer *thinks* musically. He has

---

[9] Edward McKnight Kauffer (1890–1954), American-born painter and illustrator best known for his transport posters.

[10] De Valois choreographed a version of *Rout* performed in 1927 (see *Catlogue* 8) and *Narcissus and Echo* (*Catalogue* 7), performed in 1932 and thought to have been based on the *Rhapsody* of 1919.

a real love and critical appreciation of it, so that it was possible for us to talk over the whole setting of the ballet in the most sympathetic manner.

The final problem that a composer of ballet has to face is the possible 'cutting' of some of his music. The time factor in dancing is interesting and important. A four-minute dance played in the concert hall will seem concise enough, but when danced by a solo performer in the theatre it may assume a wearisome length. So in the case of *Checkmate* eight bars were taken away here and four there, until the synthesis of music and action was complete. To the composer it is often surprising how much surgery improves his music. The weak passages necessarily disappear, and the structure becomes stronger and more firmly knit. Here, then, was the ballet finished at last and ready for Paris. Its future lay out of my hands.

BROADCAST MUSIC

I. FRENCH, ITALIAN, AND GERMAN

The Listener, 19 January 1939, p. 172.

From a week during which nearly every side of musical expression has been represented I can select but three or four items. It was a pleasurable experience to hear the dramatic work *Lakmé* presented in a broadcast edition. As long as there is no permanent opera in England there are inevitably many works that are debarred from performance, and many composers whose chief works we can only study in a somewhat mutilated form. These occasional two hours of opera presented by the BBC are valuable as an introduction to works that in foreign countries are in the normal operatic repertoire.

Delibes or, to given his full mellifluous name, Clément Philibert Léo Delibes, had the characteristic Gallic talent for charming tunes stylishly orchestrated. He could induce a nostalgia free from sentimentality, and a seriousness without profundity. A slight touch opens the right emotional door. The scene in the Brahmin Grove with which the opera starts, the Flower Duet of Lakmé and Mallika, the scenes in the second act between Lakmé and Nilakantha, Lakmé's Berceuse in the third act, and the duet between her and Gerald with distant chorus are all fine examples of this gift of Delibes for charming vocal lines and limpid orchestration.

It was interesting to welcome to this land of superb organ playing a foreign visitor in the person of Fernando Germani, though it must be admitted that his concert was a disappointment. If there is one instrument that should in performance keep its rhythmic pulse in iron control it is the organ. In the Handel concerto the quick passage work was noticeably uneven and only in the third movement did the soloist begin to give us fine rhythmic playing. His 'foot-work' was shown in all its virtuosity in the second piece, a pedal study by Manari. I am told by those who were in the hall that he played the *Canto fermo* based on *Salve Regina* with the one foot, while the busy counterpoint was the affair of the other. He ended his recital with a concerto[11] by Casella written some fifteen years ago, a rather blatant work in which the accompanying brass bay and bark in the fashion of the naughty twenties.

Bruno Walter received a great reception on Wednesday with his Mozart programme. The G minor Symphony was beautifully played, the direction being tense but natural and unforced. The *fortes* in the score were relative, not merely explosive, and the phrases were given freedom to mould themselves naturally instead of being coerced into form. Such details as the playing of the second subject and of the coda in the first movement, the flowing tempo of the second movement, the phrasing of the close to the minuet, and the dynamic quality of the staccato chords, immediately after the last repeat bar in the finale, all were intuitively right. A similarly authentic performance of the *Requiem* followed. I cannot feel much interest in the scholastic question of which sections were actually written by Mozart and which by the pen of Süssmayer.[12] The mantle of Mozart lies quite beautifully over the whole work.

Another great orchestra and conductor were heard on the air this week, namely, the Berlin Philharmonic and Wilhelm Furtwängler. The playing of the *Parsifal* excerpt and of *Also Sprach Zarathustra* which followed was characteristically spacious and majestic, and the sustained chording of the brass notably fine. One of the choicest bits of criticism would have been the printable words of Nietzsche himself on this musical analogy of his masterpiece. 'After Wagner', he wrote, 'it is essential to mediterraneanise music.' What further progress southward would he order after hearing post-Wagner?

II. TWO SYMPHONIES AND TWO SONATAS

The Listener, 26 January 1939, p. 228.

Two symphonies with which the musical public is unacquainted were heard this past week. The music of Albéric Magnard, whose Third

---

[11] *Concerto romana* (1926) for organ, brass, timpani, and strings.
[12] Mozart's pupil, who completed the *Requiem* (K. 626) left unfinished at his death.

Symphony was played by Constant Lambert, was completely unknown to me, so that the performance had the excitement of a discovery. An austere and sternly self-critical personality stood revealed.

If I had not read the name of the composer, I should at first have found it difficult to judge his nationality. The cool bare chords on the brass at the start, the reliance on architecture rather than on colour, the occasional Wagnerian flashes suggested a northerner, possibly an Englishman; the second movement, however, especially the slow dance section, contradicted this impression and the last movements were too imbued with French *sensibilité* for the country of their origin to be doubted.

The proud and retiring nature of the composer is shown in labelling the movements 'Introduction et ouverture', 'Danses', 'Pastorale', 'Finale'. This meiosis suggests a miniature suite, whereas the whole work is symphonic in the strict sense. The composer's training under Vincent d'Indy is perhaps responsible for his aristocratic use of form, witness the beautiful timing of the close to the first movement.

Deirde (A Celtic Symphony), by Rutland Boughton, was played later in the week by Clarence Raybould and provided a complete contrast. It is, indeed, not so much a symphony as a suite of tone-poems, or, as the composer himself describes it, 'a music drama without action'. The centre movement is rich in lyrical beauty and the sombre movement of the last is impressive. As in the case of some other English symphonies, I feel the need of visual aid, such as the cinema screen can give. I believe the experience would so enhance the inherent dramatic content of the music that a new art form of beauty might result.

The spell of Celtic lore does not enchant me. When, for instance, I read a sentence such as the following, 'Mananaan Mac Lir came from his wide waters shouting louder than the wind, with his daughters Cliona and Aoife, and Etain Fair-Hair, and Coll and Cecht and MacGreina, whose names are not forgotten, even Banba and Fodla and Eire, names of glory', my imagination stands on the defensive at once. It is a proof of the strength of much of Boughton's music that I can listen to its Celtic quality with admiration.

A piano recital by Philip Lévi was notable for his fine playing of an unusual programme. It consisted of works by Busoni and Szymanowski, neither of whom has as yet an abiding place in our repertoire.

The *Sonatina in diem Nativitatis Christi* is one of Busoni's most intimate and meditative works. It has a spiritual affinity with the ascetic works of Liszt written in his last years. The legitimate criticism directed against Busoni the composer cannot destroy the conviction that his personality was that of the supreme artist. Everywhere in his collected works can be found the personal record of his enquiring and finely lucid mind.

The Third Sonata of Szymanowski is a difficult work to appraise. It is as beautifully laid out for the instrument as are the Busoni pieces. Its form is clear and personal, and the fugal texture of the finale highly original. But the music itself seems composed more of nerves than of bone and muscle. The impressionistic chordal splashes, the arabesque figuration, the influence of the later Scriabin on the harmonic scheme, all give the sonata a certain monotony. At the end I was conscious of respect rather than of any warmer feeling.

III. EARLY FLOWERING, AND MATURE GROWTH

The Listener, 2 February 1939, p. 280.

The very early work of great composers has a particular charm, a charm enhanced by the knowledge that precocious musical genius is so often of short duration. Actually the number of youthful masterworks in music is fewer than in any of the other arts. Lyric poetry is the natural expression of the young, and Keats and Rimbaud are only two notable examples among many. Painting, too, is an art seemingly more quickly acquired. The greatest living painter, Picasso, was already painting masterworks before he was twenty.

But music at the outset is a complicated and difficult mode of expression and demands a long apprenticeship. The *Wunderkind* among composers is the exception. Mozart and Mendelssohn are the most famous, and it is truly wonderful that each should show at a very early age so well-defined a musical personality. The two movements of the Mozart sonata[13] played on Saturday are unmistakably Mozartian in the sense in which we now use the term. The eleventh and twelfth bars of the Andante, for example, bear his authentic fingerprint. I am sorry the first movement was not included, as it contains shortly before each double bar a beautifully personal cadence. The sonata of Mendelssohn[14] has that grace which charmed so many, though the Octet and the Overture to *A Midsummer Night's Dream* written in the following year show his genius more magnificently. In relation to Mozart and Mendelssohn horticulturists would describe the species Beethovenensis as slow growing and late flowering. The piano quartet[15] played on Wednesday is only an accomplished student's work. The Faust songs[16] of the young Schubert, however, are indicative of the highest genius.

Three English names were included: Purcell,[17] whose sense of the

[13] Sonata in G (K. 283).   [14] Sonata in E, op. 6.   [15] Quartet No. 2 in D.
[16] 'Gretchen am Spinnrade' and 'Rastlöse Liebe'.
[17] 'Elegy on the Death of Matthew Locke'.

dramatic vocal line here shows itself; Walton, whose Piano Quartet has the beauty of assured workmanship; and Wesley, whose song with violin obbligato,[18] on the score of years, was the most astonishing music of the week. It was written, it is said, when he was six years old!

The early fugue[19] by Bach still leaves one guessing. Like Shakespeare, Bach remains the eternal enigma. This is surely music writing itself.

In Busoni's music this week I found the quality necessarily lacking in these other works, a mature philosophy that can sum up the world as a stage, with the corollary that all actions lack reality. *Arlecchino* is for me an indubitable success, and why it should have taken twenty-two years for a performance to reach England is inexplicable. In this 'theatrical capriccio' the composer has breathed new life into the conventions of the old Commedia dell'Arte. Irony goes hand in hand with sentiment, and the comedy is dogged by its own shadow of tragedy. Over the whole flickers the true Latin spirit. The production under Clarence Raybould was excellent. The music was very well sung, and the part of Harlequin himself ideally cast. A witty and suitably acid translation of Busoni's own libretto by Professor Dent assured the success of the broadcast. Busoni is not too easy on his singers, though the Verdi-like ensemble at the end is splendid. The tessitura of the baritones lies high, that of the mezzo-soprano often low. His orchestration deliciously underlines the satirical dialogue and stage action. One practical point puzzles me. How is the Harlequin to get his spoken words across in an actual stage production? The speaking voice is occasionally used in other operas for asides or soliloquies, but in this work it is often combined with other singing voices. Surely this effect of duet and trio demands a common medium!

IV. MOSTLY BRAHMS

The Listener, 9 February 1939, p. 332.

Several major works of Brahms have been played this past week, including the Third Symphony, the Clarinet Quintet, a Clarinet Sonata, vocal duets, and the *Magelonelieder*. Brahms never wrote a really quick tune. If he did, I do not know it. He would often indicate that his music should be *played* quickly, but he did not *think* it quickly in the sense that Scarlatti, Mozart, Rossini, or Berlioz thought theirs. The fast movements of Brahms are really slower movements speeded up, as one might speed up a slow tune on the barrel organ by turning the handle faster. Compare the opening of

[18] 'Go my Ruth', from the oratorio *Ruth*.
[19] Fugue from *Capriccio* in Bb (on the departure of a beloved brother).

the overture *King Lear* by Berlioz—this work, by the way, was beautifully played by the LSO under Weingartner this week. Here we have an example of a musical mind habitually thinking much faster. In the same way Mozart could run like a cheetah if he wanted to, and both Rossini and Scarlatti would be more at home in an aeroplane of today than on the back of a safe hack. The normal pulse of Brahms is andante rather than vivace. His letters to his friends have much the same plodding gait. They do not skip and jump like Mozart's, or rush precipitously like those of Berlioz.

Brahms was no explorer. Throughout his long creative life his style hardly changes. The personality naturally broadens and deepens, but the expression of it is in the form of repetition rather than in experimentation. He throws out no hints for future composers, as Liszt did. There is the melancholy Brahms and the serene Brahms. His pessimism is not so easily diagnosed a malady as those described in Nicholas Breton's *Melancholick Humours*:[20] it affects one like a vague nostalgia. It is only when Brahms overcomes this and reaches serenity that his great stature is visible. Many examples of this inner harmony come to mind. I would mention the first movement of the Violin Concerto, the third movement of the First Symphony, the third movement of the Clarinet Quintet. All are really felt at the same tempo of andante.

It is difficult to imagine any music more beautiful in spirit than the second movement of Schubert's *Unfinished* Symphony, and it is high praise to say that the opening bars of the *Wozzeck* Fragments did no violence to it.

The music of Berg has always strongly moved me. It is partly due to the actual beauty of sound with which he clothes his thought. With the possible exceptions of Berlioz and Debussy he writes more subtly and beautifully for the orchestra than anyone I know. How ugly that descending passage at the start of the *Wozzeck* Fragments can sound on the piano, and how mysteriously it is transformed when played on the soft strings!

In this psychological drama Berg is absolute master of his medium. He can be as diatonic as Brahms if there is dramatic need, or more eloquent in atonality than any of his contemporaries. He has the power of evoking moods and sensations little expressed as yet in music. The poignant close to the first Fragment, with its twist towards A minor, is one example, and the horrific opening to the third another. The middle Fragment is written in more formal style. These miniature variations and fughetta are strictly worked out on a theme that Bach himself might have used.

The performance was studiously clear under the direction of Sir Adrian

---

[20] A collection of moral and reflective poems by Nicholas Breton (?1545–?1626).

Boult, and May Blyth sang the part of Marie with fine fidelity, including the jagged descent from the soprano B♭ to the alto G.

———

MODERN ENGLISH MUSIC

A lecture given by Bliss, *en route* to California to take up his Visiting Professorship at Berkeley, at the Music Teachers National Association convention, Kansas City, Missouri, 27–30 December 1939. Typescript corrected by AB, Bliss Archive, Cambridge University Library.

The word 'modern' was not originally included in the title of my short address to you today, but was apparently slipped in by your President, and though I thank him for tryng to limit my subject for me, I am going to remove that dull and deadly word 'modern' and just speak on English music.

Perhaps the most powerful influence on English music during this present century has been *not* the great work of an Elgar, a Delius, a Vaughan Williams, an Arnold Bax, or a William Walton, *not* the foundation of magnificent orchestras like the BBC under Boult or the Philharmonic under Beecham, not even the rise of London to be, till the outbreak of this war, the centre of European music, but the publication and dissemination of our sixteenth- and seventeenth-century masterpieces.

The glory of English literature in Tudor times is well known, and it was always possible to step into a bookshop and get the works of Shakespeare, Sidney, Spenser, Ben Jonson, Marlowe, Michael Drayton. But what about the musicians of that time, many of whom were working on terms of intimate friendship with their contemporary poets? It was impossible to study, much less perform, them. Only a mere handful of what is now regarded as one of the most extraordinary outpourings of music in any age was available in print.

To be able to sing only half a dozen of the works of Tallis, Tye, Gibbons, Dowland, Byrd, Morley, Weelkes, Wilbye is equivalent to being unable to purchase more than two plays of Shakespeare and half a dozen sonnets of Sidney, out of all the wealth of Elizabethan poetry.

The publication of English music from, say, 1520–1620 has had a profound influence on the conception of England as a musical nation.

It is characteristic of the English people that with a school of music dating back over 500 years, with a composer like William Byrd the equal of Palestrina, Vittoria, or Orlando di Lasso, with a song writer John Dowland as inspired as Schubert, with an original genius, Purcell, pouring out this exquisite dramatic settings before Bach or Handel were born—it is characteristic of us, I say, that we still tolerantly submit to the facile generalization that we are an unmusical country. It is as false as saying that the Frenchman is by nature volatile and the Englishman phlegmatic, when it is a well-known fact that the opposite is true.

One cannot open any contemporary history or diary without finding references to music-making. I must quote two fragments, one dealing with Queen Elizabeth and the other with King James the First. Queen Elizabeth was no faint-hearted admirer of music. She used to be regaled during dinner with twelve trumpets and two kettle drums, which together with pipes, cornets, and side drums made the hall ring for half an hour together. We read that Queen Elizabeth passed from Westminster to the Tower and the chroniclers speak of how 'the bachelors' barge of the Lord Mayor's company was in attendance with great and pleasant melody of instruments, which played in most sweet and heavenly a manner. After a loyal speech of welcome her maids danced, singing a song of six parts, with the music of an excellent consort. When Her Majesty passed through the park gate there was a company of musicians hidden in a bower.'

In 1607 when King James the First was given a solemn feast by the Merchants Taylors Company, it is recorded that 'upon either side of the hall in the windows near the upper end were galleries or seats, made for music, in either of which were seven choice musicians playing on their lutes. And in the ship which did hang aloft in the hall, three rare men and very skilful who sang to His Majesty. In the chamber where the King dined were placed a very rich pair of organs whereon Mr John Bull, Doctor of Music, did play all the dinnertime. Among the gentlemen who did sing melodious songs at the said dinner were William Byrd, William Lawes and Orlando Gibbons.'

In the diaries of Pepys and Evelyn there are constant references to the popularity of music in England. Burney's papers give an expert account of music in England in the early eighteenth century. England, in fact, was always teeming with amateurs, lovers of music. It has been described as a nest of singing birds, and so it has been and so it is, musically as well as ornithologically. If I seem to overstate my case, may I quote from two critics well known for their understatement.

John Playford, the first English publisher, in 1698 says of Purcell, 'his extraordinary talent in all sorts of music is sufficiently known, but he was especially admired for the vocal, having a peculiar genius to express the energy of English words, whereby he moved the passions of all his auditors.' Sir Donald Francis Tovey says 'almost any random quotation from Purcell might be by a composer of the calibre of Bach or Handel. Purcell is one of the greatest contrapuntalists that ever lived, one of the greatest inventors of themes, one of the greatest masters of declamation, and a completely mature master of early orchestration.'

Peter Warlock, himself a song writer and most mordant critic, says, of John Dowland, 'he is not only one of the greatest song writers that England ever produced, but he is to be placed unhesitatingly among the world's greatest song writers of all times'—*floreat* 1597 to 1612.

The English genius is rather in the direction of vocal than instrumental music. The Englishman is not born with a fiddle under his chin, but rather with the urge to sing in his bath. The great Yorkshire choirs of Huddersfield, Leeds, and Sheffield are typical of our national expression. These and other northern choruses are unsurpassed throughout the world for the beauty and virtuosity of their singing. Like Sheffield steel, they are a happy combination of experience and climatic conditions. This natural pleasure in singing has been traditional ever since the days of the madrigal, when not to be able to take part in a polyphonic vocal work at sight was regarded as barbaric ignorance and lack of education. No wonder that the masters of our Elizabethan and Restoration times and our living composers know how to set fine English words with subtlety and beauty.

I shall put before my students in Berkeley the means of studying how rightly to set the complex English language to music. In this respect no one can hope to equal Purcell, who sang his own songs in his fine tenor voice, or Campion, who was poet as well as composer. There is no excuse for faulty accents, faulty phrasing, wrong metrical stresses with a tradition so long and masterly. As Thomas Morley said in his *Plain and Easy Introduction to Practical Music*, the only textbook I know as exciting as a detective story, dated 1597, 'we must have a care to apply the notes to the words so that in singing there is no criminal barbarism committed.'

This preference for choral writing distinguishes also the third great period of English music, which can conveniently be called The Twentieth Century Renaissance. Where in the world today can such exquisite and powerful choral effects be heard as in, for instance, Elgar's *Dream of Gerontius*, Delius' *Song of the High Hills*, Vaughan Williams' *Sea Symphony*, Holst's *Hymn of Jesus*, Walton's *Belshazzar's Feast*? Are not the unaccompanied settings by Moeran as beautiful as Morley's, and the Mass of Vaughan Williams as noble as one by Tallis?

I admit the futility of naming works to you that you have not heard, but entrust me with a symphony orchestra and chorus for six concerts and I pledge myself to give you a survey of music of the English school that will have all the exciting adventures of unknown territory.

Let me try to give miniature impressions of some of our leading living English composers. Master of his art as was Elgar, and beautiful and aristocratic dreamer as was Delius, I personally believe that Vaughan Williams represents the greatest English composer since Purcell and perhaps the greatest English musical personality since William Byrd. If one wanted to point to an English composer as *echt* English as Beethoven is *echt* German or Debussy is *echt* French, one could not do better than name Vaughan Williams. His music springs from the racial and psychological roots of the English race and he is bold and daring, so that at the age of 67 he is still leader and explorer. John Ireland, his junior by seven years, is known mostly for his piano works and his songs, in which a fine personal expression is subjected to fastidious technic. His orchestral and chamber music is not so well known as it should be, but he can well afford to wait for ultimate recognition. Arnold Bax has an entirely different personality. He typifies the Celtic rather than the Anglo-Saxon strain. The nearest parallel in poetry would be the work of Yeats. His imagination kindles at the hearth of Celtic legends. He has written seven symphonies and many works in all branches of music except opera. He is an avowed lover of the romantic and is lavishly gifted.

William Walton belongs to a younger generation and his output is much smaller, but every work that he composes is final and complete. Truly classical in outlook, favouring order, lucidity, balance, he is the reverse of cold and through every work runs a high voltage of vitality. His one symphony is a work that for sustained, fine, musical thinking stands unsurpassed among contemporary symphonies.

Constant Lambert is almost kaleidoscopic in his talent. A sensitive composer, a brilliant pianist, an acid critic, and an accomplished conductor, his influence on English music is liberal and compelling. In his finest work, *Summer's Last Will and Testament*, his affinity with the Elizabethans is clearly apparent, and the final chorus with its superb ground bass is not unworthy of Purcell.

With Benjamin Britten we come to the youngest generation. Only 26, he possesses such fertility of invention and such technical dexterity that he has already won a reputation wider than Europe. The future lies with his generation and we are content to leave it with them. May fortune smile on them!

A MUSICIAN RETURNS TO ENGLAND

A talk broadcast in Canada in May or June 1941.
Recording, Canadian Broadcasting Corporation.

Two years ago almost to the day I landed my family in New York from England. I do not know which of us four was the most excited. I have lived in the States before, but find that however many times I return I am never disappointed at this first sight of the New World. My wife, being an American, felt it was like coming home, and my two young daughters, who had never crossed the Atlantic before, naturally found everything exciting —the fine boat that had been their home for a week, the voyage on which they had seen ice-bergs and whales, and then these gigantic towers in which people actually lived. We were a happy and excited quartet.

A journey is twice as good if you combine a holiday with a definite object. I had been invited to come to New York for the first performance of a new musical work of mine written for a special British concert to be given during the visit of the King and Queen to Canada. It is a concerto for piano and orchestra, and on the same boat came Sir Adrian Boult, Musical Director of the BBC, who was to conduct it, and one of our greatest pianists, Mr Solomon, who was to play it.

Already at this time the storm clouds were gathering in Europe, but the majority of men I talked with felt it was only a question of summer lightning and that sanity, statesmanship, and a sympathy with the other fellow's problem would prevent the madness of 1914. The future for my family looked very pleasant indeed. From New York we were going across the States to California, which I'm sure my children visualized as a wide-open space in which cowboys rode about firing pistols into the air, with gold to be dug up in the back garden. I was to visit the University of California and give lectures on British music, conduct the orchestra, and make myself generally musically useful for several months. The Bliss family were then to head for Canada and sail down the St Lawrence home.[21]

I have found, during my fifty-odd years, that when things look perfect it is time to beware, just as when things look very black indeed, invariably some unexpected good turns up. When in September 1939 I turned on the

[21] The original plan was in fact to return to England after a camping holiday in Maine; it was only with the declaration of war during the holiday that Bliss, for the sake of his family, decided to accept an invitation to lecture at Berkeley (see *As I Remember*, pp. 121–2).

radio and heard the King state that we were at war with Germany, my heart, as well as everyone else's, missed a beat. I knew that one epoch had ended and another begun—our family dreams shattered, and a nightmare substituted.

Many of my listeners must have vivid memories of the last war. I wonder whether some of you feel that you are actually living over the same times again, just as in several of Mr J. B. Priestley's plays the characters feel they have been there before. The other day I was sitting in a hotel in Ottawa and the band struck up a tune, the words of which begin: 'I'm Gilbert the filbert, the nut with a cane'. I haven't heard that for 25 years. And in a flash I was back in a musical hall in London—I forget its name, I think it was in Leicester Square—in a Second Lieutenant's uniform, about to leave for France with my regiment. I remember when I got to France it seemed full of Canadians, and mighty glad we were to see them. I'm hoping that when I reach England in a few weeks it too will seem full of Canadians. We shall again be mighty glad to see them.

Music is a difficult thing to get across the Atlantic. There seems to be some devilment there that sets up a crackling and a fading and a blasting, which turns finely played music at our end into an irritating noise your end. We will do our best, but even the finest engineers cannot control the weather.

And what kind of music do you most want to hear? During the last month I've asked that question of many friends. I've been given many suggestions, but I can do with more. If anybody listening to me can help with ideas, write and tell me at one of the CBC offices, and we will do our best to see that at one time or another he or she gets the music they want.

I know what kind of British music I would like you to hear. I should like you to hear, to have the chance of hearing, our great northern choruses sing. They haven't their equal in the world. The choral societies of, say, Huddersfield, Leeds, Sheffield have all the qualities of their own Sheffield steel. The power and beauty of their singing is staggering at first hearing. It's like standing under the Horseshoe Falls of Niagara. You must hear them even if we have to make special records and slip them across. All the members of big choral societies in England are amateurs. They're on their feet all day working, and then they turn up after supper and sing for a couple of hours. Britain has always had a love for singing and always will. We have many small groups of singers, too, who specialize in music written for the first of our Queen Elizabeths 350 years ago. This old music sounds just as fresh and beautiful as it did when another armada was forced aground before a smaller opponent. I would like you to hear some of that music too.

And then there are our famous brass bands. I expect many of you have heard or even seen some of them, as the prize-winning team in the annual contest tours Canada, or Australia, or South Africa as a reward for winning. And like the singers, these players are all amateurs who play for the love of it. There are 24 players in each band and there are literally hundreds of bands. They are composed of men working in different branches of industry—there are bands of miners, of electrical workers, of motor mechanics, of workers in the leather trade, there are bands in the cotton mills and in the Potteries. The brilliance of their playing has got to be heard to be believed.

Music is one of the things in life that makes life more joyous. Like light, air, food, leisure, it should be enjoyed by all—not all who can pay, but *all*. Music has strange powers. It can make you forget present anxieties, it can stir deep-seated emotions, it can inspire to action. A really fine tune never dies. Think of one of the finest of all, the *Marseillaise*. It sounds the very note of freedom and gallantry.

Music is also an international language, the only international language. One of the greatest lessons I learnt, showing the inherent understanding between men of different nations, was in 1922, when a start was made in Vienna to build up an international musical festival. I took part there at a concert in which German, French, Italian, Dutch, Polish, and British musicians all sat down together and played fine music.[22] In Geneva, at the same time, what embittered disharmony prevailed! The full effects of music and the other arts may seem in wartime to be pushed to the very background in the storms and stress of events.

MUSIC IN WARTIME

An untitled talk broadcast on the Overseas Service of BBC Radio on
3 October 1941. Bliss answered questions sent by former students at
Berkeley.
Talk script, University of California Music Library, Berkeley.

Hullo California, hullo San Francisco, hullo University of California, hullo Berkeley! It is very exciting to speak to friends and students of mine with whom I was working six months ago, and I hope that the short waves are not too choppy and that you can recognize my voice. You have sent me some very interesting questions, and I am going to try and answer them.

---

[22] A reference to the formation of the International Society for Contemporary Music after the 1922 Salzburg Festival.

Mr Schliemann asks, what are British composers doing? The answer is, musically very little. Those of military age who are fit have been called up for various kinds of military work, and those who are too old seem to find the atmosphere of a country at total war too alien to the necessary concentration. Our greatest living composer, Vaughan Williams, is the only one still producing important work. He has completed the music for a magnificent film about Canada called *The 49th Parallel*, which I hope you will see soon, and listen too to the accompanying score. He has also written, by way of contrast, a string quartet which we in London will soon hear. [23] If you could be in the town of Dorking a few miles south of London at six in the evening you might see a big man of about 65 going round in a van, collecting salvage for the Government—old iron, tin and paper and so forth. He would be Vaughan Williams, and would probably be accompanied by his brother-in-law, R. O. Morris, whose name will be known to many musical students.

Another composer writing special film music is William Walton, who is doing several propaganda films for the War Office and is ready as an ambulance driver when the need may arise.

Constant Lambert has held the Vic–Wells Ballet together, touring all over the country giving performances to large audiences—two weeks in Manchester, two weeks in Blackpool, then back to London, then up to Glasgow and so forth. He tells me he knows more of England now than even J. B. Priestley. [24] Finance does not run to an orchestra for the ballet, so you can imagine Lambert playing the piano nightly in the orchestral pit.

Two younger composers come to mind. Alan Rawsthorne is on Salisbury Plain with the Royal Artillery, and Gerald Finzi is in the Ministry of Transport. Both are trying to sketch, in their few free hours, works for the future. The character of this war, reaching out to every realm of thought and disorganizing it, makes creative work nearly impossible. It is an interim, but creative music will burst out again as soon as this madness gives way to sanity. Thank you for your question, Mr Schliemann.

Mr Ralston asks, is there *more* or *less* music than in peacetime? The answer is less. This is due not to less need for it, but simply to practical difficulties. A great many young musicians are in uniform in one or other of the Services; the supply of fine orchestral players is limited. Before the war London was the centre of European music, and through its concert halls went all the great soloists of the world. They are now all with you, enriching the musical soil of America. The blackout of large towns, starting here in London tonight at about 6.30, makes evening performances

---

[23] String Quartet No. 2 in A minor (1942–4).
[24] A reference to Priestley's *English Journey* (1934).

impossible, concerts have to be wedged in at odd times during daylight. There is no money either to spare for the organization of further concerts, and the loss of the Queen's Hall in London and the Free Trade Hall in Manchester were severe blows to a musical public. But music-making today is 100% more than what it was last year, and there will be, for instance, 60–70 concerts this season in the vast Albert Hall.

One of the most outstanding musical successes last year was the tour of the London Philharmonic Orchestra round the music halls of England. How would audiences who regularly patronized revues and musical comedies stand a full symphony concert? The results were surprising. In most towns packed audiences applauded the orchestra twice nightly. In Glasgow there was even a box-office record, and in several centres the same section of the audience came again the same night to hear the second performance. This orchestra made it a point of honour to give a concert whenever it had been announced. In Coventry and Bristol the players, under Malcolm Sargent, arrived not long after the bombing had died down, and found bigger audiences than ever before.

The BBC is of course contributing a large share of music. It has already started its fortnightly public symphony concerts. I was at the first one to hear a magnificent performance of my own *Music for Strings*, and it was good to see so many old friends playing in the orchestra. Every Sunday afternoon comes an hour of fine orchestral music, and what will interest young musicians is that a series of contemporary music will start this autumn in Cambridge. From King's College, Cambridge, we will also broadcast a series of fine Bach organ recitals. Do not think of us as barren of music—these are only a section of the short-term musical planning.

One of the interesting developments has been the founding of the RAF Symphony Orchestra and Military Band, consisting of magnificent players who give concerts at fighter and bomber stations up and down the country. It provides much lunch-time music for workers in aircraft factories. Perhaps you would like to hear them.[25]

Mr Tullis asks, does war seem to turn people to any particular composers or kind of music? I have asked a good number of people this question. They all agree about one thing. There is a very definite trend towards more serious music, and it is obvious that in times like these much frivolity in any art cannot be endured. A letter from a naval officer is on my table which might interest you. He writes: 'There are 24 of us in the Mess, and I can divide them into four categories. One, those who really dislike serious music; two, those who are not very interested but do not mind others listening to it; three, those who are interested in good music of the

---

[25] A recording of Sir Walford Davies's *Royal Air Force March: Fast*.

lighter kind but on the whole prefer dance music; and four, those who definitely demand good music and go to concerts. In the first category of music-haters we have only one man; the not very interested number seven, the politely interested six, and the actual concert-goers ten.'

In serious music there is one composer whom the people need and demand above all others, and he is Beethoven. In the recent Promenade Concerts in the Albert Hall the top galleries were filled on a Beethoven night—this generally happens only on boxing nights, or when there are great spectacular shows. Before the Queen's Hall was destroyed by bombing, Basil Cameron gave a series of five Beethoven concerts there. It was impossible to get a seat. Beethoven has supplanted Bach in general favour. Wagner has slipped well down the list of favourites, Sibelius still holds his own chosen public. The three Bs, Bach, Beethoven, and Brahms, will always draw large audiences, with Beethoven by far the most popular. This is only natural. In this war eternal truths and stark realities are there for all to see—and none can escape them. Beethoven expresses and explains them as no other composer ever has, and behind all his music is an impending sense of freedom. Thank you for your question, Mr Tullis.

I have been asked a question about American music—what American music and how much is played in England today? I am glad this question came up. I have a list here of all American music broadcast in BBC programmes since the war. It is a long one. In the past six months I see the names of John Alden Carpenter, Aaron Copland, Deems Taylor, Samuel Barber, Richard Hageman, MacDowell, Charles Griffes, Francis Hopkinson, and Leo Sowerby. Gershwin had a special concert on the anniversary of his death last July. A high spot in the recent London Promenade Concerts conducted by Sir Henry Wood in the Albert Hall was the Anglo-American concert which the American ambassador attended. We broadcast this concert to America. The chief American works were the *Song of Faith* by Carpenter, and a symphony by Samuel Barber.[26] Both went with great success. We have recently broadcast Carpenter's Violin Concerto. I think you might like to hear this American work as it was recorded from the studio with Eda Kersey playing the solo violin and Raybould conducting the BBC Orchestra.

We hope to do much more American music in the future. I want to hear again works by my friends Roy Harris and Walter Piston, and if there is a work written within the boundaries of the University of California that is suitable for us, and can be sent over, I shall be very keen to help in a performance here.

[26] Symphony No. 1 (1936).

I have time to answer one more question, and that is, how much music is available at small cost or free in the English democracy? Well, our outstanding democratic series is undoubtedly the National Gallery Concerts, organized by Myra Hess. Ever since the start of the war, every day at one o'clock you see queues lining up at the National Gallery in Trafalgar Square to listen to an hour's lunch-time concert of chamber music. It costs a shilling to get in, and there you hear the finest music, though you may be exceedingly crowded. Here again Beethoven is to the fore, the complete cycle of his quartets having been given several times. The five hundredth concert was reached last month, and there is no slackening in enthusiasm.[27] These concerts have been given every day, regardless of how bad war conditions are. Similar concerts have started weekly in Oxford, Bath, Cheltenham, and Liverpool. I am going down to Oxford myself to take part in one in a few weeks.

Music for the people is in the air, but we have a lot to learn from you in this respect. We envy you your Hollywood Bowl, your New York Stadium, and your Ravinia Park,[28] and your many festivals, but we are determined to regain the ground we have lost here.

Goodbye to all my friends in California.

———

MUSIC POLICY

Bliss assisted in the Overseas Music Department of the BBC 1941–2 and was Director of Music 1942–4. This is his reply, in a memorandum of 30 December 1941, to a discussion paper by B. E. Nicholls, Controller of Programmes. A slightly edited version appears in *As I Remember*, pp. 149–52. Typescript, BBC Written Archives.

Your policy contains so much wisdom arising from broadcasting experience that I am naturally in agreement with its main drift, but there are details in it in which you seem to adopt a certain 'cat on hot bricks' attitude which I would like to question, and as you have asked for a frank reply, I give it.

Truism

A sense of music is a primal thing in mankind, and a tremendous force, either for good or for evil.

[27] The number of concerts (Oct. 1939–Apr. 1946) eventually reached 1,698. The substantial proceeds went to the Musicians' Benevolent Fund.

[28] In suburban Chicago, the site of a summer festival since 1936.

Threefold Function of Broadcast Music
1. Inexorably to continue and expand the principle of great music as an ultimate value, indeed a justification of life.
2. Faithfully to enrich leisure hours with entertainment.
3. Physically and mentally to stimulate tired bodies and worn nerves.

N.B. It betrays its trust if it debases the spiritual value of music, acts as a narcotic or drug, or bores by sheer inanity.

Coaxing Caliban
The danger of the theory of the maximum audience for music is that it can so soon degenerate into wooing the lowest common denominator of that audience. We are apt to be a timid nation, aesthetically and intellectually, and a bit shamefaced when appealing to the finer instincts of people. Just as the pace of a convoy is determined by its slowest ship, so often is the level of a programme determined by consideration for the lowest common intelligence. You cannot coax Caliban without losing the interest and respect of Ferdinand and Miranda. It is to the brave new world that future programmes must inevitably appeal.

Popular Rising Values
There are two ways in which you can no more popularize great music than you can popularize Christianity.

(a) The cinema organ. The delight Caliban takes in this is its evocative power to recall the holding-hands atmosphere of a cinema, where he can enjoy, suffer, and live vicariously. Certain successions of chords free the tear glands; the music starts a physical sensation of a cloying kind, offensive to a vigorous mind. The cinema organ exploits with skill its red plush quality. The Germans prohibit what they know is a depressant and not a stimulant. It is a dope as insidious as opium; it is certainly not educative, winning the masses over to fine music.

Your policy as regards the cinema organ is not comparable with that of Sir Henry Wood in the early Promenade programmes, in which he included separate movements of classical symphonies in an otherwise light entertaining programme—because these symphonic movements truly reproduce the composer's genius, while the cinema organ only exudes *Ersatz*. This has no more relation to, say, Beethoven, than has a highly coloured copy of Titian, done by a pavement artist, to the real achievement. All the cinema organ does when it grasps the classics is to prettify and debase values, and end can never justify means when that end is crippled and dwarfed by the very means employed.

(b) Jazzing J.S.B. What applies to the cinema organ applies even more strongly to the jazz band. 'Mr Christ comes to town'[29] will win no more adherents to the Sermon on the Mount. The missionary aim is defeated by the vulgarity of the Hollywood setting. When you hear a messenger boy whistling the first eight bars of Mozart's Piano Sonata in C major, he is not necessarily a convert to Mozart, but simply a convert to swing. After hearing the *Unfinished* Symphony magnificently swung by a prize jazz band at the top of the Regis Hotel in New York, I cannot easily listen to the original Schubert, the former sounds so much more contemporary and exciting. I have had a dose of Benzedrine, and naturally want some more. The jazz band can be used for artificial excitement and aphrodisiacal purposes, but not for spreading eternal truths.

Transcriptions

The above criticisms do not apply to transcription of well-known classics. Liszt and Busoni have transcribed masterpieces from one medium to another, and enlarged the scope of appreciation. Present-day arrangers for military band are doing a similar service. This is not simpering at classical music, like the cinema organ, or leering like the jazz band, but is an honest translation, and as such, is commendable.

Note. There is a place for both the cinema organ and the jazz band in our programmes to provide entertainment, and your suggestion that they should be included in the policy of the Music Department is the right one.

Condensed Opera

Due to the 'vision limitation' there is a valid case for some adjustment and compression in performance of broadcast opera, and the finely rehearsed and spirited performances I have heard will justify the experiment, but I should like it remembered:

1. That a whole opera is relayed through the USA from the Metropolitan Opera House in New York every week, and that the audience that listens to this is one of the largest in the States. *Ergo* broadcasting limitations may be overcome.

2. That in many cases an alternative to mangling the form of an opera is to give one act at a time complete. Opera is an art form that cannot stand much mutilation, and sometimes the effect produced is not unlike that of the Lyon's Popular Café 2/6*d*. dinner, masquerading as a Ritz Carlton one.

Crush the Girlish Crooner

This is obviously a case for the application of *peine forte et dure*. Has this actually been done?

---

[29] A reference to Alec Templeton's popular jazz pastiche *Mr Bach Goes to Town* and works in a similar vein.

Music Policy

Let the Air Breathe
In war time the BBC must be kept on the air, but in peace time these breathing moments of silence are indispensable for life. These pauses should avoid such frequent instances as:

Announcer: I think we just have time to play you the beautiful sonata by Scarlatti, etc., etc.

After thirty seconds the beautiful sonata of Scarlatti is faded out, one more bleeding chunk[30] from the knacker's yard.

Announcer: I am sorry we have no time to finish this beautiful sonata by Scarlatti, etc., etc.

Music and Defeatism
A certain type of music I believe to be debilitating—the recent plugging of such songs as 'Russian Rose' and 'My Sister and I'. Their appeal in mawkish and forced. Again, the 'Sincerely Yours, Vera Lynn' type of programme is effective just because it is a sure tear-jerker. Does this kind of broadcast regularly given soften or stiffen an army's morale?[31]

Scrappy-Mindedness
A glance at the *Radio Times* is like looking at a jigsaw puzzle. A paper like the *Daily Mail* will give the same impression to the eye. The Harmsworth Press years ago decided that sensationalism sold a paper. To induce love of sensationalism, a reader must be prevented from concentrating his attention on any one subject more than a minute or so. Hence the birth of paragraph technique, and headline announcements. A word to the wise!

A Fantasy
The ideal method of broadcasting throughout this country would be to have three separate channels. Available for all citizens that are worth fighting for would be two contrasted services, so that at any minute of the day he or she could draw on two of the three categories in my note on functions. For the Calibans, there would be a third service, 'the dirt track', a continual stream of noise and nonsense put on by untouchables with the use of records.[32]

---

[30] Michael Kennedy in *The Concise Oxford Dictionary of Music* (3rd edn., Oxford, 1980) attributes the phrase 'bleeding chunks' in musical usage to Sir Donald Tovey, who in his *Essays in Musical Analysis* (London, 1935) refers to 'listeners who profess to enjoy the bleeding chunks of butcher's meat chopped from Wagner's operas and served up on Wagner nights'.

[31] The last two sentences are deleted in *As I Remember*.

[32] An anticipation of present-day BBC Radio 1 (pop music). Another part of the 'fantasy' became a reality with the formation in 1946 of the Third Programme (now Radio 3) 'for cultivated tastes and interests'.

THE CASE FOR LIVE MUSIC

Memorandum to the Overseas Music Director of the BBC
22 January 1942.
Typescript, BBC Written Archives.

1. You can only hold your overseas audiences by the *personal* touch. 'Live' must speak to 'live'. Commercial canned music will hold no one, because the same discs are obtainable all over the world and are constantly heard on local stations.

2. We must continue to proclaim in music, as in every other way, what this country stands for, what it has done in the past, what it is doing now, and what its efforts will lead to. We must have in mind the position music holds in most other countries. It is our misfortune if by comparison we are uncouth, and we must not broadcast this fact. We must initiate a standard of culture at least equal to that advertised by Germany. Our own great music and our own great poetry must be broadcast by our *living* artists, who should be proud to do this service at any hour, day or night.

3. We must continue to use music as a friendly complimentary gesture, *e.g.* we must broadcast the scores of Canadian composers sent us by the CBC, and those that arrive from South Africa, New Zealand, and Australia. Dominion artists in this country must be used. Other examples of complimentary concerts have been weekly series 'Music of the Allies', the proposed Latin-American concert, and the Stalin and Roosevelt birthday concerts. There is no compliment in commercial recordings.

4. 'Live' music will always remain of potent use for:

(a) Evoking memories in exiled audiences
(b) Encouraging and stirring countries whose own music has been forbidden by the enemy.

Note 1
Engineers must conquer the short-wave difficulties. Overseas listening to German stations is caused more by the clarity of their transmissions than by the matter transmitted or the methods employed.

Note 2
Without 'live' music, we shall simply become a talking shop, and anyhow, what are we all talking about?

BÉLA BARTÓK

A tribute to Bartók, who had died on 26 September, broadcast on
BBC Radio on 29 September 1945.
Talk script, BBC Written Archives.

When we musicians in England hear the name Béla Bartók, we immediately see a vision of Hungary. Like Sibelius, Vaughan Williams, de Falla, Bartók can conjure up in a few bars a whole country. Even for those of us who have never seen Hungary his music fixes vivid and precious memories in the imagination. We feel that the folk songs of Hungary, Slovakia, and Roumania have never before found so authentic an interpreter.

But it would be setting too great a limit to his musical genius to think of him only as a product of nationalism in music. He is one of the most individual of all twentieth-century composers, and at each festival of modern music throughout Europe it was *his* work round which ranged the greatest controversy.

I first came across Bartók's music when as a young man I found a copy of his ballet *The Wooden Prince*. How I wish I had seen it in Budapest! Here was music so markedly personal that I can only compare its impact with that of the first Debussy pieces that I heard. I tried to get all the music of this Hungarian composer that I could—his early *Bagatelles*, the *Roumanian Dances*, the *Elegies*, the children's pieces. A new star had risen for me in the musical sky and I studied these piano pieces with excitement and admiration.

His music I find quite uncompromising. There are few concessions offered to those who go to a concert primarily for entertainment. What Bartók has to offer is the truth as he saw it, and those of us who wish to discover it must go with hearts prepared. But when his message has been grasped, how rich the reward!—the lovely Violin Concerto, the dazzling Sonata for two pianos with percussion, the moving *Music for Strings, Percussion, and Celesta.*

Bartók was always sure of an enthusiastic welcome here in England. His dignity and modesty, his dislike of publicity, his refusal to wear the air of a great man heightened respect for one so richly gifted.

It was always memorable to hear Bartók play the piano either in his own works or in music such as the Scarlatti sonatas that he loved. It was playing of an impeccable clarity—precise and balanced, with a highly polished style in rhythm and phrasing.

To fumble myself through the collection of short pieces he called *Mikrokosmos* and then to hear him play them on his last visit to London was to receive an object lesson in how a sense of style and tonal balance can make music live and glitter. I remember Bartók playing his Second Piano Concerto with Sir Henry Wood in the Queen's Hall. I sat close to him and could observe the concentration of his beautifully formed head, and the look of splendid intelligence in his eyes. The last time I saw him was in California during the first year of the war. A refugee from his own country, his face had assumed a tragic mask, and it was only when he spoke of music that it took on serenity.

The world is the loser when a great artist dies, and in Béla Bartók we have lost a great artist. His work remains to enrich succeeding generations.

FILM MUSIC

Bliss had recently written the score for his third film, *Men of Two Worlds* (1945).
Untitled contribution to a symposium in John Humphrey, *British Film Music* (London, 1947), p. 160.

I'm afraid I have to be brutally frank and say that the chief incentive to write for the screen is £. *s. d.*, because a composer is likely to make far more money in a little time by this sort of work than he is from the casual and not-too-frequent performances of his works in the concert hall or over the radio. But even while working against all the mechanical restrictions on inspiration imposed by this form of composition, it may still be possible for a musician to preserve his artistic integrity. But he must bear several things in mind; one is that the atmosphere of the film studio may encourage complacency, because film people have a way of exaggerating and bestowing praise that is not always justified by hard artistic standards. Secondly, it must be remembered that the dramatic quality of a piece of film music is enhanced by the correspondingly dramatic content of the picture itself. The person watching the film is already in an emotionally responsive condition and will tend to invest the music with wonderful qualities that it doesn't really possess. My argument is that in the last resort film music should be judged solely as music—that is to say, by the ears alone, and the question of its value depends on whether it can stand up to this test.

———

GRACE NOTES ON BALLET

After *Checkmate* came the ballets *Miracle in the Gorbals* (1944) and *Adam Zero* (1946), both to scenarios by Michael Benthall and first performed by the Sadler's Wells Ballet conducted by Constant Lambert, to whom *Adam Zero*, with its Night Club Scene, was appropriately dedicated.
Contribution to *British Ballet*, ed. Peter Noble (London, 1949), pp. 129–30.

The most desirable music for ballet is music which can have no complete or logical life apart from its association with dancing.

*

All great classical symphonies and concertos live by their own self-imposed laws and are complete, vital, satisfying entities. Why superimpose another art? Would you add the tail of a peacock to the body of a lion?

*

Of all classical forms the most fitted for choreography is the variation, which can be treated choreographically without aesthetic confusion. Frederick Ashton acknowledges the aesthetic truth of this in his beautiful ballet, *Symphonic Variations*.[33]

*

Ballet is a visual rather than an oral art. Opera is an oral rather than a visual art. *Verb. sap. comp*.[34]

*

In ballet the synthesis of several arts advocated as an ideal by Wagner can be obtained. A composer, a choreographer, and a painter can, from the start, work on equal terms and create together a new form of art—intelligible dialectic!

[33] Music by César Franck.
[34] 'A word to the wise is sufficient'.

The most powerful imaginative movement in ballet is often the simplest —the moment when a physical gesture and a musical phrase indissolubly blend. If each is performed separately, mystery evaporates.

*

The composer for ballet is severely limited by a 'time factor'. How long, for instance, can a solo dancer sustain his difficult role? Music for ballet should often be epigrammatic.

*

Robert Helpmann breathes the dust of the theatre like hydrogen. His quickness to seize on the dramatic possibilities of music is mercurial. I was not at all surprised to hear him sing in *Les Sirènes*.[35] It would seem quite natural to see him walk on to the Albert Hall platform one day to play a violin concerto.

*

Ninette de Valois is the one choreographer to experiment with Bach's *Art of Fugue*, so beautifully clear and logical is her mind. I was exhilarated by working with her in *Checkmate*; she moved the pieces like an Alekhine.

———

CHRISTOPHER COLUMBUS

An account of the music for the film, directed by David Macdonald
and released in June 1949. Bliss did not make a suite from his score,
though two short extracts were broadcast by the BBC in July 1949.
In 1979 Marcus Dods edited a three-movement suite and recorded
it with the City of Birmingham Symphony Orchestra
(HMV ASD 3797).
Film Music Notes, 9 (November–December 1949), p. 16.

The whole of the first half of the picture, *Christopher Columbus*, is laid in Spain, mostly at the Spanish court, and shows Columbus's frustration at the delay and lack of interest in his first adventure. It is difficult with American and English actors to suggest the atmosphere of Spain—that is what the music has to do—so I have tried using Spanish idioms and tunes akin to those of Spain which convey the feeling and atmosphere of the age in which Columbus set forth from Spain.

---

[35] Music by Lord Berners (1946).

The first two climaxes in the film for music are naturally the first sight of the New World and later the return of Columbus with the triumphant news in Spain. In the voyage across I tried to convey the long suspense as confidence gives way to dejection, leading to mutiny aboard. After many trials, land is finally sighted and apprehension gives way to thanks-giving as the New World is reached. The voyage back rises rapidly to a crescendo of excitement as Columbus's ship, the *Nina*, approaches Spain. A small boy sights it from the cliff tops and rushes into the town spreading the news 'Columbus is back'. The music re-echoes his cries. The townspeople gather at the harbour; the excitement grows intense. The *Nina* sails into the harbour—and now the scene changes to the Court of Ferdinand and Isabella. The court trumpeters blow a fanfare and, to a triumphant march, Columbus makes his entry into the grand hall and up to the thrones of the King and Queen of Spain. Musically I found the picture extremely interesting.[36]

CONCERTO FOR TWO PIANOS AND ORCHESTRA

From an introductory talk to a BBC Radio concert broadcast on
18 July 1950 which also included *Introduction and Allegro* and
Music for Strings. The concerto was revised in 1950, though it is
not clear whether this performance was of the revised version.
See *Catalogue* 110.
Typescript, Bliss Archive, Cambridge University Library.

The Concerto for two pianos and orchestra which ends this concert was the earliest of the three works to be composed. It began its career in 1920, though in a very different guise. In that year my friends Myra Hess, the pianist, and Steuart Wilson, the tenor, planned to give a concert with me in London. To mark the occasion I wrote an experimental work for them both to appear in together, a Concerto for piano, tenor voice and string orchestra. I also added a third soloist in the shape of a xylophone player. The words for the tenor, abstract and philosophic, I wrote myself.[37]

[36] In later life Bliss often admitted that parts of the film were unintentionally comic, in particular Columbus's arrival in America, but he remained impressed by its spectacular features and proud of his score: 'I saw it on television about two years ago, and I must say that the sound-track was superb . . . we didn't have a lot of extraneous talking or noises . . . there were big sweeps of music without anything else . . . It was comic, but at the same time the pageantry was splendidly done and the colour gorgeous' (from an interview with Muir Mathieson recorded in 1974 for the Granada Television Historical Record archive).
[37] See p. 4, n. 4 above.

The actual performance was encored and we played it straight through again. There seemed, however, little likelihood of a third performance, as this unusual combination was almost impossible to fit into any normal programme. But I was fond of the work and did not want to see it wholly neglected. I determined therefore to rethink it for a different combination of players, and a few years later I rewrote the whole concerto for the two American pianists Maier and Pattison, to be accompanied by a full orchestra.[38] They played it for the first time in its new habit with Koussevitzky in Boston. The xylophone still remained an important third personage, but the part for tenor voice was woven into the orchestral texture.

As in the *Introduction and Allegro*, the opening theme, here given out in octaves by both pianists, forms the motto for the whole work, appearing in many disguises throughout. The concerto is in one continuous movement, bright and percussive in character, but there is a slow middle section which gives quiet relief, and permits the two pianists a lyrical flow. I feel now that this thirty-year-old work foreshadows, in its preoccupation with rhythm and colour, the later ballets, *Checkmate*, *Miracle in the Gorbals*, and *Adam Zero*.

———

THINGS TO COME

An introductory talk to a BBC Radio concert broadcast on
15 November 1950.
Typescript, Bliss Archive, Cambridge University Library.

It was in 1935 that I got my first experience in writing music for the films. During that year Sir Alexander Korda produced in his Denham Studios, near London, the film version of H. G. Wells' book *The Shape of Things to Come*, and Wells asked me to provide the musical score. This invitation brought me six months of adventure. To begin with, it was an adventure to see Wells himself at work. He was a man of tireless curiosity. For him, as for me, it was a plunge into a new world, and he was always interested in the new. He was constantly in the studios, suggesting, criticizing, stimulating all and sundry.

Although he knew next to nothing about musical technique, he had a genius for putting his finger on a weak spot, for pointing out a slack

[38] See p. 48 above.

thought. I treasure letters and postcards from him during that time, written in his small and squiggly hand, and containing a mass of directions and hints, some of which, I fear, were frankly unpractical.

It was an adventure too to watch the army of technicians at work on the gigantic sets, and to have a magnificent orchestra like the London Symphony on the spot to record what I had just written. Directing the orchestra was a young Scottish conductor who has long been famous in the world of film music, Muir Mathieson.

In the thirties Wells wrote *The Shape of Things to Come* as a prophetic warning of what one day might happen to our world. The story starts in a great capital city—Wells called it Everytown—at Christmas time. Suddenly, without warning, an enemy country launches a devastating attack from the air. This is the spark which sets alight a world conflagration. In the course of long years of war, civilization as we know it is virtually destroyed. The survivors live like men in some primitive age, deprived of any of the material comforts of life which we usually take for granted. From this barbarism there slowly emerges a group of men who are determined to build a new world, one from which war will be banished and in which security and happiness will seem assured to mankind. The film shows a view into the far future when this plan is realized, and we glimpse its order and beauty. But Wells did not believe that man ever rested on past achievement, and so in the final scene two young volunteers, a boy and a girl, are shown setting out on a dangerous quest to reach the moon.

I have chosen six selections from my music to this film. The first accompanies the Christmas scene at the outset. Young children are playing round a Christmas tree, while their elders are examining with amusement some of the toys, among them models of tanks and aeroplanes. This leads them to discuss whether war were possible with such destructive weapons. I call this first piece 'Ballet for Children'.

This Christmas scene is interrupted by the sudden air attack. The scene changes to a crowded street in a theatre district (it might be Piccadilly Circus or Broadway), and the film, accompanied by realistic sound as well as by the music, shows bombs falling and buildings crashing ('The Attack').

Wells wished to show that, whether victors or vanquished, all suffer equally from the destruction of scientific knowledge and the break-up of medical safeguards. The long years of war bring a pestilence ('The Pestilence').

The remaining three pieces in this suite deal with the new world as seen through Wells' imagination. The first attempts to regain order and sanity are accompanied by the following 'Theme of Reconstruction'.

Gigantic machines rebuild the world anew. We see hills levelled, the earth mined, houses built, power supplied, all apparently without the visible control of human beings. Wells was particularly keen to secure the appropriate music to this sequence, and I have a note from him in which he wrote, 'Remember that the machines of the future will be absolutely noiseless.' I couldn't solve that puzzle, so I contented myself with trying to express the calm unhurried rhythm of these almost-human monsters ('The Machines').

The final movement is a March, which served as a motto theme for the whole film.

STRING QUARTET NO. 2

Although Bliss had written two quartets previously, in *c*.1914 (later withdrawn) and 1923, he began his numbering with the String Quartet in Bb (1941); see 'A Note on the String Quartets', *Catalogue*, p. 44. String Quartet No. 2 was first performed by the Griller Quartet at the Edinburgh Festival on 1 September 1950. Typescript, Bliss Archive, Cambridge University Library.

This Second String Quartet was composed ten years after the first quartet, and was written during the spring and summer of 1950. It is dedicated to the Griller String Quartet, and is a tribute to those players on the twentieth anniversary year of their coming together.

The work is in four movements.

The first movement, marked 'allegro con spirito', is forceful in character, and opens with an energetic theme played in unison by the three upper strings:

This is heard in different guises throughout the movement, either in *legato cantabile* form, or in augmented notes, or in an inverted shape. It is most often treated contrapuntally.

Two other themes complete the first group of subjects; the first quietly harmonized:

the second rhythmic and percussive in effect:

A contrasting section follows, marked by a gently flowing tune of seventeen bars starting with the first violin over a pedal bass:

The cello plays a varied version of this, and there immediately follows a clearly recognizable development of **A**. Much use is made of the upward leap of a major seventh. The music grows in force and dynamic power, and the climax is reached with a powerful statement of **B**. A classical recapitulation of **A**, **B**, **C**, **D** is heard with different scoring, and the movement is brought to a close in a quiet coda anchoring itself firmly in F minor.

The second movement is slow and contemplative in character. It starts with a quiet dissonance, the rhythm and spread of which is characteristic of the first theme:

All strings are muted, and harmonic clashes add to the veiled effect. A second section, quicker in pace, is announced by the first and second violins playing in thirds, and later in fifths, over a staccato rhythmical figure in the cello:

After a return to the mood of **E** the cello without mute has a solo, declamatory in style, accompanied by the other three strings tremolando and still muted. The music quietens to a further variation of **E**, and a threefold repetition of the opening dissonance, very softly played, ends this slow movement.

The third movement, marked 'vivo e con brio', has the spirit of a scherzo and is played at top speed. After an upward rush for the four instruments in turn, later to be an important feature,

the following rhythmic pattern is heard:

From this fragment most of the movement grows, though the following snatch of jagged tune is developed later:

A contrasting section is formed by the quartet playing a somewhat harshly harmonized version of the following fragment:

A fugato on **G** follows, and there is an extended solo for the viola, found on **J**.

Other characteristics of the remaining pages are: (a) **K** heard quietly on the viola above a pizzicato bass and below harmonics on the two violins; (b) a combination of **K** and **G**. After a fortissimo statement of **G** in dissonance the movement ends quietly and unexpectedly.

The last movement is laid out in alternate sections. A section of each main theme is given:

L is first heard on the viola; on its second appearance later in the movement both first violin and cello have a chance to play it. It also forms the quiet coda with which the movement ends. In the last few bars the tonality, after hovering between F minor and F major, finally comes to rest in the latter.

VERDI

Contribution to 'Verdi—A Symposium', *Opera*, February 1951,
pp. 112–13.

The star of Verdi's genius rose somewhat slowly on the musical horizon which I faced as a boy. Other brilliant stars there were—Bach, the Viennese classical school, Wagner, French and Russian contemporaries —but the great Italian was low in my heavens and cloud-covered. The cloud was the indifference shown to opera by the musical world of England at that time. Oratorio was the one satisfying form, and it was therefore natural that my first experience of Verdi's music should come from singing in the choruses of his *Requiem* while I was at Cambridge.

The Latin genius is invariably seductive to an Englishman, and this first glimpse of Vesuvian fire and Mediterranean serenity acted on me like a sunny Italian wine. I got the orchestral score of *Otello* and studied it deeply. Had not Stanford told his pupils that *this* was the model score for all who wanted to write for the opera house?

It was many years, however, before I had a chance to see this opera on the stage. Among its many wonders, one struck me with special amazement: Verdi had here triumphantly solved the subtle and difficult problem of the time factor. In the first twenty minutes, with rapid decisive stroke Verdi sets before us, in music, every ingredient for the tragedy that is to follow. I tried to calculate how long in actual time the interim between the storm and the disgrace of Cassio would take. The two dimensions, Verdi's time-in-music and the time of the world, have little relation. How has he so successfully persuaded us to this paradox, especially when, in the exquisite love-duet which ends this act, he makes the radiant minutes slip by as in real life? Only a genius who had truly taken infinite pains over his art could so easily and unobtrusively master this problem of inexorable time.

'I am not a learned composer,' he said, 'but I am a very experienced one.' Experienced indeed! Some twenty-eight operas go to build his pyramid of fame, and then at the last two masterpieces crown it. In *Otello* and *Falstaff* Verdi, the master, solves the problem that daunts all writers of opera. We go to an opera house, first and foremost, to hear fine singing, because the human voice is capable of more expressive beauty than the finest Stradivarius. We also go to experience drama manifested in music.

Our first wish is satisfied by a lyric style that demands for its effect a more or less static situation. Our latter wish can only be satisfied when rapid action and crossfire argument result in tense dramatic events. Eloquence of melody must in this way be allied to dramatic musical declamation, *must* if the total result is to have unity, flow, and cohesion.

Verdi had taken over in his youth the artificial and rigid scheme of recitative and aria, together with the traditional demands by singers for repetition, cadenzas, long held high notes, and other easy tricks for winning applause. Gradually and painstakingly Verdi forged a new and flexible style in which the transition from lyric to dramatic was effected without a jolt. We can see him well on the way to a solution in such a passage as opens Act I of *La forza del destino*, where the Marquis of Calatrava is bidding his daughter Leonora goodnight. A splendid example of the fusion of irreconcilables—the lyric and the dramatic—is found in Act III of *Aïda*, from the moment Aïda is heard tragically declaiming 'O patria mia' right through the act to the final cry of Radames: 'Sacerdotes, io resto a te'.

But it is in *Falstaff*, the last opera of all, that Verdi, in his eightieth year, sets the crown on this technical accomplishment. The old alchemist mixes for the last time the opposing elements of drama, words, action, and music, bringing forth imperishable gold, aglitter with wit, gaiety, and life.

PROMS CONCERTS

A talk, illustrated by recordings, broadcast on BBC Radio on
22 July 1951.
Talk script, BBC Written Archives.

In six days from now the fifty-seventh season of the Proms starts in the Albert Hall, and once more that great musical patchwork quilt is spread before us. Once more in these skilfully varied programmes an audience is taken, as it were, for a tour through a National Gallery of music, a Tate Gallery, and also given a glimpse of some private exhibition where present-day work is being shown.

When Sir Henry Wood started the Proms, he slowly but inexorably imposed *his* musical ideas on the public. Now, perhaps, it is truer to say that the musical public is slowly and inexorably imposing *its* choice on those who plan the feast. The result looks like some Gallup poll taken from a wide section of intelligent listeners.

As can be expected, the first votes are given for the most familiar classics, and the most popular soloists. I say 'as can be expected', but it might be argued that now there are so many opportunities of hearing the best-known classics at others times of the year, some of these could be dropped from this particular season without loss of audience, and less familiar music of the eighteenth and nineteenth centuries substituted.

When it comes to our own times the net is flung fairly wide, within the remaining space left, and a good many representative names are included; but there are some curious omissions that will interest a future historian.

Obviously the two most discussed figures in the world of music during the past forty years have been Schoenberg and Stravinsky. These comments were written before the death of Schoenberg in Los Angeles this last week. Wherever music was talked of, whether in Vienna, Berlin, Rome, London, Paris, New York, or a hundred other centres, these two names inevitably cropped up in the discussion. Each one has laid a violent hand on twentieth-century music, and each is leaving a lasting mark. Why is it therefore that in the present series of Promenade programmes no work of Schoenberg appears, and no characteristic example of the later Stravinsky, later, that is, than 1912? Why not include, for instance, Stravinsky's *Symphony of Psalms*?

A German critic writing recently on the English novel said that seldom is an intellectual literary event identical with the interests of the general reader. Are the works of Schoenberg and his many followers, and those of the mature Stravinsky, simply intellectual events for the professional musician? I should have liked this put to the test by including a fine example of each in the present year's programmes.

Other famous foreign names fare rather poorly too. Bartók, Hindemith, Prokofiev have one work each (in the case of the last two names not a very important one). There is no work by an living Frenchman or by any living American composer. In this prospectus marked 'Festival Year 1951' I should have liked to see one concert a week devoted to music written during our own century.

British music gets, rightly, major representation, but I notice here one odd thing. There are only three composers under the age of 46. These three are Benjamin Britten, and two younger men, Daniel Jones, whose *Five Pieces for Orchestra* will be welcomed on August 31st, and Racine Fricker, whose First Symphony will be given on September 14th. This symphony has already had several performances outside London, and I advise all those who want to hear an authoritative voice from the new generation to be there in the hall. It is steely and purposeful music and speaks with a cosmopolitan voice. It will be interesting to see how the

Promenade audience responds to this stern exhortation to tighten the emotional belt.

There should, I think, be more music included that can be labelled 'difficult': that means, to a great extent, more music by the younger men, as indeed there used to be. This audience is largely a youthful one, and it might well welcome more music by unknown names that speak to it in accents of its own age, and this goes for players too.

Mr Herbage[39] has asked me which of the many programmes I should choose to go to, if I could only come up from the country for a single concert. I would pick August 13th. I should be able to hear an overture, an operatic aria, two concertos, a symphony, and a piece of programme music. In the course of it I should be hearing English music, Italian, French, Austrian and Russian-cum-Spanish: not a bad variety both in form and style.

The symphony is William Walton's, to be conducted by Sir Malcolm Sargent. I heard the first performance of this, or rather of the first three movements, when Hamilton Harty introduced it in the Queen's Hall.[40] I think Harty made up his mind to play it then in its unfinished form mainly to give the composer a quickened urge successfully to complete the final movement. Judging from the finished work, he was fully justified. Harty told me after the performance that he had never conducted any work at its first playing that made so deep an impression on him. Critics often use terms like 'voltage' or 'electrical force' to describe the effect of some of Walton's music. These symbols seem to be apt, for in truth I often feel as if I had been in contact with a live battery.

'High voltage' is a suitable word too for the dramatic aria of Verdi which I shall be hearing at this same concert. Nothing in opera makes a more powerful impact than *Otello*, and nothing in it is more electric (as in the heart of a thundercloud) than Iago's monologue in Act II, his creed of nihilism. This year is Verdi's year and it is good to salute him with this masterpiece.

The two concertos (both for piano) on August 13th have one thing in common. They are both written expressly for the left hand, and will be played at this concert by Paul Wittgenstein. The first is by Ravel, the second is by Benjamin Britten.[41] Both composers are master craftsmen, and indeed Britten seems to find inspiration in the very act of solving technical difficulties. The concerto must not sound as if two hands would make it more effective. A stylish solution of this same problem can be

---

[39] Julian Herbage (1904–76), on the staff of the BBC 1927–76 as programme planner and presenter, notably of the weekly *Music Magazine* for which the present talk was written.

[40] In 1934. Walton added the finale in the following year.

[41] *Diversions on a Theme* (1940).

heard a few nights earlier when Harriet Cohen plays a concertante for solo piano by Arnold Bax.

But now that I am in London for this concert on the 13th, why not stay over for the 14th too? I shall then be able to recall the morning when I first heard this music, with the composer listening, in the Maida Vale Studios of the BBC—the morning of the first rehearsal of Vaughan Williams' Fifth Symphony, in an inspired vision of peace in a world at war. This music has added interest now, for its themes and spirit recur in the composer's recent morality *The Pilgrim's Progress*. I can think of only one other composer, Beethoven, who has explored this distant world of the human spirit.

I find I have struck a very good week in the Albert Hall, for if I stay up Tuesday the 14th, why not remain Wednesday and hear Dennis Brain play the last of the four Mozart horn concertos? I believe Mozart scored this one with red, blue, black, and green inks and added numerous jokes in the margin to confuse his good friend Leitgeb, a horn player in Salzburg. I shall also be able to see Constant Lambert conduct his perennially fresh *Rio Grande* the same evening. And what about the unusual programme of Bach and Mahler on the 15th? It is really hopeless to begin choosing.

Much better get a ticket for whole series!

SOME ANSWERS TO SOME QUESTIONS

Music, December 1951, pp. 17–19.

1. *Do you think composing is a full-time job? Do you think that a composer can gain by (a) teaching, (b) playing in an orchestra, (c) making one or other his main job?*

Composing is not a job at all. It is a function, one for which certain human beings are designed. You might as well ask 'Has a lighthouse a full-time job, or should it be doing something else during its daylight hours?'

Perhaps by teaching a composer *may* be able to focus more clearly certain problems in his own compositions, and by looking through the eye of a pupil find the solution to his own difficulties. Perhaps by playing in an orchestra a composer will more quickly learn practical details in orchestration. It would be interesting to find out what Eugene Goossens, Eric Coates, Philip Sainton, Malcolm Arnold, for instance, say about this. But as a rule a composer only undertakes teaching or continuous playing in an orchestra for severely practical reasons. He has to provide himself with the means of living, which composing by itself may not do. Most outside activities soon become a positive drudgery, and if persisted in stifle the creative impulse altogether.

This economic dilemma in which talented composers find themselves is one that state patronage of the arts can and should solve; there are too many instances in the past of tragedy caused by necessity killing invention. Creative effort in any branch of the arts means a lifetime of work. Whether awake or asleep the mind continuously strives to convert experience into sound. Hence the traditional and correct estimate of the artist as someone vague and undependable, someone only half there. Exactly so. If a composer becomes sharp and business-like, punctual and all there, he has deliberately turned off the current. The lighthouse is not functioning; it has become for the time being a seaside bungalow.

2. *In your journeys to the USA have you noticed any difference in (a) the composer's approach to music, (b) the audience's approach to music, compared with your own?*

I think the music of the younger American composers, on the whole, shows more cosmopolitan influences than does our own. I am not thinking of men like Roy Harris or Aaron Copland, whose finest work seems to me in its spaciousness and vigour to have a definitely American character, but of their more youthful contemporaries.

In so large a continent, with stock from so many races, it would be strange to find a homogeneous mode of expression, to be able to say 'American music' and know what we mean, as without question we do when we say 'French music'. I am excepting American dance music, which has a unique character all its own. It indeed directs the fashions in world dance halls, as does the American film in world cinemas. There may be emerging in America a 'New England School', a 'Middle Western School', a 'Southern School', a 'Pacific Coast school', but if there are, I am sure they will have markedly different characteristics. It must be remembered that in recent years the most influential teachers of composition in America have settled there from Europe and brought their musical traditions with them.

When I was on the Pacific Coast at the outbreak of war, Schoenberg, Bloch, and Milhaud all held important teaching posts there, and although Stravinsky has never, I believe, taken pupils, his presence in California was bound to make a strong appeal. The influence of these men on their pupils would not be of a kind to foster a national American school as such.

Beyond these considerations it is my belief that music today is searching for a more international language. The invisible guardian of music is seeking to form some common bond of conventions to which most all composers can subscribe. Its power works through the recent scientific methods of making music everywhere easily heard. In the days when Bach had to walk 30 miles to Hamburg to hear Reinken on the organ it would be inconceivable to talk about cosmopolitanism in music. But when by turning a knob I can be in the Fenice in Venice, blind indeed but not deaf, the inconceivable may well become the commonplace.

As to audiences in America, I found them very lively in their attitude to contemporary music. Like the Athenians they appreciate, even demand, a quality of newness in the arts. Just as they will tear down buildings only newly built, because they have discovered newer, and to them therefore better, designs or materials to replace them, so they tend by disposition to search for new approaches to the problem of musical expression. Fashions in art change quickly there. Whatever the advantage this may be, it certainly makes the concert programmes look more varied and enterprising than our own (I except the BBC from this stricture).

On entering the Festival Hall on the South Bank for the first time, I immediately felt that new music must be written to be heard there. Its vivid appearance stimulated creation. It seemed exactly right that it should originate a long line of new works. In America the eye is constantly being compelled by the grandeur of new projects, and it is natural that audiences there are less prejudiced against strangeness.

3. *What influences are the achievements of Schoenberg having?*

During a period of world upheaval and revolution there manifests itself a natural longing to find in the inner kingdom of art the stability and order denied to the outer world. I believe much of the popular appreciation of Bach in this country can be traced to this conscious need for serenity and order. Bach stands to us all as a symbol of peace and constructive work.

With his very different musical utterance Schoenberg too, in his mature works, appeals to our love of inner discipline and order. He was first and foremost a great teacher, and it may be in the works of his pupils in many countries that his influence will be most secure. He insisted on every piece of music being composed as perfectly as possible, seeking always for its final and inevitable form. Just as in the craft of carpentry there must be no lie, so in the architecture of sounds there must be no falsity.

He demanded a great deal from those he taught. He told me in California that his greatest difficulty was to combat the American desire for short cuts. His pupils were always demanding some abracadabra that would enable them to write a completely contemporary work ready for immediate performance. He insisted on a logical study of musical procedure from A to Z, A being the traditional practice of harmony and counterpoint. His pupils invariably wanted to start at Z.

By contrast, Hindemith, whose influence as a teacher in America is great, makes use of this American love of quick accomplishment to teach his pupils facility and free them from too much restraint. He likes to give them in the morning a problem in composition to complete, and make them perform it that same day to test its worth in sound. There is something very attractive in this practical approach, especially when the master himself can do it with such impeccable skill.

Schoenberg has certainly not made composition any less difficult a task by his teaching or by his example. He viewed the art of music from the same elevated and aristocratic platform as did Tovey, and its dignity has been enhanced. Of the strict application of his twelve-note system I am decidedly suspicious.[42] Could not any educated man, who had mastered the calculus and taken the diploma of the RIBA,[43] construct an atonal work of integrity, even if he lacked a specific musical gift?

4. *Does writing music for the films affect a composer's style?*

This depends on the individual composer's attitude to such work. Symphonies, chamber music, operas, ballets, films live in totally different worlds, and a composer must change his clothes when going from one to another.

Writing for the films is first and foremost a means of livelihood, and those film music directors who have introduced our composers to the industry are benefactors. I found the experience fascinating. It is a dream world, quite bogus, but one in which all concerned work as though it were reality itself. The technical processes dealing with music interested me, the recording, the dubbing, the cutting. Every technician seemed set on perfecting his part of the film, even if such perfection was thrown away on mere ephemeral stuff. The composer in the studio has the finest opportunity possible for learning by trial and error what is effective and what is not. Each tiny section of music is rehearsed, recorded, and then played back to him. In the concert hall there never seems the time to perfect details; in the studio, surprisingly, there is plenty.

Above all the composer learns the virtue there is in the blue pencil. Cutting because he must, he finds the slack phrase become a pregnant epigram.

How many works, I wonder, in the existing concert repertoire would not benefit by this necessary compression?

[42] In the previous month Bliss had written: 'Respect and awe are my paramount feelings for Schoenberg and his works: respect for his will in forging new tools for composition, awe for his monumental achievements in that workshop. But love? No! I love a *Figaro*, a *Meistersinger*, a *Falstaff* for the wealth of human spirit that transfigures them. Behind the works of Schoenberg I see only an inhuman lunar landscape; and I cannot warm to it' (contribution to 'Arnold Schoenberg 1874–1951', *Music and Letters* (Oct. 1951), p. 307).

[43] The Royal Institute of British Architects.

5. *Now early did you feel the need to become a composer?*

I cannot remember any time when music was not a part of my life. My mother was a fine pianist, and although she died when I was very young, the sound of music must have entered my ears from earliest days. As a child I began to learn the piano, and my two younger brothers also began to play instruments, one the clarinet, and the other the cello. An elder half-brother was already a violinist, so that the playing of music was a natural instinct in the family.

I cannot recall when I first started putting notes down on paper. It cannot have been very early, as my first ambition was to be a solo pianist. For better or worse I have kept no diaries, preferring the past to bury its past, and each new day to start without much burden of reminiscence. So my memories of those early years are vague. But I do call to mind a childish trio in E♭, a set of pieces for clarinet and piano, and more ambitious, a set of variations in C minor for piano, clarinet, cello, and drums, which was performed when I was at Rugby. I suppose I was fifteen or sixteen at the time. It was my first startling experience that what looks well enough on paper can have a strangely unbalanced effect when heard.

6. *What is the greatest problem of the composer?*

Composition is self-expression: it is an attempt to record in musical notation the jumble of feelings and experiences, of impressions and stimulations, of passions and prejudices accumulated by the I. It is as personal a thing as one's hair, and the music is the man. If it is not, there is some definable reason for the disguise. How then to chisel from the block a self-portrait?

The problem is the same as it was when Apollo admonished from the temple at Delphi 'Know Thyself'!

IS MUSIC USELESS?

Sunday Times, 19 October 1952, p. 9.

In reply to the birthday welcome given to him by the Incorporated Society of Musicians, Dr Vaughan Williams gave us one of his periodic apophthegms and told us that 'the honour and glory of our great art is that it is absolutely and entirely useless.'

He went on to enact the part of some town councillor complaining to fellow members of his committee that whereas they could at a pinch sell the oil painting by X, purchased by them ten years before, they could raise absolutely nothing on the performance of Y's symphony given the same year. It was a dead loss, in fact absolutely and entirely useless.

If there be such an official, let him go a little below the hard surface of debit and credit, and explore a less practical function of music.

Of all the arts, music can best create, store, and at will re-create memories. Every musician knows that his unconscious mind is filled with countless memories of listening, and that those which most readily rise to the surface conjure up not the personalities, places, journeys, or other vaguer contacts with performances, but the very sound itself as it was played or sung. Consequently I seldom want to remember gramophone or radio performances, because even at their best they are mere substitutes where the ear is concerned, mere dried eggs in place of fresh. I cannot imagine a listener to even the finest radio or gramophone having the same glint in his eye as the violinist has when he first tries a newly-acquired Stradivarius: or if the listener *has*, he is already beginning to lose the sensitivity of his ear.

The quality of sound *qua* sound is the first requirement for musical performance, the true hallmark of its value. True intonation from the strings, perfect chording among the woodwind and brass, subtle gradation of tone and style in the percussion are obvious essentials before an orchestral performance can be enjoyed at all. An orchestra must produce many varieties of tone colour, for a score by Debussy demands a completely different sound approach from that demanded by a score by Brahms. Perhaps for really fine stylistic performances a concert should always be shared by two conductors.

The place of performance, too, must favour the beauty or drama of the score. I am glad, for instance, that I have heard the music of *L'Après-midi d'un faune* floating up to me from the shell in the Hollywood Bowl. I am thankful, too, to have heard *Le Sacre du printemps* for the first time in the old Queen's Hall, whose acoustical properties let me enjoy a real physical impact of sound.

When it comes to exercising my analytical powers, rather than listen to Kant or sit studying him in musical notation, I prefer to read him. Some composers—and, after studying his important book of essays, *A Composer's World* (Cumberlege, 24s.), I take Hindemith to be one of them —think rather lightly of this sensuous approach to music. Myself, I am getting more and more to value it. I believe that the ear today is clearly in need of treatment, and should be nursed back to health by concentrated doses of indisputably musical sounds.

A little while ago I was listening to some French recordings of contrived noises, ranging from pops and whirrings produced by accidental imperfections in the material to watery slappings and gurgles caused by running a film track of dialogue at abnormal speeds. These sounds had been transcribed by Olivier Messiaen for various percussion instruments and cleverly moved into a rhythmic pattern.

It was an interesting clinical experiment and on a par with the many blackboard demonstrations in music produced in the last twenty years. But the ear must not surrender to a variety of jet-engine sounds, or different types of traffic noises, or, coming closer to music, to this kind of *musique concrète*. I read with a new passion the slogan 'There is no substitute for wool'.

But the ear is not the only organ in the body to seek satisfaction in music: there is another, less easily located. Some put it in the upper vertebral column, some in the solar plexus. It manifests its presence by an unmistakable shiver. This *frisson* seems to be occasioned when in the arts some quite remarkable beauty is divined. In music it may be a moment in a Mozart symphony when by chromatic alternation Mozart darkens the hitherto limpidly clear diatonic tune. It may denote the moment in ballet when musical phrase and balletic mime so intertwine that a third element of beauty is born. In opera there are many instances where synthesis of three arts produces an overwhelming sense of mystery.

This aesthetic pleasure, evanescent but intense, is perhaps the purest given to man, and like its kin in the physical world, is inexpressible except by the poet.

In some subtle way these satisfactions are linked with the belief expressed by Dr Vaughan Williams at his birthday dinner that as he grew older he found that music enabled him more and more to glimpse the Reality behind the Appearance. Can music then really be as useless as our supposed town councillor thought?

1953–1963

INTRODUCTION

IN 1953, the year of the coronation of Queen Elizabeth II, Bliss was appointed Master of the Queen's Musick (he preferred the archaic spelling) on the death of Arnold Bax. With his sense of occasion and his love of spectacle he proved an ideal choice. His contributions to the coronation were a *Processional* for organ and orchestra and a choral *Aubade for Coronation Morning*, and in 1954 he wrote *A Song of Welcome* and an Elgarian march, *Welcome the Queen*, for the Queen's return from her tour of the Commonwealth. In this year he became President of the Performing Right Society and presented Stravinsky with the Royal Philharmonic Society's Gold Medal. He was also at work on a Violin Concerto (1953–5) commissioned by the BBC. Then in 1955, a year after he and his wife had sold their Somerset home and moved to St John's Wood in London, came a set of orchestral variations, *Meditations on a Theme by John Blow*, of which he later said, quoting Elgar's inscription on the score of *The Dream of Gerontius*, 'This is the best of me'.[1] In 1956 he contributed the music to his last film, *Seven Waves Away*, and wrote the signature and interval tune for the inauguration of the ABC (later ITV) television service.

As a recognized ambassador of English music, Bliss was asked by the British Council in 1956 to lead a party of musicians on a concert tour in the USSR, where he met Shostakovich for the first time. He returned to Moscow two years later, at Shostakovich's invitation, to help in the judging of the International Tchaikovsky Piano Competition. There were other trips abroad in these years and more administrative duties, but he always managed to find time for new projects. He wrote the overture *Edinburgh* for the Edinburgh Festival of 1956, *Discourse for Orchestra* (1957) for the Louisville Orchestra, and the last of his ballets, *The Lady of Shalott* (1958), for the University of California at Berkeley. The birth of Prince Andrew

---

[1] See 'A Testament', pp. 281–2 below.

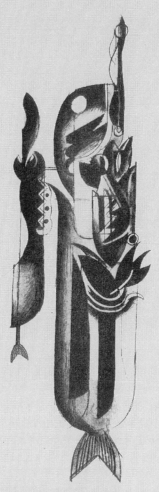

 1922 ARTHUR BLISS. A COLOUR SYMPHONY

and the wedding of Princess Margaret in 1960 were occasions for further official contributions. An opera specially written for television, *Tobias and the Angel* (1959), showed his pioneering spirit still strong at the age of nearly seventy, and was the first of several major works on biblical subjects. The cantata *The Beatitudes* (1961) was commissioned for the opening of the new Coventry Cathedral in 1962. As with certain of his other major works, from the time of *A Colour Symphony* on, the first performance was marred by practical difficulties, and this most beautiful of cantatas remains largely unknown. A second cantata, *Mary of Magdala* (1962), was followed in 1963 by *A Knot of Riddles*, a song-cycle based on Old English texts. In this year, having presented it to many other musicians in the past, Bliss received the Gold Medal of the Royal Philharmonic Society. He said on this occasion:

I don't claim to have done more than light a small taper at the shrine of music. I do not upbraid Fate for not having given me greater gifts. Endeavour has been the joy.[2]

'IN THE QUICK FORGE AND WORKING-HOUSE OF THOUGHT'

This piece, written in 1953, was apparently intended for publication or broadcast, but no record of its appearance has been found. The title is from Shakespeare's *Henry V*.
Typescript corrected by AB, Bliss Archive, Cambridge University Library.

This might well be a description of musical activity in this country today. In no previous year have there been so many concerts announced, so many festivals offered, so many summer schools organized, so many composers at work, so many plans for everything musical from grand opera to local competitive festivals. The place has accelerated from the mere *andante poco pesante* of forty years ago to the *vivace precipitato* of today.

For this increasing complexity in the music machine two factors seem mainly responsible: one, the purposeful broadcasting of serious music on a grand scale, and two, the influence of our own professional musicians, this remarkably powerful phalanx of composers and executants in our midst.

---

[2] Quoted in 'Counterpoint', *Music and Musicians*, 11 (Mar. 1963), p. 24.

With urbane buffoonery Sir Thomas Beecham denies that there has been a single good tune written since 1928. On the contrary, there have seldom been so many good ones. If you take the trouble to examine the concert programmes of forty years ago, you will be probably most struck by their restricted and unambitious scope. Only a tiny arc of the whole musical circle was thought worthy of attention. It takes no keen eye to see nowadays that almost anything, from the latest exotic to music of the remote past, can be heard somewhere and at some time. No wonder the audience grows in numbers when every taste is catered for.

It was not so long ago that if you questioned that the best came from abroad, you brought on your head the accusation of being either ignorant or pigheadedly chauvinistic. If you wanted to attend some musical festival, it must of course be somewhere in Central Europe. If you decided that you needed that extra finish that enrolment in a master class gave, obviously you had to travel across the Channel to get it. But in 1953, without spending any of your foreign allowance, you can enjoy in your own country a plethora of festivals or schools simply by zigzagging up and down the land. I might suggest you start by visiting a Cinderella of these festivals, who makes her debut at St Ives on the north coast of Cornwall early in June. Here, at a spot made famous in recent years by the presence of distinguished painters and sculptors, a week will be devoted to music and the arts with programmes of an uncommonly attractive kind. If you have sufficient money left you could well finish up in a blaze of floodlight at Edinburgh some three months later.

These festivals, whether young and specialized or mature and international, are sure proof of the vigour of our musical life today. So is the growth of the summer school movement. These holiday courses are a practical preparation for the festivals. Students can analyse, sing, or play the repertoire of music that later they will enjoy hearing under gala conditions. Quite close to me in Dorset is an outstanding example, the Bryanston Summer School, where for several years past students have been accommodated. Here in informal surroundings they have made music, and received instruction from some of the most famous musicians in the world.

I believe that enterprises of this professional standard are a comparatively recent feature in our musical life.

It might be asked, where is all this continuous activity leading, what will be the state of music in England in, say, fifty years' time? The answerer can well pause before replying. Dr Vaughan Williams is reported to have once said 'Music is a rum go'. It certainly *is*, a *very* rum go. Our art will not do the expected, *i.e.* develop comfortably along the same lines as before, only perhaps with accelerated pace.

The history of music cannot be used as an argument to prove any theory of evolution, of perpetual progress, of happy and controlled development. It rather proceeds by a series of more or less violent jerks, and these spasmodic convulsions are mainly caused by the emergence from time to time of musical personalities of marked individuality. At their appearance on the scene music shakes and shivers and later re-settles herself, but in a slightly different position. It is as impossible to prophesy who these personalities will be or when they will come as to forecast an entirely new vegetable. It would seem that every so often the musical apple cart must be upset, and that in picking up the apples again some very strange fruit is found lodged among them.

In purely technical matters, I can venture a supposition or two. I think the next division of our art on which composers will concentrate for hard thinking may well be the question of 'form'. While the sister arts, notably sculpture, have found new definitions for the shapes in which 'ideas' can be carved or cast, music has remained largely dependent on forms handed down by tradition. These traditional forms are still in general use, although the musical ideas of today are often in total variance to the moulds into which they are forced. Some of Paul Klee's delicate pictures have been compared to 'going for a walk with a line'.[3] Perhaps we want fresh directions in which musical phrases can ramble.

I think too that in fifty years' time the orchestra as now composed may seem an anachronism. Its composition is mainly held steady in balance by the overwhelming weight of classical music that requires instruments of a certain tone in a certain proportion. But there is no natural acoustical law that demands just this instrumentation.

During the last thirty years a good deal of empirical work has been done in the realms of sound; new instruments will be invented, and new textures of sound will require quite different orchestral organization. Perhaps even the conductor who for years has so successfully competed with singer and pianist for the honours of primadonnadom may himself be superseded, but by whom?

[3] Bliss often used this phrase to describe the opening theme of his *Music for Strings*.

HINDEMITH

Contribution to 'Studies in Music Criticism 5: Hindemith', a
symposium on BBC Radio introduced by William Glock and
broadcast on 14 May 1953. The talk included musical examples.
Typescript, BBC Written Archives.

A composer is not a very trustworthy guide to the music of his contemporaries. He views them too suspiciously from the narrow ledge of his own aesthetic. Climbing as he does towards a goal dimly seen, the only fellow travellers that he can admire are those who toil with him in the same stony track. If he should look around him too inquisitively, he would fall.

His introspection makes him less broad-minded than a professional writer on music, or indeed a conductor or performer. These latter should try to like as many kinds of music as possible. A composer tends to enjoy only the music to which his nature makes him akin. Hazlitt says 'critics must be tasters for the public'; composers, on the other hand, need eat only what they like. When, therefore, I was asked to join a symposium on the music of Hindemith, I had to admit to myself and my colleagues that I would be in danger of uncovering my own prejudices and blind spots rather than illuminating the work of a distinguished musician like Hindemith.

Some years ago Mr T. S. Eliot with radar-like precision defined the processes of creative development in a simple exposition, this in a preface to the poems of Ezra Pound. He wrote that a creative artist's work 'may proceed along two lines on an imaginary graph, one of the lines being his conscious and continuous effort in technical excellence, that is, in continually developing his medium for the moment when he really has something to say. The other line is just his normal human course of development, his accumulation and digestion of experience, and by experience I mean the results of reading and reflection, varied interests of all sorts, contacts and acquaintances, as well as passion and adventure; and then the two lines converge at a high peak, so that we get a masterpiece.'

If I may add to what Mr Eliot has written, I will say that in music the first of these lines leads to a mastery of style or manner of composing, while the second ensures a richness and diversity of matter. At the high peak, manner and matter become one. Now I am on absolutely sure ground when I acclaim Hindemith for his mastery of technique. I know of no other living composer with such command of every technical resource. He never fails to solve the problems which he sets himself, and his facility and authority make him a commanding teacher.

I have heard it said that Hindemith encourages his pupils to write quickly in the morning and perform what they have written in the afternoon. This practical approach is characteristic. Much of his own music is written to interest the players, and I have yet to meet one who does not enjoy playing a typical Hindemith passage. Like Strauss, he seems to know the psychology of every instrument. His approach to his art is very German. He has a genius for organization and a deep earnestness which includes the conviction that music has a moral purpose. His view of 'form' is traditional; he prefers the clear-cut designs inherited from former masters, from Bach to Reger. His movements in sonata form, his many essays in fugal texture are as easily analysed as similar ones in the German classics. He believes in the necessity of counterpoint at all costs—and if this all sounds like a description of any typical *Kapellmeister* let me quickly add that he speaks with an entirely personal voice. His music cannot be mistaken in manner for anyone else's, so original is the baroque shape of his themes, and the unsensuous harmonic character he can give them. If, as has been objected, his music approximates to some sort of tonal engineering, the graphs of his melodies drawn on a blueprint would immediately establish his personal utterance.

This music of Hindemith with its drive, logic, and intellectual grip comes to me as the music of a contented, extroverted composer, in complete contrast to so much other Central European music over which the Freudian shadow of Schoenberg has passed, leaving neuroticism.

Now as to the second of the lines mentioned by Mr Eliot in his words on creative activity, how rich is the inner life of this music, a life which should warm and colour what the perfected technique is so capable of translating? In estimating the value of Hindemith's mature work in terms of human experience I find myself on much more debatable ground. I like to play it. I like to study it. How much do I really enjoy listening to it as an experience? Is it stone or bread?

Hindemith himself has no doubts on this point. In his recent book, *A Composer's World*, he writes: 'A composer cannot be far-reaching enough; his desire to know, to comprehend, must incite, inspire, and drench every phase of his work. Storming the heavens with artistic wisdom and practical skill must be his last ambition.' Agreed, but why, I ask myself, in listening to his music do I feel neither incited, inspired, or drenched with emotion? To my disappointment I feel I am getting not an emotional experience, but a lecture.

A lecture can be brilliant, provocative, masterly in form, and eloquent in delivery, but it remains a lecture. I demand something more from music, from painting, poetry, the drama than an appeal to my analytical powers, I demand mystery, some vision of the truth. Hindemith may believe that he can say with Blake 'for thou hast touched my five senses and they answered thee'. But far from sensing mystery in Hindemith's music, I find only a portrayal of a world which I apprehend here every day.

You may answer that I entirely fail to understand Hindemith's aims, and that in this sonata for four hands that we have heard, all he wants to do is to create an architecture of rich sound for a percussive instrument, and that in this he has wholly succeeded. Perhaps, but I doubt whether Hindemith would be satisfied with this limitation.

What about another example played this evening, the Symphonic Interlude from the opera *Mathis der Mahler*? Here surely Hindemith is not content to storm the heavens only with artistic wisdom and practical skill. I tested my theory of 'bread and stone' by playing after this record excerpts from two other composers, both of whom, like Hindemith, use a contrapuntal texture for the expression of deep feeling. One was a movement from Michael Tippett's Concerto for Double String Orchestra, and the other a movement from Edmund Rubbra's Second String Quartet. Both composers might take such a subject as 'the Entombment' and portray it with compassionate and tragic music. After replaying the Hindemith I ended with the slow movement from Vaughan Williams' Fifth Symphony. My impression was that the music of Hindemith sounded in comparison impersonal, even detached, less expressive, less generously suffused with human experience. It may be salutary at times to adopt a French aesthetic and hate *le moi*; but one must have an 'I' before it can be an object of hate. In the last analysis it is personality alone that can touch the heart.

I believe that if some sensitive seismographic instrument could register the oscillations of the human heart during performances of great music, we could better distinguish between that music which produces a real aesthetic *frisson* and that which only interests the analysing mind.

I feel that in the music of Tippett, of Rubbra, and of Vaughan Williams that I have played there is a higher voltage of emotion and a more urgent need for expression than is vouchsafed to Hindemith. When a composer is subjected to such a degree of intensity that the music seems to write itself, we call it inspiration. Between those composers, who at times act as a medium for music, and those others, however highly endowed, who only manufacture it, there is a very wide gulf.

I ask myself, can Hindemith's great gift of technique by itself generate enough heat to produce works of lasting significance?

======

NOEL MEWTON-WOOD

A talk broadcast on BBC Radio on 24 January 1954, following the
death, by suicide, of the Australian pianist (1922–53) to whom Bliss
had dedicated his Piano Sonata (1952), and who had given its first
performance in a BBC Radio broadcast on 24 April 1953.
Typescript, BBC Written Archives.

When a young player with many splendid gifts dies before those gifts can
be brought to full accomplishment, his friends and admiring colleagues in
the musical world feel a very special loss. This is markedly so in the case of
Noel Mewton-Wood, whose death at the age of 31 robbed us of a young
man likely in his next few years to become one of the great players of our
time. I used the word 'splendid' to describe his gifts, for their brilliance
must have seemed dazzling to his young fellow pupils in Melbourne.

The facts of his life are easily told. He comes from a musical family, his
mother being his first teacher. He came to this country from Australia
when he was fourteen, and at seventeen made his first appearance as a
concerto player in the Old Queen's Hall, when he played Beethoven's C
minor Concerto with Sir Thomas Beecham conducting. He started as a
prodigy, and a providence in the guise of a wise mother watched over this
particular prodigy and let him steadily develop into an artist.

If I have said that his gifts had not come to full accomplishment, it was
simply because every time he played he seemed to me to be growing in
stature. For a time he was at the Royal Academy of Music, and he studied
later with both Clifford Curzon and Schnabel. The years following were
filled with the ever-widening circle of concert engagements and tours
abroad.

Before talking about him further, I would like you to hear him for
yourselves, hear him as the virtuoso pianist playing in the grand manner.
He was always original in his choice of works, and he often liked to rescue
from temporary oblivion music that took his fancy. In this instance it is
Tchaikovsky's rarely-played *Concert Fantasy.* I have chosen the cadenza,
and in this we can hear him playing with all his youthful exuberance and
joyous vitality.

Mewton-Wood was much more than an outstanding pianist. His was
one of the most inquiring and far-reaching minds I have met in a young
man. A study of his bookshelves would show the serious and varied range

of his reading. He had a great love of poetry. He admired modern painting, and knew how to add to the collection left him by his uncle, the poet Walter Turner.

Here were some of his other interests. I am indebted to a close friend of his for many of these, to me, unexpected hobbies. He was deeply interested in certain aspects of science, especially medical subjects. He was knowledgeable on the breeding of Alsatian dogs. He was a good mechanic, the only pianist I have ever met who could repair his own piano. He was an excellent cook; his speciality was sauces. He liked the mechanism of clocks: at eight years of age with sure, sensitive fingers he could take a watch apart and, what is more difficult, assemble it again (what other pianist kept a bottle of clock oil?). He built a marionette theatre and wrote little plays for it. I feel I might be describing some young Goethe.

This variety of interests together with his analytical powers—seeing how the clock works—made his interpretation of music intellectually very satisfying. He indeed felt the music from the composer's standpoint. His appreciation of a 'style' was unusually keen. I would like you to hear his recent recording of one of Liszt's *Petrarch Sonnets*, Sonnet 47. The secure and quiet happiness he always felt in playing is evident throughout.

Noel Mewton-Wood's repertoire was a very wide one. He was a staunch exponent of modern music. It is rare to get a great virtuoso who will play modern music with understanding and enthusiasm, and with his death we composers of today have lost one of our greatest champions. I remember wonderfully authentic performances of Bartók's Sonata for two pianos and percussion, of Stravinsky's Concerto and *Capriccio*, of Michael Tippett's Sonata, of Hindemith's *Ludus Tonalis*. I heard him play this last work at Morley College a few years back. With its twelve fugues and interludes, it is a long and formidable work to learn; but Mewton-Wood played it by memory with apparent ease, a very stern test for brain and fingers. Like his master, Schnabel, he enjoyed playing chamber music, and again like his master he called from his partner in ensemble the finest playing of which the other was capable. I want you to hear part of Busoni's Second Violin Sonata played by Max Rostal and Mewton-Wood. Mewton-Wood was an ardent admirer of Busoni's music, and had mastered Busoni's great Piano Concerto as well as his *Fantasia contrappuntistica*.

I have chosen from Busoni's Violin Sonata the Presto and the succeeding Andante Grave, and close with the statement of the Bach chorale on which Busoni, for his final section, builds a structure of variation.

Earlier on I said that Noel Mewton-Wood felt music from a composer's standpoint. It may be news to many that he was himself a composer of many works. I confess I did not know this myself. He was so modest both on the platform and off that I never knew what really lay behind that keen mind. Thanks to his mother, who has shown me his scores, I now know that he had written two symphonies (the second was composed during a South African tour), three piano concertos, two string quartets, piano and violin sonatas, and many songs. Remember his age—31.

When he was studying with Schnabel he sketched out a two-act opera on *Alice in Wonderland*, and more recently he had written a film score, *Tawny Pipit*, and music for the radio. No wonder he had such a grasp of modern music, since he wrote it too. I am sorry this evening we have no examples of his work to play. But I would like you to hear him again as an impeccable ensemble player, this time in partnership with Peter Pears. I chose this particular song partly because it is one of the last records he made, and partly because the music is by Michael Tippett, himself a close friend of Mewton-Wood. This comes from a song-cycle called *The Heart's Assurance*, and is the song from which the cycle takes its name. The words are by Sidney Keyes.

If I may be allowed, I will end this tribute on a more personal note. I had known Noel for some twelve years, and had recently conducted my own Piano Concerto with him as soloist. Quite recently, in admiration for his gifts, I asked him to accept the dedication of my first Piano Sonata. In his personality there was a blend of truly youthful and driving enthusiasm with a surprising maturity of feeling and seriousness. This made him not only an inspiring player to make music with, but a lovable companion to be with.

His impulses were invariably generous; he was always ready to give help quickly. As an artist he was the complete professional, untouched by humbug or conceit. He is a great loss to our music.

I would like to hear him play once more the slow movement of my own concerto, which he recorded with Walter Goehr last year.[4] It brings back to me many happy memories of him, for which I shall always be grateful.

MUSIC AND IMAGINATION

A review of Aaron Copland, *Music and Imagination* (1952).
Musical Times, January 1954, pp. 21–2.

Few composers of distinction have written lucidly about their methods of composing, however entertainingly they may have told us about their personal lives and loves. Either a sense of self-preservation or an

[4] Concerto for piano and orchestra in B♭ (1939), recorded by Mewton-Wood and the Utrecht Symphony Orchestra conducted by Walter Goehr (Nixa CLP 1167).

insufficiently facile pen has stopped most of them. A description of the mental processes by which a music work is composed needs the use not only of analytical powers of a high order, but of an objectivity of approach and a skill in words, given to few. It is all the more remarkable therefore that recently two books[5] have appeared in which these gifts are shown. One is Hindemith's *A Composer's World,* and the other is Aaron Copland's *Music and Imagination.* It is with the second book that I am here concerned.

This is a reprint of the six Charles Eliot Norton lectures that Mr Copland delivered at Harvard University during the academic year 1951–52. The composer modestly describes them as 'a free improvisation on the general theme of the role imagination plays in the art of music', but his subject matter is so logically varied and consistently developed that 'symphonic' would be a more adequate musical description.

In the first three lectures he discusses the importance of the gift of imagination first to the listener, then to the performer and composer. Mr Copland has a good deal to say throughout the book on the thorny subject of communication between modern composer and modern listener; and for his theories he postulates an ideal listener, who shall combine 'the preparation of the trained professional with the innocence of the intuitive amateur'.

This type of listener has a right to experience the music of every age.

Does he get this experience in America? Mr Copland thinks not: 'for', he says, 'there exists a universal preponderance of old music on concert programmes. Concert halls have been turned into musical museums.' I remember reading the same complaint in one of Mr Virgil Thomson's notices where, referring to the civically supported symphony orchestras, he claims they are less open to experiment than American churches or banks. We know all about this disadvantage here too.

The most suggestive pages in the first half of Mr Copland's book are concerned with his own feelings as a composer. Reading these pages and the later ones where he describes his early enthusiasms in Brooklyn, I feel he is lucky in his disposition, 'head' and 'heart' being so nicely in equipoise. His native romanticism and warm-heartedness are tactfully controlled by the Gallic taste he acquired when studying as a young man in Paris.

His account of why he is impelled to compose, how it feels to be in the throes, and why later he seems so detached during performances of his music is admirably convincing. His attitude to sound as such, the 'sonorous image' as he terms it, is that of an Athenian. He enjoys anything new,

5 Since reading these two books I have come across a third, equally illuminating—*The Musical Experience* by Roger Sessions. [AB]

everything new. He revels as much in the 'hard-as-nails' performances of a band of Argentinian accordion players, or the percussive sonorities of Varèse's *Arcana*, as in the effect of quarter tones in an Alois Haba quartet, or the sound of the Brazilian *berimbau*.[6] This may seem the belated stage of a musical adolescence, but it also explains why much of Copland's own music comes to the ear so fresh and personal in sound.

In his last three lectures he is on more debatable ground. He acts as guide and takes us on a short tour round Europe, followed by a more extensive one throughout the Americas. In the course of these he gives us his personal opinions on the composers he thinks important. He is mostly fair and generous, and is aware that *his* is just one opinion among many.

He has some trenchant things to say about tradition and innovation. I suspect that he supports the view of Busoni, whom he quotes: 'Creative power may be the more readily recognized, the more it shakes itself loose from tradition.' In studying this fourth lecture of Mr Copland I could not help contrasting his thesis with that of another Charles Eliot Norton lecturer, Mr T. S. Eliot, who has written: 'The artist's concern with originality may be considered as largely negative: he wishes only to avoid saying what has already been said as well as it can be.' I shall like to think that this provocative lecture of Mr Copland in Cambridge led to fierce discussion, public and private.

To point his remarks Mr Copland arranged six short recitals of music, the programmes of which, printed at the end of the book, show the sophisticated taste and wide sympathies of the lecturer. *Music and Imagination* is a short book, some 110 pages of text, but it is a valuable one. It certainly makes me eager to study and hear more of the work of this remarkable composer.

CONCERTO FOR VIOLIN AND ORCHESTRA

Musical Times, June 1955, pp. 304–5.

This violin concerto is the result of an invitation given me some two years ago by the BBC. I have had to interrupt my work on it from time to time in order to write several *pièces d'occasion*, but perhaps this very sidetracking

---

[6] 'A Brazilian gourd-resonated musical bow of African origin, with a single wire string. The player holds a stick and a *caxixi* (wicker maraca) in his right hand and strikes the string with the stick' (*The New Grove Dictionary of Music and Musicians*, ed. Stanley Sadie (20 vols, London, 1980), ii. 553).

has enabled me to see my main musical path the more clearly. Taking a comfortable tempo for its composition, I completed the score at the beginning of this year.

It is designed with the customary three movements, takes about forty minutes to perform, and conspicuously displays the soloist as the protagonist throughout. In my first movement I have followed classical precedent and made its structure depend on clearly defined and contrasting themes, with interlocking sections in which these themes, or most of them, show growth. The pace is allegro non troppo, with the ♪ = 108–120. A blackboard diagram of its design would look something like this:

First group of themes:

N.B.—Each of these themes I found capable of proliferation. Second contrasting theme:

N.B.—This lyrical theme of sixteen bars occurs but once more in the movement, when it is heard on the full orchestra.

Development of Ex. 1, Ex. 2, Ex. 3.
Short accompanied cadenza founded on a fragment of Ex. 1.
Restatement of Ex. 4.
Coda founded mostly on Ex. 2.

I should also mention a 'motto' theme of six bars' length, which introduces the soloist at the outset, ushers in the lyrical theme, Ex. 4, starts the 'development' section, and finally leads to the short cadenza.

Between the quarter-of-an-hour movements I and III comes a shorter movement marked 'vivo'. It is unmistakably a scherzo. If I had 'Queen Mab' in my mind as I wrote it, it was chiefly in order to keep Berlioz's exquisite scoring before me as a warning against overemphasis. This movement is light fingered (Ex. 5) and develops a series of dance rhythms (Ex. 6, Ex. 7).

Ex. 5

Ex. 6

Ex. 7

Ex. 8

The initial quick tempo $\flat. = 144$ is varied by a more sustained section (Ex. 8), into which, however, the capricious scherzo keeps breaking. At the conclusion of this movement, the notes of the solo violin disappear into the sky.

Without imitating a recent Russian example of self-criticism, I must say the third movement gave me considerable trouble. There were several problems to reconcile. Up to this moment there had been no slow movement. This finale had to start with complete change of mood and tempo. I felt, however, that the character of the concerto as a whole demanded a brilliant finish, and, for balance, a considerable cadenza for the violin without accompaniment.

Here the length of time I permitted myself in writing the concerto was of benefit. I began rehearsing the first two movements with my soloist, while deeply considering the third. I let myself be swayed by the style of playing of my chosen soloist, just as a playwright might be influenced by a great actor in his leading role. Campoli and I have had many rehearsals together. He has been tireless in discussing the work—almost bar by bar—in suggesting how difficult and awkward passages can be made more amenable, and in giving me, by his masterly playing, stimulation to further work. It is with the most sincere gratitude that I place his name on the title page.

An analysis of the finale might be shown thus:

Slow introduction.

Slow theme and variation:

Ex. 9

Ex. 10

N.B.—The gipsy feeling is a tribute to my soloist's temperament!
Bridge passage to second lively theme:

Ex. 11

Main cadenza, unaccompanied.

N.B.—This is founded largely on Ex. 9 and 11, and especially the bridge passage leading to Ex. 11.

Restatement of theme and variation (Ex. 9).

Coda founded on Ex. 11.

After completing the concerto I spent a week's holiday near Genoa. I went into the famous port to see one of its treasures, Paganini's own violin. I learnt with pleasurable surprise that Campoli himself had recently given a broadcast there on this famous instrument. May this coincidence prove of good omen for our concerto!

MEDITATIONS ON A THEME BY JOHN BLOW

Programme note for the first performance, Birmingham Town Hall,
13 December 1955.

Introduction: 'The Lord is my Shepherd.' 'I will fear no evil.'
Meditation I: 'He leadeth me beside the still waters.'
Meditation II: 'Thy rod and staff they comfort me.'
Meditation III: The Lambs.
Meditation IV: 'He restoreth my soul.'
Meditation V: 'In green pastures.'
Interlude: 'Through the valley of the shadow of death.'
Finale: 'In the House of the Lord.'

Shortly after receiving the welcome invitation from the City of Birmingham Orchestra to write a new work specially for them, and while thinking over what form this might take, I was sent a second present from Birmingham. This came from Professor Anthony Lewis[7] and was a copy of John Blow's *Coronation Anthems* and *Anthems with Strings* published in the collection *Musica Britannica*, edited by Mr Harold Watkins Shaw and Professor Lewis himself. I happened to open the volume at the verse anthem 'The Lord is my Shepherd' and found this noble tune. I give it just as it appears in the violins at the opening ritornello in this edition.

[7] Professor of Music, University of Birmingham, 1947–68.

I felt a signal omen had been granted me, and it was accordingly on this theme that I began to build my new work. I have used the title 'Meditations' in spite of the energetic, almost violent, character of some of the music, because I have been aware of dwelling in thought on the varied imagery used in this psalm, and of allowing myself to compose freely on different fragments of Blow's melody. Indeed, its full statement does not make itself apparent until the Finale section of the work.

The Introduction starts as a pastoral. First an oboe, and then two flutes and a piccolo play a long free melody.

Two contrasting moods are depicted in this Introduction, one of comfort and assurance, the presence of the Shepherd,

and the other of peril and lurking evil.

MEDITATION I: 'He leadeth me beside the still waters.'

This is a flowing treatment of the theme, with special reference to bars 6, 7, 8, and 9, though the contours of all the four symmetrical sections are found. The scoring is mainly confined to woodwind, horns and strings. The opening bars show the character.

MEDITATION II: 'Thy rod and staff they comfort me.'

This is based on a strongly rhythmic version of the theme, scored for full orchestra. Confidence and pride are expressed.

MEDITATION III: The Lambs.

As a contrast, this miniature scherzo is pianissimo throughout, with muted strings, woodwind, harp, and glockenspiel. The first eleven bars emphasize the truism that sheep move 'in close imitation'. The musical basis for this meditation is found in bars 14, 15, 29, and 30 of Blow's melody.

MEDITATION IV: 'He restoreth my soul.'

A quick triplet appearance of the theme

alternates with a rising progression of brass chords.

The character of the whole is joyful and confident.

MEDITATION V: 'In green pastures.'

This is concerned with a quiet re-statement of (1). From the sound of the introductory and closing bars of this meditation it may be adduced that gently flowing streams keep these fields lush and green. The peace of this section is crudely broken into with the interruption of (3),

and over a quiet percussive rhythm (full percussion is only employed in this part of the work), the Interlude 'Through the valley of the shadow of death' begins. At the end of this Interlude there is a sudden hush and the bass clarinet, still playing a version of (3), begins a quiet climb from the 'valley'. The first four bars of Blow's theme are played by the trombones and the Finale begins.

In this there are two statements of the theme. In the first, each eight-bar section is played by itself with a few bars' ritornello between. The theme is heard in the order of voices: bass, tenor, soprano, alto, and then bass again. In the second statement, the whole thirty bars are played straight through in the dominant. Over the brass tutti, the violins keep up a florid descant.

The coda consists of a return to the pastoral feeling of the Introduction. Just before the end there is one more premonition of peril, but the final chord brings complete assurance.

A COLOUR SYMPHONY

Sleeve note for a Decca recording (LXT 5170) issued in 1956, with the London Symphony Orchestra conducted by Bliss.

In 1921 Elgar invited me to write a new work for the Three Choirs Festival to be held the following year. This symphony was the result, and I conducted the first performance with the London Symphony Orchestra in Gloucester Cathedral on September 7, 1922.

The name *Colour Symphony* resulted from my accidentally coming across a book on heraldry in which I read of the symbolical meaning associated with the various colours, purple, red, blue, green, etc. Influenced by this I gave each movement of the symphony a character corresponding to a particular colour and its heraldic significance.

First Movement: Purple—the colour of Amethysts, Pageantry, Royalty, and Death

The first movement is slow in pace and ceremonial in character. Its shape is of the simplest: three short sections, each with its own theme; a rise to a climax in the centre of the movement, and then a return of the themes, slightly varied, in reverse order. A procession, in fact, the audience as onlooker watching the approach and later seeing the disappearance. The final chord is ominous.

Second Movement: Red—the colour of Rubies, Wine, Revelry, Furnaces, Courage, and Magic

A scherzo, rhythmical, gay, glittering, percussive. The sparkling opening is followed by two trios, one in flowing 6/8 time, the other a rough outburst in irregular bar rhythm. A reprise of the scherzo leads to a riotous coda. In 1932, ten years after the first performance, I revised the codas of both the first and second movements, and it is these revisions which are always played now.[8]

Third Movement: Blue—*the colour of Sapphires, Deep Water, Skies, Loyalty, and Melancholy*

The main slow movement of the symphony. At many places throughout is heard a rhythm of chords that I liken to the lapping of water against a moored boat, or stone pier:

Above this rhythm there appear arabesques on the flute, and then a long descending chromatic line for the trumpet. Later both arabesques and chromatic descent are heard together, the latter no longer played by the shrill trumpet, but on a solo violin which quietly comes from the heights. In the centre of the movement the cor anglais plays a melancholy little tune below the trillings of flutes.

Fourth Movement: Green—*the colour of Emeralds, Hope, Youth, Joy, Spring, and Victory*

The finale can roughly be described as a double fugue. The first subject is given at the outset to the violas, and the exposition is mainly on the strings:

[8] Bliss wrote at the time that 'the revision mostly refers to touches of orchestration and harmonic clarity. The only really new things will be codas for the 1st and 2nd movement. The pruning-knife has been used judiciously throughout the whole work, but the material remains as it was, and the whole spirit of the work is untouched. It is in no way a re-composition—simply a revision in the light of more mature years' (quoted by Robert H. Hull, 'Bliss's "Colour" Symphony Reconsidered', *Monthly Musical Record*, 1 July 1931, p. 200).

The second subject, in contrast, is a light, rapid theme given first to the clarinet, and then developed mainly by the woodwind section of the orchestra:

Later both subjects are combined, and the entrance of six timpani playing the rhythm of the second fugue subject heralds the climax of the symphony.

═══════

NOTES ON A MUSICAL TRIP TO THE USSR
APRIL 14th–MAY 8th, 1956

In the spring of 1956 Bliss led a party of musicians sponsored by the
British Council on a concert tour of the Soviet Union. Extracts from
his diary of the visit appeared as 'A Musical Embassy to the USSR:
Russia through English Eyes', *The Times*, 1 June 1956, pp. 11–12.
Typescript, Bliss Archive, Cambridge University Library.

This is a diary of a three weeks' concert tour in the USSR undertaken by
eight English musicians. The party consisted of Clarence Raybould,
Campoli, Cyril Smith and Phyllis Sellick, Jennifer Vyvyan, Leon Goossens, Gerald Moore, and myself; the ninth member of the party was my
wife.

April 14th. We left London together by air for Moscow via Copenhagen
and Helsinki (still snow-covered amid scenery that can only be described
as Sibelian). Arrived at Moscow airport just before midnight, to be
welcomed in the hospitable manner well known to visiting delegations.
Strong lights were thrown on us, moving cameras levelled, and a gathering
of musicians including the composers Kabalevsky and Khatchaturyan, the
violinist Kogan, the pianist Tatyana Nikolayeva, representatives of the
Ministry of Culture and the Philharmonic Society advanced with bou-
quets. Kabalevsky, the President of the Union of Soviet Composers, spoke
over the microphone, incidentally giving us the news that every seat for
our sixteen concerts had been taken, and I briefly replied for our party,
throwing somewhat rashly on the air my few Russian phrases of thanks.

April 15th. This day was allotted to 'acclimatization' and practice. We
visited two historic places associated in our minds with Moussorgsky's
operas—the Novo-Dievitchy Convent, the scene of the First Act of *Boris
Godounov*, and the Cathedral of St Basil pictured in *Khovantschina*. In
the evening we attended a concert of the music of Khatchaturyan,
conducted by the composer. The programme was unusual, consisting as it
did of three concertos, for cello, piano, and violin. Khatchaturyan's music
enjoys great popularity in the USSR, as well it might, with its melodic and
rhythmic freshness and its strong flavour of Armenian folk music.

April 16th. The powerful personality of Boris Godounov haunted us
again this morning during our visit to the Kremlin. We saw his coronation
throne in gold and precious stones, his gold saddle decorated with lion

heads, his breast plate of 2000 links, each engraved with the motto 'God with us, and nobody against us', and the splendid carriage given to him by our Queen Elizabeth.

Dazed by the barbaric splendour of the treasures in the Kremlin we took it easy in the afternoon, and prepared ourselves for the evening's invitation. This was to hear a performance of Mozart's *Requiem* given by the students of the Conservatoire. Under the direction of Sveshnikov these young players and singers gave a disciplined and sensitive performance. We could have been sitting in the concert hall of the RAM or RCM except that all the sopranos and contraltos had identical hair-dos, plaits braided round the head, and wore similar white costumes—a pretty picture to the eye. We were struck by the real pianissimo attained by the orchestra, and by some fine playing by a young trombonist.

April 17th. Our first rehearsal with the State Symphony Orchestra of Moscow in the Tchaikovsky Hall. The programme contained Elgar's *Cockaigne*, my own Violin Concerto, Arnold Cooke's Oboe Concerto, the aria 'Marten aller Arten' from *Il Seraglio*, and Kabalevsky's suite *Colas Breugnon*.

I had aksed for twelve hours' rehearsal and was generously given thirteen. Raybould with his easy and authoritative manner *and* linguistic ability immediately secure the goodwill of the players, and hardly needed the brilliant interpreter who was such a godsend to me in rehearsals.

I was interested to discover how a Russian orchestra would read music in an unfamiliar idiom. To my relief they were as fluent as our players here. At a later rehearsal Raybould bet the orchestra that they could not get through the rhythmic puzzles of Walton's *Portsmouth Point* the first time through, but he lost his bet. The string playing was particularly satisfying, the prize going to the really splendid basses. We came away from our first rehearsal in Russia with confidence.

In the evening Cyril Smith and Phyllis Sellick opened 'our season' with a recital in the Conservatoire Hall. This seats 1700 people, and is acoustically excellent. Marble columns, brilliantly lit chandeliers, and gold curtains give it an air of festivity. The hall was overcrowded, the majority of the audience being young; and as in all our following concerts appreciation of our music and our players was most generous. In response to prolonged 'slow clapping' numerous encores had to be given. We were all pleased to meet the daughter of Chaliapin among the musicians present, and to recall, to her evident delight, London memories of her famous father.

April 18th. While Jennifer Vyvyan, Leon Goossens, and Gerald Moore were giving their recital in the same hall, the others of us were invited to an evening at the Club of Art Workers, an association of writers, painters, musicians, actors, and technicians associated with film and television. The evening was devoted to a discussion on the influence of English literature and art on the Russian mind. The novelist Boris Polevoi was in the chair, and actors declaimed Russian translations of poems by Byron, Burns, and Dylan Thomas. A musical programme was given later which included a performance of Bax's *Fantasy Sonata* for viola and harp, and by the insistence of the audience Cyril Smith and Phyllis Sellick contributed soli. We sat throughout the evening in the glare of television lights and got back to our hotel too late to learn of our second recital's resounding success.

April 19th. The day of our first orchestral concert in the Tchaikovsky Hall. This is a comparatively modern building with a glass roof that can be illuminated in various colours, and seats 1600. From the platform the audience looked like one of our own Saturday night Promenade audiences. The corridors on each side of the stalls were filled with young people, who, as at other of our concerts, press forward at the end, often holding out slips of paper with musical requests or words of thanks. I saw Oistrakh sitting in front listening to Campoli. These two fine players became great friends. I was glad too to meet the composers Glière and Shaporin and the conductors of the Bolshoi Theatre. All expressed admiration for the technical mastery of the three English soloists performing tonight.

April 20th. This morning Shostakovich came to see me, and we spent nearly two hours talking together. I had asked him to bring sketches of his new symphony[9] to show me, but he claimed that they were not sufficiently advanced yet, so we discussed general musical subjects—the problems of symphonic finales, the unconscious influence of audiences on the composer, atonality, and, that inevitable topic when composers meet, the role of the critic. I felt very attracted to this shy, modest, sensitive, and highly gifted musician. He left me to lay a wreath on the grave of Miaskovsky, his master in composition, whose birth anniversary it was.

In the evening Campoli and Gerald Moore gave their first recital, an exacting programme for which both artists received enthusiastic press notices. For the rest of us it was an evening of ballet in the Bolshoi Theatre. The ballet, a new one, was based on a play of Lope de Vega, and the music was written by the Georgian composer Krein.[10] The leading role of Laurentia was danced by Plisetskaya,[11] who will certainly take London by storm when the Bolshoi Ballet visits us. To me the most notable feature of this ballet, as of others I saw in Russia, was the intensity and force of the miming and dancing at dramatic climaxes. Gestures seem more commanding than those seen here, and the faces of the dancers, like those

---

[9] Symphony No. 11, 'The Year 1905' (1957).

[10] Alexander Krein (1883–1951) was Russian, and his ballet *Laurencia* was written in 1938.

[11] Maya Plisetskaya (1925–   ), wife of the composer Rodion Shchedrin.

of Chinese actors, convey emotions of rage, hate, longing, and despair with vivid extravagance.

The conductor Fraier[12] told me how much he looked forward to presenting the Bolshoi Theatre's version of *Romeo and Juliet* in Shakespeare's own country. I am sure the high moments of dramatic action will surprise us by their power.

April 22nd. Our second orchestral concert: Walton's *Portsmouth Point*, Vaughan Williams' *London Symphony*, Lennox Berkeley's two-piano concerto, and my own dances from *Checkmate*.

For this concert, the State Orchestra of Moscow had requested an extra hour rehearsal in order to do justice to the *London Symphony*— Raybould's poetical and authentic performance of this was one of the successes of the tour. The music seemed to cast a spell on the audience, broken only when the reference to the Westminster chimes caused a rustle to pass through the hall. Berkeley's beautiful and subtle variations likewise aroused admiration among all musicians, and I doubt whether this concerto has ever had so detailed and careful preparation.

Directly after the concert we prepared to leave for Leningrad. We drove through streets busily preparing for the May 1st celebrations, and at midnight we were in the 'Red Arrow' smoothly and swiftly moving north. As day dawned we caught a glimpse of the Russian countryside— interminable flatlands thickly planted with birches and poplars under which the snow was melting. My wife said the landscape reminded her of Wisconsin. Members of the Leningrad Philharmonic Society were at the station to meet us, and we were driven to our hotel opposite the Philharmonic Hall, where posters showed our strange-looking names in the Russian lettering. We went almost at once into rehearsal.

The Philharmonic Hall seats about 2000, most of whom sit on a sloping ground floor. The stage is rather narrow, and with so many string players as they have the back desks seem far off. Once again we admired the quick and accurate reading of this new music and the players' interest in what we wanted.

April 24th. Armed with cameras we all went for a walk along the Neva. Ice blocks were still moving swiftly downstream towards the Gulf of Finland, and it was cold. Leningrad with its imposing vistas must be one of the finest laid-out cities in the world. We looked across at the Fortress of Peter and Paul, and then went to take pictures of the Dvortsovaya Square decorated with huge pictures of Lenin and Marx. Women were busily putting gold paint on the saluting base in preparation for May 1st.

For light relief we were invited in the evening to a music hall to see the

---

12 Yuri Fraier (1890–1971).

comedian Arcady Raikin. He is the Russian Charlie Chaplin, a winning personality who can depict 'the little man' facing undeserved difficulties. Most of the sketches hit at officialdom, its laborious slowness and pomposity, or showed the more humorous side of domestic life when both partners have day-long jobs. The audience did not respond with the loud bursts of laughter that seemed called for; they appeared a little shy of letting themselves go. In the middle of the fun a serious pep sketch was suddenly inserted about a good and bad worker.

April 25th. At our opening concert Goossens introduced the new concerto written for him by Gordon Jacob; the parts had luckily just arrived in time. This work proved a distinguished addition to our repertoire. I hope the composer did not mind my muting the strings in certain sections of the work after hearing the rehearsal in the over-resonant hall.

Two soloists came all the way from Talinn to see Goossens play, after having heard him on the radio, and to learn next morning at his hotel how he managed certain technical difficulties. At the concert we met the orchestra's two conductors, Mravinsky and Yansons, who were both eagerly looking forward to the proposed visit to England with their players.

April 26th. We had a chance this morning to tour the city. I was interested to see two of the places made famous by Pushkin and Tchaikovsky in the *Queen of Spades*: the saloon where Hermann gambled, and the bridge from which poor Lisa threw herself into the Neva. In Leningrad as in Moscow I had to become used to a new scale of dimension. Everything looks a little more than life size, the streets, the squares, the new buildings, the rivers, the stadiums. Only the modest house of Peter the Great seemed of normal size, and he was a giant himself.

Moored in the Neva, as a training ship and historical symbol, is the cruiser *Aurora* which fired the signal shot for the rising on October 25th, 1917. We went on board and met one of the original crew, Deputy Commissar now Lt. Col. Lipatov, who showed us the primitive radio apparatus from which Lenin's slogans were broadcast. It was disappointing not to have more free time in Leningrad, and so to have to hustle through such incomparable collections as are to be found in the Hermitage and Winter Palace. Our recitals here were crowded and broadcast. Among the English composers represented were Vaughan Williams, Holst, Bax, Dunhill, Ireland, Howard Ferguson, Malcolm Arnold, and Purcell, and folk song in Britten's realizations. Our final concert in Leningrad was on Saturday, April 28th, and early next morning we flew into Kiev and into the spring.

One of the charming arrangements for welcome was that we each met our opposite number, so at the Kiev airport there was a Ukrainian conductor, composer, pianist, violinist, and instrumentalist bearing flowers. In some ways we liked Kiev the best of all the four cities we visited. Perhaps this was due to the glorious spring weather after the rather sullen skies we had been seeing, or perhaps the stir in the city as May 1st approached made for spontaneity. Whatever the cause, we recall Kiev with particular pleasure.

We had been noticing several small details common to Russian cities. For example, there is no litter in the principal streets and parks, and no sign of any advertising hoarding or poster. Kiev has had largely to be rebuilt, and now resembles an American town in its public buildings and boulevards. Yet alongside this contemporary look is its medieval past.

The monastery of Lavra, the most revered convent in Russia, was mined by the Germans, but survives as a glorious ruin showing many traces of its frescoes and paintings. Nearby are the 11th-century catacombs in which are buried saintly persons who spent their lives in these tiny cells and chapels. Taper in hand we felt our way round this underground labyrinth, and learnt that on the previous day a pilgrim had arrived on foot all the way from the Volga to pay his tribute at these shrines.

May 1st. There were no rehearsals on this day. Instead we watched the May Day procession from a raised platform near the saluting base. Right opposite us was one of the largest bands I have ever seen. I counted in the front row sixteen cymbal players, whose highly polished discs caught the sun as they clashed. Between troops lining the broad thoroughfare two cars slowly approached from different directions. One contained the commander of the Kiev forces, the other the defender of Stalingrad, Marshal Chuvikov, who took the salute that morning. As guns fired, the Ukrainian flag slowly floated up to a barrage balloon moored high in the air. The military march past followed the pattern made familiar by films of the Red Square parade. In succession came detachments, some 24 abreast, of cadres from the Suvorov School, of the air force, liaison, infantry, tank and medical corps, of naval forces from the Dnieper, and of artillery. The step was very quick, similar to that of our light infantry regiments, and the method of marching resembled the goose-step. It was disciplined and precise from start to finish.

Then for three hours came in two parallel waves what looked like the whole population of Kiev. Actually there were about 350,000, I was told, men, women, and children, many of the latter carried on the shoulders of their parents. Everybody carried something—flags, banners, slogans, pictures of the Soviet leaders, artificial flowers. Every activity, every district of the city was represented. Many amateur bands came along playing, adding to the confused din of loudspeakers announcing each group of workers. Several of our musicians had been televised the day before and were recognized by the young students in the procession. This

gave us a personal and amused interest in the procession as we stood from
10.30 a.m. to 2 p.m. to watch it go by. At the end a magnificent march of
athletes of both sexes galvanized us into attention, and finally the heroic
band wheeled into position and marched away still playing.

In the evening we saw a performance of *Swan Lake* at the opera. It was
the only occasion when I saw a comparatively poor house. Perhaps the
day's festivities had tired everyone. We got a model performance by the
orchestra, but the dancing was somewhat disappointing. As we stepped
out into the fine May evening we saw the huge Ukrainian flag picked out in
the sky by searchlight, a final touch to a dramatic day.

May 2nd. A nice compliment was paid at our orchestral concert this
evening by the Ukrainian conductor Lyatoshinsky, who came onto the
platform to pay a tribute to English music. Russian and English musical
scores were exchanged.

May 3rd. We flew to Kharkov, and it was here that to our great anxiety
Cyril Smith fell seriously ill.[13] He had played brilliantly throughout the
tour, and was always ready to give his services at informal gatherings of
musicians. This sudden ill stroke of luck cast a gloom over what had
hitherto been the happiest of journeys.

Two concerts were given on the stage of the Opera House in Kharkov,
and by 7.30 on the morning of May 6th we were on the plane for Moscow.
Even at this early hour representatives of the Symphony Orchestra were
at the airport to give us a friendly send-off.

We had offered to give an additional farewell concert in Moscow before
we left for England. Although officially it was their free day, the Moscow
State Symphony Orchestra volunteered to join in this concert with us. We
gave a frankly popular programme. We started and ended with Russian
music, Glinka's Overture to *Russlan and Ludmilla* and Tchaikovsky's
Theme and Variations from the Suite in G. In between Campoli played the
Mendelssohn Violin Concerto, Jennifer Vyvyan sang Purcell and Mozart
with Gerald Moore, Goossens played the Jacob concerto (new to Moscow),
and I added my March from *Things to Come*. The hall was decorated with
the Union Jack and the Red Flag, and Mr Bulganin and Mr Kruschchev sat
with the British Ambassador and Lady Hayter in a box.

The evening ended with characteristic Russian hospitality at a banquet
at which many toasts were given.

One of our aims in going to Russia was to further the opportunity for
others to follow us. Russian audiences and players want our music, but at

---

[13] Smith suffered a stroke which incapacitated one arm. Later he and his wife, Phyllis Sellick,
continued playing duets for three hands. In 1968 Bliss collaborated with Clifford Phillips in
arranging his Concerto for two pianos for them.

present they cannot get it. I sat next to Mr Mikhailov, Minister of Culture, at the banquet and took the opportunity of telling him how difficult it was from the copyright point of view to ensure a free flow of music between the two countries. At the same table sat the delegation from the BBC under the leadership of J. B. Clark. As he was conferring with the Minister on parallel problems it is to be hoped that a solution will be found by which British music in Russia and Russian music in England can freely be performed on an equitable basis.

———

OVERTURE *EDINBURGH*

A talk broadcast on BBC Radio on 27 July 1956. Bliss gave the first
performance with the Royal Philharmonic Orchestra at the
Edinburgh Festival on 20 August.
Typescript, Bliss Archive, Cambridge University Library.

When, last autumn, I got an invitation to write a concert overture for this year's Edinburgh Festival, I was very pleased indeed, for by writing a special work I could at last say a musical 'thank you' to Scotland for the two honours I have received from Scottish universities. I greatly prize being a Doctor of Music at Edinburgh, and a Doctor of Law at Glasgow, and though this work of mine is a short and modest one, it allows me at any rate to do something in return.

I call it simply Overture *Edinburgh* because there are certain elements in it that bind it to the city of Edinburgh. First of all, the opening, which carries the rhythm of the word 'Edinburgh' itself. This rhythm occurs frequently throughout the work, sometimes in slow tempo, and some-times in fast. You have it in the first bars. With its massive scoring, and the rhythm pounded out by side drums, it may perhaps suggest a vision of the castle itself on the heights.

Shortly after this opening section, listeners will recognize a tune from the Scottish Psalter, a metrical version of Psalm 124: 'Now Israel may say, and that truly, if that the Lord had not our cause maintained . . . then certainly they had devoured us all'. The tune is taken from the French Psalter of 1551. Of course, I use my own harmonies, and also through it surges a tempestuous rhythm, but you will at once recognize the splendid tune. I like to think that it may have been sung in the Church of St Giles during the middle of the sixteenth century, for it would then—in terms of time—provide the link to the middle section of the overture. This is devoted to Mary Stuart, and has the heading 'Pavane in memory of Mary Queen of Scots'. I recall Dr Johnson's words: 'Such a Queen as every man of any gallantry of spirit would have sacrificed his life for'.

No music for Edinburgh can leave out a reference to dancing, so the final section of my overture is characterized by reel and strathspey rhythms. I cannot possibly compete with Scotland's magnificent pipers in this, nor do I pretend that anyone not born in Scotland can give you the authentic spirit, but I feel this dance section is needed to bring the overture to a gay end.

ON BEING MASTER OF THE QUEEN'S MUSICK

A talk broadcast on BBC Radio on 2 August 1956, Bliss's sixty-fifth birthday.
Typescript, BBC Written Archives.

The title 'Master of the Musick' is quite an old one. It is first found in one of the Lord Chamberlain's Records for June 13th, 1626. We can see here an entry which authorizes the giving of livery to one Nicholas Lanier, Master of Musick. This first holder of the office was a much more versatile man than I am. He not only sang, played the flute, composed, and produced court masques, but he painted the scenery as well. He held office under Charles I and Charles II, and under the latter had many more privileges too than I have now.

It is stated in the Lord Chamberlain's Records that 'he shall not be arrested, nor warned to attend at assizes nor impanelled on juries, nor charged with any contributions, taxes or payments.' This is one of the conditions I should certainly like back today! For these privileges he was kept busy. He had to lead the Royal Band when playing to the King at meals and state ceremonies, accompany the King on his travels, and join with the Chapel Royal to celebrate all royal occasions.

Until we come to Victorian times there are not many names of Masters that mean very much today. But there was John Eccles, who wrote incidental music to Congreve's plays; William Boyce and Maurice Greene, with distinguished contributions to church music; and there was the blind organist John Stanley, whose music is becoming known these days through the scholarship of the English composer, Gerald Finzi, who has rescued much of his work from oblivion. But by and large the others were not composers of much consequence, and music in general was not helped by the total lack of interest in it shown by the majority of our rulers.

It is not really until the time of the Prince Consort that music at court became fashionable. Prince Albert reorganized the Royal Band into a good-sized orchestra, and it was used for state concerts and entertainments. He also championed the music of Mendelssohn and later supported the cause of Wagner.

Unfortunately after his death the office of the Master of Musick again declined, until it became just a name without any specific duties. Edward VII disbanded the Royal Orchestra, and it has never been re-formed. This is a pity, I think. With our fine instrumentalists, we could summon a Royal Band for state occasions unrivalled in the world. Perhaps this ancient custom can be revived.

Today we are fortunate to have a royal family who by going to opera, ballet, and concerts show their personal interest in the world of music.

It is one of the duties of the Master of Musick to urge the claims of music on behalf of his fellow musicians. He must also be able to write appropriate music for special occasions. I have always found these occasional pieces an interesting problem rather than a tedious chore, especially when the occasions have colour and ceremony. The Coronation was a supreme example, and a galaxy of English composers wrote for it. Then there was the return of the Queen and the Duke of Edinburgh from their Empire Tour in May 1954. This obviously called for a 'Welcome Ode', and Purcell and Dryden had shown the way. I was lucky to have the poet Day Lewis to write the words, and with Sir Malcolm Sargent conducting, this *Song of Welcome* was broadcast on the night of the return.[14]

My immediate predecessors, Elgar, Walford Davies, and Bax, also wrote music for the royal children of their day, and it would be within the duties of my office to present the present royal children with a work, especially if later they could play it themselves.

Today the widespread world of music has its own problems and worries. I think the most valuable contribution the Master of Musick can make is to throw whatever influence his post gives him into helping to solve these. Surprisingly, musicians are generally unanimous over their practical problems. What I must do is continually to hold up before the powers that be the great part that music now plays in the social life of our community.

---

[14] In a BBC Radio broadcast on 15 May 1954, with Joan Sutherland (soprano), Ian Wallace (baritone), and the BBC Chorus and Concert Orchestra conducted by Sir Malcolm Sargent.

━━━━━

HAROLD BROOKE: AN APPRECIATION

Harold Brooke (1880–1956) was a publishing director of Novello's,
the music publisher.
Musical Times, November 1956, p. 578.

Harold Brooke was a close friend of mine for nearly thirty years. At this distance of time I cannot remember exactly how this long friendship started. I know he disapproved of my early works, and only felt an inclination towards my music later; so my first clear picture of him must be towards the end of the twenties, when I began to visit him in Novello's, in that room of his which surely needs the pen of Dickens to describe. I can see Harold at that desk of his, a desk which maliciously seemed to abstract any object immediately needed. I had drawn up a chair alongside him, uncomfortably close, too, to the gas fire in the corner. While the printing machines across the narrow way made the room hum, and every so often a buzzer sounded through the building, Harold proceeded carefully and methodically to go through the proof sheets of my *Pastoral* with me.

At that time he directed a small and expert chorus which gave public concerts in the City, and was named the Harold Brooke Choir. I had written this work especially for his singers. He was a good chorus trainer and conductor, and I look back on the first performance of this *Pastoral* in May 1929 as being one of the most poetical it has ever received.

Harold was a good practical musician. He could have been, if he had wished, a competent pianist (as a young man he studied with Teichmüller in Leipzig). He read scores with ease, and he was a musical editor of distinction. I have learnt a great deal from him as to how music should actually *look* on paper. His object was always to simplify. He tried many ways, for instance, of making difficult cross-rhythms look easier and more natural in print. The layout must never appear more complex than absolutely necessary. He had a quick eye for mistakes in manuscript, and I was always aware of his critical attitude to the music itself during our work together. He would suddenly rap out, 'I can't understand what *that* has to do with this passage', or 'You will never get altos to take *that* leap in tune'.

I had an admiring respect for his judgment on music of mine that he knew almost as well as I did, and as a result I have often used the blue pencil in time, and to advantage.

He was a man with definite blind spots where modern music was concerned, and it was no use trying to convince him, when he sat listening to it bored or irritated. But he eagerly sought for new talent to enrich his own catalogue. I recall the enthusiasm with which he mentioned Kenneth Leighton's Violin Concerto to me, and the pride he took in the performances of Joubert's works.

Harold Brooke entered my life at a time when I needed encouragement; as a wise counsellor he came to the first performances of all my music associated with his publishing house. By my dedication on the first page of *The Olympians*, 'To my friend and colleague of many years', I have tried in some part to acknowledge my indebtedness.

I wish I could have seen him once more at the Festival in Gloucester this September, where he always felt among intimate friends.

But I rejoice that the last music he ever heard was music for which he had a special love, the *Hymnus Paradisi* of Herbert Howells. Here was a fitting requiem to a man who loved music and laboured many years to serve it.

WRITING MUSIC FOR THE FILMS

Untitled contribution to Roger Manvell and John Huntley, *The Technique of Film Music* (London, 1957), pp. 209–10.

I came to my first assignment (to write music for the films) with all the excitement and pleasure that contact with an entirely new medium brings. That was in 1935; the film was *Things to Come*, and the invitation to collaborate came from H. G. Wells and Sir Alexander Korda.

Later, it was interest in some particular film that finally persuaded me to write the music. A conspicuous instance was the film *Men of Two Worlds*[15]—I admired Thorold Dickinson's direction; the photography was beautiful; the story of the coloured West African pianist and composer appealed to me.

There have also been at least two films where the pull was distinctly a financial one. So I suppose a graph would show a downward slope: enthusiasm and curiosity for the new thing—admiration for a particular picture—greed.

[15] Released in Britain in 1946 but refused in the USA until 1952, when it appeared under the title *Kisenga, Man of Africa* (a.k.a. *Witch Doctor*). The central item is a lively concert piece for piano, orchestra, and male voices entitled *Baraza*, 'a Swahili word meaning a discussion in council between an African chief and his head man' (note to the Novello score, 1946).

I soon found out that music in the final synthesis took a very humble position. In opera its influence is paramount and all pervasive, in ballet it is, at least, of equal importance with the choreography and the decor, but in the films it is subservient, and at the first sign of opposition disappears out of hearing.

Sometimes it is the invisible producer who exerts the restricting influence, concerned as he must be with what the lowest common denominator (the paying multitude) would like.

Often too the director of the picture is too unmusical to imagine how greatly music could enhance and sometimes even save sections of his film.

I have had unforgettable experiences with one director who, where music was concerned, with a certifiable lunatic, [16] and I had to discontinue collaboration. On the other hand there are many others who instinctively understand the value of a musical score, though untrained themselves. They leave a composer free; and so work with them becomes pleasurable and worth while.

Before I decide to write the music, I like to see as many of the early 'rushes' as I can. I want to be brought in at an early stage, and have an opportunity for round-table talks with the others concerned. I like to feel I am sure about the 'general treatment' before I start my score.

Heaven help me from having a director who works by 'inspiration' and who changes his mind every time he hears of some success or some novelty elsewhere, and who switches from a tragic to a comic treatment as nonchalantly as if he were stepping out of his bath!

I like a full three months to prepare my score. I am told many composers today have their own orchestrator at the end of the telephone line. I am sure the most original composers do not; for in the films it is often the actual texture of sound made that is the important factor, and only the composer himself can manipulate this.

Abetted by directors who once thought that the bigger the orchestra the better the film, I started by using a full symphony orchestra. I soon found out my mistake. Indeed, the smaller the number of players, the better is the recording and the greater the variety of tone colour obtained. I now prefer a picked band of soloists, with which sounds can be fabricated in the most effective way for the film. I believe the composer should not think of either concert hall or opera house in determining these.

Today you find yourself more and more in healthy competition with the sound-effects technicians. I do not know whether they have already

---

[16] Gabriel Pascal, the director of *Caesar and Cleopatra* (1945). Bliss wrote a quantity of music (see *Catlogue* 103), which has never been performed, before withdrawing from the project. The score was subsequently provided by Georges Auric.

taken over *musique concrète*—if so, this determined and resourceful department is a threat to music's own independence.

I do not seriously think we are in danger, as pure musical sound will always have a wide importance in the films. It is powerfully expressive. It can bring nostalgia to a landscape, drama to any hour of day or night; it can express undercurrents of human emotion when the actors involved show little of it outwardly. It can suggest what is going to happen, it can recall what has happened; most important of all, perhaps, it can make what has turned dead and dull in a picture come alive and exciting.

And yet, music must not obstinately intrude, as at any time it can. Someone said that the best film music is that which is not consciously heard at all. There is a truth in the paradox. The music should do its work so smoothly and perfectly that it is only when you see the same picture run through in the studio without it that you realize its irreplaceable importance.

ARTURO TOSCANINI

A tribute to Toscanini, who had died on 16 January, broadcast on
BBC Radio on 17 January 1957.
Talk script, BBC Written Archives.

We in England haven't seen as much of Arturo Toscanini as we should have wished. He came to London three times in the thirties, and he paid us what was virtually a farewell visit in 1952.

I shall never forget the first concerts he gave here in the old Queen's Hall: no library of gramophone recordings can ever really conjure up those rehearsals. They had to be seen and lived through. I see today as vividly as then the orchestral players on the Queen's Hall platform. In the circle of the auditorium there are groups of prominent musicians, all silent, all waiting for that one man, who suddenly, a slight figure, enters, carrying his baton. He quickly mounts the rostrum, flicks his stick against the metal stand, and launches straight into rehearsal. His beat seems big; his baton carves geometrical figures in the air; he uses it like a rapier or stiletto. There is no difference in intensity between rehearsal and concert performance—no relaxation of effort. At the end of a movement or section Toscanini lifts the score close to his eyes and in a quiet, determined way expresses what he wants.

Toscanini worked his magic partly through his qualities as a man, and partly through his authority as a musician.

We know how in his career he fought for what he believed was humanly right, as well as politically right. We also know that he thought great music was one of the noblest expressions of man's soul, and should always be played as perfectly as humanly possible.

Toscanini was born with rare musical gifts. His prodigious memory was famous. He could, as it were, photograph on his mind the exact replica of a symphony score. Being born near the Mediterranean he naturally conceived music as something to be sung, and one could hear him humming in his light tenor voice as he conducted. His vitality gave enormous drive to the rhythmic pulse. He created great tension in those who listened to him.

I met Toscanini during his first London visits. One night he invited my wife and myself to have supper with him and Madam Toscanini at his hotel. It was an unexpected compliment, and I had many qualms about going. Could I interest him at all, or pass the test of those searching eyes?

Like other great men Toscanini was at heart a modest man and quickly sensitive to the feelings of others. He saw at once that I was nervous, and to put me at ease he settled me down on the sofa beside him and said, 'Tell me, Mr Bliss, do you as an Englishman think that I, an Italian, take the slow movements of Beethoven symphonies too fast?' This kindly appeal to put me at my ease was something I have always remembered.

The name Toscanini is only another word for single-minded artistic integrity. Whenever English musicians speak of him it will be with reverence.

EDWARD ELGAR

A talk given in the Assembly Room of Worcester Guildhall on
5 June 1957, the centenary of Elgar's birth.
Berrow's Journal, June 1957, pp. 7–9.

I am greatly privileged on this centenary occasion to pay tribute to Elgar in the city with which his name will ever be associated, and in the room in which he was made a Freeman fifty-one years ago. I find that the Mayor of that year, seconded by the High Sheriff, moved that this honour should be conferred on him 'In recognition of the eminent position which he, a citizen of the Faithful City, has attained in the Musical World.'

You must pardon me if in opening my tribute to Elgar I first recall some personal recollections. It is not only that I am proud of them, but also I feel they may make my inadequate words more convincing.

In the early years of this century when I was a boy at school, my father during the summer holidays used to take a house in the country for my brothers and myself, and as luck would have it, he fixed on Worcestershire, Herefordshire, and Gloucestershire as the preferred counties. One of the peaks of those lovely summer holidays was a visit to the Three Choirs Festival. Under Sinclair, Brewer, and Atkins, I heard much great music played at these annual festivals, but none made a greater impression on me than the *Dream of Gerontius*. I got to know the music of this master work very well, for, with great daring, a performance was organized at Rugby when I was a boy at school there, and not only did I sing in the rehearsals, but, at the performance, filled in (on the piano) several parts for which we did not have the necessary players.

Like all young admirers of an older man's power, I determined to meet the composer face to face. It was not easy; Lady Elgar quite rightly protected him from those who wanted to waste his time. But sincere and sheer persistence often gets its own reward, and, through the kindness of a mutual friend, I was invited one day (during the First World War)[17] to tea at Severn House, Hampstead, where Elgar was then living. I remember the day very well: the long tramp up Netherhall Gardens, asking a passer-by the way, being told 'if it was that music fellow I was looking for, it was the big house at the top, on the right', my almost surreptitious entry, and hearing, as I stood in the long corridor, a phrase on the piano being played over and over again. I remember the kindness of Lady Elgar, and her efforts to put me at my ease, and her daughter's too. Mrs Elgar Blake was good enough to tell me recently that she remembered me distinctly as the 'slim young man in uniform'. I cannot remember *anything* that Elgar said on that occasion. I was overwhelmed by the fact that this was the composer of the *Dream of Gerontius*, of the Violin Concerto, of which I had heard the first performance, and of the Second Symphony, of which again I had heard the first performance.

When I returned to France, Elgar wrote me several letters, and one of my most precious possessions is a miniature score of *Cockaigne* which he sent me, and which—in its now brilliant binding—retains the mud marks of the trenches.

In later years I was present at the first performance in the Queen's Hall of the Cello Concerto, and, in the intimate surroundings of his Hampstead music room, I heard the first run-through of the Violin Sonata with W. H. Reed playing the solo part, Elgar at the piano, while I sat alongside turning over for him.

---

[17] The meeting described here occurred in 1912 (see *As I Remember*, p. 23). Bliss visited Elgar again in 1917 while waiting to return to active duty in France.

Three main impressions come to my mind as I think of Elgar's music: (1) his *mastery of the sound* that he wants. His orchestral scores are wonderful examples of consummate craftsmanship. No wonder orchestral players, whether string, woodwind, brass, or percussion, delight to play them. Each is given passages to play which seem to be a personal compliment to the player. There are innumerable touches of colour that give variety and vitality. I have recently been recording the five *Pomp and Circumstance Marches*.[18] Now, a march is a comparatively humble form of music, but a detailed study of *these* five very different marches gives a remarkable insight into what Elgar can do in the manipulation of sound. His instrumentation is (as Donald Francis Tovey once wrote) 'astoundingly subtle, uncannily efficient, and utterly original'.

This brings me to my second impression, (2) his *originality*. Musical phrases of Elgar's are very much his own. They are like personal gestures, so much so that, as you know, we have had to coin the word 'Elgarian' to describe them. The conviction that a very marked individual is speaking to us is all the more pronounced when we remember that his vocabulary was the one generally in use in the Europe of his day. He made use of the same technical procedures as Brahms and Wagner, and *yet*, what he says is his own.

To achieve this indicates, I believe, greater strength of personality than if (as many composers do today) he had invented a consciously new and esoteric style. What it *is* that Elgar is expressing in his music can, perhaps, only be suggested—in words—by a poet. Cecil Day Lewis, the poet, told me the other day that, springing from his admiration of the music, he wanted to write an ode to Elgar. I asked him what moods Elgar evoked in him, and he said that Elgar's strongest magic was to call up vividly the landscape of the countryside that lies just about us here; as Constable immortalized Suffolk, so has Elgar immortalized those counties that border on Wales, enshrining their great beauty, and, because of the evanescence of beauty, tingeing this expression with a certain sadness.

For my part, I find in Elgar's work something as rare in today's music as unselfconscious originality, and that is (3) a delight in the inexhaustible vitality of nature and life. He may have written at the head of his Second Symphony 'Rarely, rarely comest thou, Spirit of Delight'. But this is surely regret that he could not grasp more of the beauty of life he apprehended in everything around him. His music abounds in vitality, and is continually leaping forward, moving swiftly like a mountain torrent, or like the Severn when the tidal wave sweeps up it. It is characteristic that he should choose

---

[18] For an RCA recording (SB 2026) with the London Symphony Orchestra, released in 1959, on which he also conducted his own *Welcome the Queen* and the Suite from *Things to Come*.

Falstaff (that mountain of zest) rather than the melancholy Dane as a subject for musical portraiture.

Perhaps Elgar's inmost thoughts are revealed to his friends at the end of the slow movement of his First Symphony, which we are to hear tonight. Perhaps the autumnal sadness of the Cello Concerto evokes for Cecil Day Lewis, and other poets, Elgar's early love for his countryside. For me, the predominant effect of Elgar's music is an enhancement of life. That is why I give thanks for the appearance in England of this great composer; that is why I rejoice to celebrate his genius during this week; and that is why I believe that, after fine performances of his music, we emerge better, stronger, and more sensitive human beings.

THE OLYMPIANS

Programme note for a performance of excerpts from Act II by the
London Symphony Orchestra and the Royal Choral Society, Royal
Albert Hall, 28 November 1957.

The story of the opera is based on the legend that when men ceased to believe in the deities of Olympus, some of these gods and goddesses became members of a troupe of strolling players, travelling the roads of Europe century after century. It is assumed, for the purposes of the story, that every hundred years or so on Midsummer Night, for a few hours, these gods-turned-players find themselves again in the possession of their divine powers.

The action of the opera takes place in a small town in the south of France in midsummer, 1836. The main human characters are Lavatte, a rich bourgeois; his daughter Madeleine, whom he intends to marry to an elderly nobleman; Hector, a young poet with whom she falls in love at an accidental meeting. The gods-turned-players are engaged by Lavatte to entertain the guests at a party to celebrate his daughter's engagement to the nobleman. This happens to fall on Midsummer's Day in the very year when the gods are due to regain their divine powers. They take a hand in the human story, casting a spell on Madeleine and Hector, bewitching the house-guests and thoroughly frightening Lavatte. The latter is eventually persuaded by the young lovers, aided and abetted by the local curé, to permit their marriage. He announces their engagement to the tired guests in the early morning. The gods' powers fade with the morning light and the opera closes as the gods, once more in the guise of old and weary players, start out again on their travels.

The portion of the opera to be performed tonight contains some of its most dramatic music. It commences at a moment when the party is at its height and the guests have begun to feel the effects of the magic of the gods. The women come crowding excitedly out of the house and Diana, now the goddess, appears in the courtyard and invokes the moon. She sings of the joys of the hunt in the moonlight and the chorus joyfully respond. Finally she awakens Madeleine, who is sleeping under the influence of a spell cast by Mercury, and together they lead the whole rout over the hills. At the close, their voices are heard high and clear on the hills. Other guests swarm out of the house and Bacchus, dragging a great wine cask, makes his appearance. The cask is broached as Bacchus and the chorus sing of the youth of the world, of wine and the delights of love, leading into an Ode to Venus, who now appears in the full glory of her beauty. Hector is bewitched by the appearance of Venus, despite the protests of Madeleine, and joins Bacchus and the chorus in a further salutation to her. Finally, Jupiter himself, the father of the gods, appears in majesty, and gravely addresses the mortals, asking them to remember the old power of the gods and telling them not to desert the ancient ways of mankind. Thus will they re-make the Age of Gold.

RALPH VAUGHAN WILLIAMS

A tribute to Vaughan Williams, who had died on 26 August,
broadcast on BBC Radio on 14 September 1958.
BBC Sound Archives.

When Vaughan Williams died, many notable tributes came from all over the world to his memory. They came from famous conductors and orchestras, from famous composers, from his devoted colleagues in the Leith Hill Festival[19] and other English choruses, and from men and women who had met him casually during his humble services in both wars. He was a man universally admired, and a composer widely honoured.

It's more than forty-five years since I first came across his name. I was shown a snapshot of him taken about 1910. It showed him walking over the

---

[19] Founded in 1905 by Vaughan Williams's sister, Margaret, and Lady Farrer, originally for the benefit of local choirs and later a festival of national importance under Vaughan Williams.

downs. He was striding along, deep in thought, and just behind him came his friend Gustav Holst. The horizon facing him might have been the setting for his opera *The Shepherds of the Delectable Mountains*. Vaughan Williams had a Wordsworthian love of the country. In it he found much of his inspiration. Only a short time before his death, after an evening concert in London, he asked to be driven into the country, where in the early hours he watched the dawn break and listened to the June chorus of birds. His own music has much of the strong, slow rhythm of nature in it.

My first glimpse of him was at Cambridge in 1911. His two volumes of *Songs of Travel* were on all our pianos, and it was a great event when we heard that he was coming to a performance of his song-cycle *On Wenlock Edge* at the University Musical Club. He sat in the front row in tweeds, smoking a short pipe. As always since, he was embarrassingly modest, rather blunt in speech, acknowledging our enthusiasm with a short bow and vague gestures of both hands.

We followed this work of his with a performance of his *Sea Symphony*. I can't remember now whether Vaughan Williams actually conducted this or only came to a rehearsal, but I do know his personality seemed present all the time. As we in the chorus leapt from Bb minor to D major on the words 'Behold the sea', we knew something new had come into our music.

Vaughan Williams had deep and strange things to say in music, and it was perhaps natural that it took him many years to find his own method of expression.

Vaughan Williams grew in stature as the years went by, like some magnificent tree. At the end his mind was still filled with music. He was always an explorer, a searcher. He was a great man, as we judge great men, and it was wholly fitting that he should be laid to rest in the Abbey beside Purcell and Handel.

TOBIAS AND THE ANGEL

Bliss's second opera, based on the Apocryphal Book of Tobit, was
commissioned by BBC Television and broadcast on 19 May 1960.
To date the stage version has not been performed.
From 'Sir Arthur Bliss Discusses his New Opera for Television',
The Times, 29 April 1959, p. 7.

I'm sorry now that I didn't turn my hand to opera much earlier, because it's a form that suits my inclinations. I've written four ballets, and a good deal of music for the theatre. The chief difficulty is to find a good libretto, and a librettist who isn't too parental about his text to alter passages when the composer feels the need.

I must say that Christopher Hassall,[20] who's written the libretto of *Tobias and the Angel* for me, has been a perfect collaborator. Sometimes he's written a beautiful verse, and I've asked him to change it because there's a word that doesn't set to music easily, or a thought that's too complicated to be sung; and he hasn't complained at all. It's very important that the thought should be simple, and the words short, in sung music. And at one point in this new opera I wrote the music of a vocal quintet before the words, and sent it to him, and he made a text that perfectly expressed the different feelings of the five characters.

I wouldn't care to write an opera on a contemporary subject, though Menotti has brought it off wonderfully well in *The Consul*. I once planned a contemporary opera with Wyndham Lewis; the first scene was going to take place in St Pancras station. But we had to give it up because such realism didn't seem suitable for opera: people would laugh if they heard a soprano singing 'Porter, porter!'

What's so interesting about working on *Tobias and the Angel* is that, since it's intended for television, the time-scale has to be much smaller. It isn't simply that they don't want an extended opera, and only partly that they're afraid people will switch off the set unless they're held in suspense. Audiences of today don't want to be told everything in detail, as in Wagner's symphonic monologues, and they certainly don't need to be told it a second time, as in the old formal aria with recapitulation—once is enough.

There's a moment of climax in *Tobias and the Angel* where a servant is suddenly revealed as the angel Gabriel. An earlier opera composer would have expatiated at this point on the reactions and feelings of everybody present, and even a modern composer wants to make this an impressive moment. When I asked how long this passage should last, I was astonished when the music representative of BBC television insisted that it must on no account take longer than one minute. Another thing I've discovered while writing this opera: it's generally accepted that music moves more slowly than the spoken word, but for the intimacy of television presentation I've found it advisable to set the text almost at the tempo of speech.

[20] English poet (1912–63) who contributed the lyrics to several Ivor Novello musicals in 1930s and was the librettist for Walton's *Troilus and Cressida* (1954). He collaborated with Bliss also on the cantatas *The Beautitudes* (1961) and *Mary of Magdala* (1962), which is dedicated to his memory.

REPLY TO A WORK STUDY OFFICER

A reply to a whimsical 'report' written by Bliss's son-in-law,
Christopher Sellick.
Typescript dated 30 July 1960, Bliss Archive, Cambridge University
Library.

THE REPORT

It is interesting to note that all those who are Work Study operators automatically become enthusiasts and their attitude of mind changes considerably after a short time. For example, some weeks ago one of our Work Study officers attended a symphony concert in London. A few days later his clerk found the following notes, which had doubtless been inspired by the concert, scribbled on his blotting pad:

For considerable periods the four oboe players had nothing to do. The number should be reduced and the work spread more evenly over the whole of the concert, thus eliminating peaks of activity. All the twelve violins were playing identical notes. This seems unnecessary duplication. The staff of this section should be drastically cut. If a large volume of sound is required it could be obtained by electronic apparatus. Much effort was absorbed in the playing of demisemiquavers. This seems an unnecessary refinement. It is recommended that all notes should be rounded off to the nearest semiquaver. If this were done it would be possible to use trainees and lower-grade operators more extensively. No useful purpose is served by repeating on the horns a passage which has already been handled by the strings. It is estimated that if all redundant passages were eliminated, the whole concert time of two hours could be reduced to twenty minutes and there would have been no need for an intermission.

THE REPLY

The report of your Work Study Officer's Clerk, interesting and enthusiastic as it is, is inevitably a total ignorance of the conditions under which orchestral musicians work—yes, *work*. May I explain some facts to him?

For considerable periods the four oboe players had nothing to do.

He should know that oboe players invariably live to a very advanced age, and by the rules of the Union *cannot* be superseded. When therefore *four* players are seen, *two* are probably past the age of being able to make any sound and simply hold the instrument from time to time in their mouth (M.U. Con. Ch. IV Para. 3). The other two, presumably younger, actually play (or should) the notes before them. They certainly should *not* have been *inactive over a considerable period*. This might have been due, on the occasional notes, to this:

(a) Having lost their places.
(b) Becoming sleepy after 'interval' in concert (see later note).
(c) Simply disliking certain passages given them by the composer.

Much effort was absorbed in the playing of demisemiquavers.

Your Clerk has a good point here.

Players dislike a lot of small black notes, especially in the old well-used part in which it is difficult often to distinguish a semiquaver from a squashed fly and other foreign bodies. A maximum of 8 semiquavers a page is suggested to prevent bows of string instruments getting 'stuck'.

No useful purpose is served by repeating on the strings a passage etc.

Quite right—but beware! The converse is incorrect.

There is *every* reason for repeating on the strings a passage which has been already handled (a good technical word for stopped (+) notes —bravo, Clerk—on the horns). A horn player, especially after the interval (see below) will 'bubble' or 'squeak' a note so that the passage comes faultily to the audience. In these cases the strings *correct*, not repeat the passage, for the information of the hearer.

The whole concert time of 2 hours could be reduced to 20 minutes and there would have been no need for an intermission.

This statement, together with an earlier reference to 'peaks of activity', shows that the writer has never entered a concert hall, and that by 'attending a symphony concert' he meant lying at home on a sofa listening to the radionic transmission. For the peak of activity for every orchestral player *is* the intermission, in which he can refresh himself and gird himself for further efforts—whether misapplied (see horn) or not. Even if the concert should, as your clerk wishes, last only 20 minutes, there *must* be 15 minutes in the middle for 'the peak of activity' referred to above. So we have:

2½ minutes music
15 minutes peak activity or intermission
2½ minutes music

This would greatly appeal to the player but might prove unsympathetic to an audience—especially to late-comers.

NB. This comment about all the 12 violins playing identical notes arises from sheer lack of experience. Anyone who has sat among the first or second violins knows that not *one* of them is playing the exact note of his neighbour. One is a little higher, one a little lower, one a little faster, one a little slower, *ad inf*. This is known among conductors as allowing the individual personality 'to tell'.

———

A PERSONAL REMINISCENCE OF SHOSTAKOVICH

An article commissioned to coincide with the release of a recording
of Shostakovich's Ninth Symphony.
World of Music, March 1962, p. 6.

I have always admired the music of Shostakovich ever since I heard, many years ago, his First Symphony, an astonishing work to be written by a young student then at the Leningrad Conservatoire. It was, therefore, with great interest that I looked forward to meeting him when the opportunity came in 1956 for me to lead a group of English musicians to give concerts in Soviet Russia. Our first concert was on April 19th of that year in the Tchaikovsky Hall in Moscow, and next morning Shostakovich came to see me at my hotel. I took an immediate liking to this shy, sensitive, modest, and highly gifted man. I had hoped that he would bring me the sketches of his new symphony on which he was working, for there was a piano in my room, and Shostakovich is an accomplished pianist. But he explained that the symphony was not yet sufficiently advanced to be seen, so we went on to talk on general musical problems. Even through the unsatisfactory medium of an interpreter it was, for me, a most stimulating experience. He reminded me a little of Arnold Bax in manner, hesitant in speaking on other topics but music, but on his own art downright and authoritative.

I recall, for instance, saying that in much of Prokofiev's music I caught glimpses of the *gamin*; he would have none of this—'deeply serious', he insisted. We discussed the difficulties of finding the right solution for the symphonic finale; the impression that a tonality gives of being confined to the more neurotic emotional moods; the unconscious influence of an imagined audience; and, of course, as happens always when composers meet, the proper role of the critic.

Two hours passed swiftly, and then Shostakovich left me to lay a wreath on the grave of Miaskovsky, whose birth anniversary it was.

I visited the Soviet Union again in the spring of 1958 at Shostakovich's invitation, to take part in the judging of the International Tchaikovsky Piano Competition. He was that year's President, and often sat in a box in the Tchaikovsky Hall to hear the competitors, many of whom played one or other of his own preludes and fugues. One evening Madame Shostakovich and he invited my wife and myself to dinner in their apartment. It was the first time I had ever been in a Russian home. We were ushered into a big living room with two grand pianos in it. Our host was playing a self-invented game of Patience with two packs of cards. Shostakovich is proud of his reputation as one of the finest poker players in the Soviet Union, and says that the manipulation of cards calms and rests him. Other musicians came in including two old friends of mine, the composers Kabalevsky and Khatchaturyan. Our hosts could not have been more generous, and their table was heaped with Russian delicacies. Alas! We had only time to sample a few of these, for, in the Russian custom, frequent toasts and speeches intervened, and then Shostakovich suddenly rose and said we had been bidden to a reception at the Kremlin and must hurry away. I perfectly understood at that moment the sensations of Tantalus.

A year or so later Shostakovich paid a visit to London and my wife and I were naturally anxious to repay his former kindness to us. He came with a counsellor from the Soviet Embassy to dinner at our house, and then we took him to a concert of English madrigals sung by the Golden Age Singers, and given in the chapel of the Royal Hospital, Chelsea. It was unfortunately a very stormy night and he saw little of the Wren architecture, but he enjoyed the music immensely. He told me he had never heard our sixteenth-century music, and as I had procured copies of everything sung, he followed the idiom with ease though he knows no English.

Shostakovich is the musical mouthpiece of Soviet Russia, a figure greatly honoured and loved there. It is obviously necessary that his music should be widely known elsewhere through authoritative and fine recordings.

THE ROYAL PHILHARMONIC SOCIETY 1813–1963

Bliss received the Gold Medal of the Society on 24 January 1963.
Foreword to the programme book of the Royal Philharmonic
Society's 1962–3 season.

The foundation of the Philharmonic Society one hundred and fifty years ago led to the first continuous fine orchestral concerts that London ever had. Two features of this society were significant. Firstly, it consisted wholly of professional musicians who at the outset gave their services gratuitously. Even after 150 years the Society retains the characteristics of a musical club, and those who are elected as officials to guide it serve without financial recompense. During all this time the Society, the second oldest of its kind in the world—only the Leipzig Gewandhaus is its senior—has continued its activities undismayed by wars and ever-recurring hard times. It must be placed on record that the present Chairman, Mr George Baker, has served the Society for forty years, for nearly a quarter of its whole life. This wonderful devotion to music is eloquent testimony to the position the Royal Philharmonic Society holds in the hearts of professional musicians.

Secondly, from the start the Society announced a policy of introducing new music to England and of commissioning new works from the leading composers of the time. The long list of first performances in its programmes fairly glitters. How we should have enjoyed seeing Mendelssohn conduct his *Italian* Symphony, Berlioz his *Harold in Italy*, Wagner a whole concert of his music, Dvořák his D minor Symphony,[21] Tchaikovsky his B-flat minor Piano Concerto!—and then of course there is the greatest name of all, Beethoven's Ninth Symphony. As we approach our own epoch, the names of many British composers appear with new works that have now passed into the general repertoire. For the cumulative effect of this policy of enterprise we have to thank what is now the Royal Philharmonic Society.

This season, to celebrate its 150th birthday, the Royal Philharmonic Society has invited four of its oldest orchestral colleagues to contribute to

---

21 Dvořák conducted two of his symphonies in D minor at Philharmonic concerts: No. 4 in 1884, and No. 7, specially written for the occasion, in the following year.

the anniversary series of concerts: the Royal Liverpool Philharmonic, founded in 1840, the Vienna Philharmonic and New York Philharmonic, both founded two years later, and the Hallé, which dates from 1857. Conductors include three Gold Medallists of the Society, Sir John Barbirolli, Sir Adrian Boult, and Sir Malcolm Sargent, together with Pierre Monteux, doyen of international conductors, Herbert von Karajan, and Leonard Bernstein. Soloists include two of the Society's most distinguished Gold Medallists, Yehudi Menuhin and Artur Rubinstein. Programmes consist largely of works written for, or performed for the first time in England at, a Philharmonic concert. The names of their composers alone—Beethoven, Brahms, Dvořák, Holst, Mendelssohn, Ravel, Sibelius, Walton, and Weber—show the scope of the Society's achievement.

So much for the past and the present, but what of the future? The curse of the lack of money hangs heavily over the musical world: orchestral players are underpaid and have to resort to wearisome drudgery to make up an adequate income; proper rehearsal time is too expensive and has to be cancelled; the price of seats rises and prevents the participation of the younger generation: concerts that show adventure in their programmes lose too heavily for the experiment to be repeated. This woeful story is only too well known.

Authority when hard pressed gives a bit here and a bit there, but in reality and indeed in comparison with some of our fortunate neighbours, the amount is insignificant.

Supposing as in a dream Authority were to take seriously the benefits that music can give, and make permanently secure that which now operates on a hand-to-mouth basis. What in such a case would be the true function of our oldest musical society? It could then continue to fulfill the high aims with which it started in 1813—an impeccable professional standard and a stimulating and adventurous policy. It might for instance plan two seasons of concerts every year, one in the spring and one in the autumn, each of ten or twelve programmes, placed well together to secure logical sequence. Each programme would be allotted not less than four rehearsals; let it not be forgotten than an initial purpose was to promote performances 'in the most perfect manner possible'. In each programme there would be one new work given under the happiest auspices.

Should Authority by some sudden and startling experiment make this dream a reality, the rewarding result would be inspiration and delight to future generations.

1964–1975

Written by Bliss in Greek on the title page of the original manuscript of
Hymn to Apollo.

But he who without the divine madness comes to the doors of the
Muses, confident that he will be a good poet by art, meets with no
success, and the poetry of the sane man vanishes into nothingness
before that of the inspired madman.

INTRODUCTION

BLISS completed a third cantata, *The Golden Cantata* (1963), for the
quincentenary celebrations in 1964 of the first degree in music granted by
Cambridge University, which made him an honorary Doctor of Music.
There were also, as ever, smaller occasional pieces—in this and the
following year a cradle song for the birth of Prince Edward, a fanfare for the
Shakespeare quatercentenary, a prelude for the 900th anniversary of
Westminster Abbey, a march for the funeral of Sir Winston Churchill
—and an increasing number of children's songs and religious hymns and
anthems. The autumn of 1964 was spent visiting his daughter in Australia
and giving concerts there and in Japan, concluding with visits to Hong
Kong and Ceylon. Among the many tributes to Bliss in 1966, on his
seventy-fifth birthday, was a BBC television documentary on his musical
life, which prompted him to begin work on his autobiography, *As I
Remember*. In the next three years he made several trips abroad on
concert tours: to Malta, Canada, and Florida in 1967, to New York in 1968
to conduct *The Beatitudes*, and to Princeton, New Jersey, in 1969 to
conduct *Mary of Magdala*. A song cycle, *Angels of the Mind*, and a fourth

cantata, *The World is Charged with the Grandeur of God*, appeared in 1969, as did the music for the Investiture of the Prince of Wales in Caernarvon Castle, a technical challenge Bliss particularly enjoyed. In the same year he was made a KCVO and in 1971, as a special mark of royal gratitude, a Companion of Honour.

At the age of almost eighty another man might well have basked in the glow of honours and disengaged himself from administrative duties, but Bliss's energy and creative impulse remained undiminished. In the stream of songs, fanfares, and other occasional pieces came perhaps the finest of all his concertos, for cello and orchestra (1970), the orchestral *Metamorphic Variations* (1972), and a final cantata, *Shield of Faith* (1974), composed for the Quincentenary of St George's Chapel, Windsor. Fittingly, his last project was the music for a BBC Television series entitled *Spirit of the Age* (1975). Arthur Bliss died at his home in St John's Wood on 27 March 1975.

———

A SYMPHONY OF COMPOSERS

An account of the work of the Composer's Guild of Great Britain, founded in 1944 to represent the interests of British composers. Bliss was President of the Guild from 1950.
Occasion (Connaught Rooms Review), 6 (1964), pp. 10–11. A portion of the text also appeared as 'Let Us Take the Initiative', *Composer*, 14 (1964), p. 3, with additional paragraphs enclosed here in square brackets.

The Composer's Guild of Great Britain is an association of 300 British composers founded 18 years ago to protect their rights and further their professional welfare. It was formed of necessity. Few composers have the dispositon or means actively to battle against indifference or neglect, and the chances of a young composer emerging by his own efforts from our musical jungle are pretty slim.

There is strength in unity, and though British composers are individualists who do not willingly combine into groups and parties as they do, for instance, in France, the experiment was tried and has proved singularly successful.

The success has been due to the generous and successful work of those members who are chosen annually to act as Chairman and Council—and how composers hate administration duties! I want to mention here the names of Theodore Holland and Alan Bush, who were the first two chairmen to launch this enterprise.

A Symphony of Composers

Our policy is that of any good watch dog: to be alert to conditions in which contemporary British music is being set aside, and to attack the sources of the neglect.

A watchful eye, for instance, scans the programmes of the BBC, the most powerful patron of music that the world has ever known. The BBC has done great service to British music, but, can it do more? The Guild thinks it can. To this end periodic meetings and consultations are held with their leading personalities.

The Guild also inspects the annual programmes issued by the leading musical organizations throughout the country. These are generally disappointing, British music being conspicuous by its sheer rarity. Letters regretting this go to those responsible, politely and firmly asking for more consideration. In these letters British composers speak with a collective voice.

The Guild also gives its members legal advice, puts their point of view to the Music Publishers' Association and to the Musicians' Union, issues a comprehensive catalogue of British orchestral works, encourages universities to give extramural lectures on British music, and brings amateur players and composers together to their mutual advantage.

Its activities are not confined to this country alone. It has sent leading figures to a recent international conference in Stockholm, and in four successive years two different eminent composers have visited the Soviet Union, this welcome gesture being reciprocated by Soviet composers.

Among the 300 members of the Guild are composers of every kind of music: the Guild does not limit its membership to any particular category. Some write for the opera stage, others for the concert hall, for big choruses, for church choirs, for our chamber ensembles, for our instrumental and vocal soloists; still others seek a wider public by writing 'light' and 'popular' music. I have to adopt these slightly absurd descriptions as they are fixed in common usage.

The style of composition is equally varied, ranging from the tonal, the modal, the atonal to the electronic. Our Annual General Meeting after the Luncheon is apt to be a lively affair, if it touches on the manner in which music should be written today. But all agree that fair opportunity must be given to *every* kind of musical talent.

These annual luncheons and later meetings at the Connaught Rooms combine pleasure with very practical business. At the last one held on October 14th, there was a full gathering of our leading composers, with Mr John Gardner in the chair. Each year a special guest of honour is invited, and on this occasion the lot fell on the distinguished conductor, Mr Basil Cameron, who in his 80th year can look back on long service to British music both here and in the United States.

He spoke feelingly of his friendship with Sibelius, and solved for us the mystery of his Eighth Symphony, which was promised to Cameron for its first performance, but, alas, never completed. Thanking the Guild on behalf of the guests, Mr Peter Pears spoke modestly of singers 'being the servants of composers'. The applause that greeted him must have shown him how faithful and inspired a servant he has been.

British music has never had an easy time in this country. We are still obsessed by the snobbish attitude of our grandfathers who were convinced that the only music worth hearing came from foreign countries where, of course, they do everything so much better than we do—play better, sing better, conduct better, and have the only composers worth listening to. British music they said (and indeed their grandsons still say it) is 'parochial', whereas the music from abroad is of truly international interest. Personally, I am bored with being international with everyone else: it gives me the feeling of walking down a main street in Everytown during the busy hours. The French music I admire is not international at all; it is redolent of France. What I like about Italian music is its national character (or, if you like, its 'parochial' character). If I were a Jugoslavian I should probably admire the British music that reminded me most forcibly of a British way of thought and expression.

I wish our leading musical organizations showed a greater pride in what has been written since, say, the days of Elgar, and a greater courage in performing it. Faith and pertinacity seldom fail, even if the initial effort is costly.

We have amassed an astonishingly fine corpus of British music in the last 60 years, and it is time that the masochistic streak in the national consciousness regarding it disappeared.

[I think that the Guild should try and get support for a series of concerts, to be arranged by its own members: that is to say that it should set an example by *actively* promoting new British music, and not simply exist to urge others to perform it.

I should like to see concerts planned not only of this country's music but also of Commonwealth composers and of our foreign contemporaries. The Guild, which represents the whole of Britain's creative activity, surely has the authority to do this. What is needed is the money guaranteed to put the project into orbit. If only some sponsor would say 'Say what you plan, and I will underwrite it', the dream of impeccable performances with picked artists and lavish rehearsals could be realized.

It would add dignity to such a scheme if it was carried out in conjunction with the Royal Philharmonic Society, whose traditional support of British music is memorable. But let the Guild itself be the spearpoint of an aggressive policy.]

GREAT MUSIC SHOULD BE SEEN AS WELL AS HEARD

TV Times, 31 January 1964, p. 11.

The best television programme, as we know, is one that immediately rivets your eye and then compels you to go on watching. The ear comes a good second and, therefore, any programme that demands a listener rather than a viewer is better on radio. Hence the immediate response of a television producer: 'Why *should* I bother with a Bach chorale or a Beethoven symphony, a song of Schubert, and opera by Mozart, Verdi, or Wagner?'

Well, perhaps if you run a fine radio programme as well, *that* is a fair question, but if you have only *one* programme, and this article is devoted wholly to Independent Television, there is another side to the argument. Television authorities well know that there is no such person as 'the average viewer'. What there *is* is a very large number of individuals, all watching their programmes. They comprise a great number with different interests and enthusiasms. The serious music lovers are one such section of the public, and not a particularly small one either. How has Independent Television catered for them?

Remember that only a handful of these will ever see the inside of Covent Garden Opera House, Sadler's Wells, or the Royal Festival Hall. Very few can ever hear an opera or symphony in actual performance or see world-famous singers, players, and conductors as a member of their audience. The large majority of enthusiasts, prevented as they are by the distance, expense, and any one of the many weekly problems, have to accept the next best thing, and watch on television. If they cannot go to opera house and concert hall, then opera house and concert hall must be brought to them.

What has Independent Television done in past years to satisfy the lovers of fine music? Frankly, it doesn't have a very generous record for a country like ours. There must be reasons apart from the anxiety (if you depart from the ephemeral and offer a programme of more enduring value) of losing your maximum audience.

Of course there are, and these are bound up with the limitations of the small screen itself. Even with future colour and a larger screen there are still problems to solve if a sufficiently large audience is to be held watching the performance of serious music.

It is comparatively easy to put over the world of jazz and 'pop music'; all items are short, all make immediate effect, and the personality of singer or player is brought close to you and the cameras. In opera, full length ballet, and music for the concert hall, the first difficulty to be overcome is the 'time factor'. One minute on the screen equals at least five minutes on the stage; in television opera the plot must be tightened up and the music edited; its tempo must be much quicker than stage opera.

The second difficulty is the limitation of the small screen. The big dramatic moments in *Aïda*, for example, lose their effect if characters appear as tiny as puppets; on the other hand a 'close up' of the singers in full voice can be disastrous. The presentation of opera not specially written for television is a real challenge to the inventive minds at work in the televison world, but surely nothing is really insoluble. The viewer should feel that he is sitting in the best seat in the house with a good pair of opera glasses to hand.

Ballet does not involve similar difficulties. Opera is written primarily for the ear, while ballet is concerned almost wholly with the eye.

I suggest that an interesting experiment would be to take the audience to a *rehearsal* of opera and ballet. Most of us like to look in at the making of something, and to see professional personalities at work. Look at the success of the gramophone record that Bruno Walter made while rehearsing a Mozart symphony! To those who had no idea how a great conductor 'shaped' the music at rehearsal, this record proved enthralling.

It is the concert hall that presents the greatest difficulty to television directors. How can the attention of a big audience be held during the performance of fine symphonic music? This is just the same problem, by the way, that faced Sir Henry Wood and his colleagues at the start of the Promenade Concerts. The key lies in the imagination exerted by great personalities.

Beethoven was, of course, one such towering personality and if it could be announced that he would appear in the Albert Hall next spring, you would not be able to get into London for the stream of visitors from all parts of the world.

In default of this there are a number of great living conductors who can present him to us in his music, and here the camera must act as a magic medium. For instance, while listening to his *Pastoral* Symphony I should much enjoy walking in the woods near Vienna. I might actually be following Beethoven's footsteps. I would likewise welcome views of Fingal's Cave during a performance of Mendelssohn's *Hebrides Overture*, remembering that the composer sketched the first 20 bars of the music there and wrote to a friend: 'how extraordinarily the place affected me.'

The film *Fantasia* showed, though in a somewhat perverse and exaggerated manner, what could be done by the marrying of sound with sight. There is, for example, the wide interest taken in modern art especially by the young; if this is doubted, try and get into the Tate Gallery one day when there is a notable exhibition there. It might be worthwhile acknowledging this interest and linking a series of (say) abstract paintings with the sound patterns of Stockhausen, Berio, or Nono. The programme would come as a shock; a shock provokes reaction, reaction causes heated comment, and heated comment provides wide advertisement for the originator of the idea, in this case Independent Television.

Even if, as I hope, Independent Television could play *one* adult programme of fine music each week, this still would not affect the size of audiences elsewhere. There will always be something missing on your home screen. You miss the added excitement of being a participator in an eager audience; you are only an outisde spectator and even if you shout your criticism or express your enthusiasm to your television set, it releases very little pent-up feeling!

Also I feel, and perhaps a Puritan ancestry speaks here, that the more effort that is made by the listener the greater the reward. I do not think that the boy Johann Sebastian Bach, who walked 30 miles to Hamburg to hear the famous Reinken play the organ, would have valued the experience as much if he had just stayed at home and 'tuned in'.

This article is a plea for more fine music on Independent Television programmes. Expect at the outset that the index figure for listening will be a low one, but also expect that this figure will rise and that persistence will bring a young and important new 'promenade' audience.

———

HYMN TO APOLLO

A talk broadcast on BBC Radio on 30 June 1965. The revised version
of the *Hymn* was first performed at the Cheltenham Festival on 5
July by the BBC Northern Orchestra conducted by Bliss.
BBC Sound Archives.

I wrote this short orchestral piece, the *Hymn to Apollo*, in 1926 as a 'thank you' to Pierre Monteux, who had introduced my *Colour Symphony* to audiences in Boston and New York. With Monteux I travelled to Amsterdam to hear him give the first performance.

And it was after a second hearing at a Royal Philharmonic concert in London that I began to have some doubts, both about the proportions of the work and the actual sound of my orchestration. It didn't really fulfil what I had in mind. It was hopeless to tinker with it so soon after completing it, so I just put it by.

But recently, after nearly forty years, I took it up again, and while using the same musical material throughout, I have rescored it for a smaller orchestra and modified its form. I am sure that this is a case where second thoughts are best.

The *Hymn* is an invocation to Apollo as the god of healing, and the music moves like a procession of suppliants.

―――

DISCOURSE FOR ORCHESTRA

Programme note for the first performance of the revised version, by the London Symphony Orchestra conducted by Bliss, at the Royal Festival Hall on 28 September 1965.
Manuscript, Bliss Archive, Cambridge University Library.

This *Discourse for Orchestra* was written for the Louisville Orchestra and first given in Louisville's Columbia Auditorium by that orchestra under its conductor, Robert Wh 'ney, on 23 October 1957. Later I had second thoughts about this wo k and kept it from performance during the intervening years. This year I devised an entirely new score for slightly larger orchestra and altered the proportions of the work, cutting out one section altogether.

The subject of this 20-minute dissertation is announced in the first few bars. The work can be divided into five clearly-defined sections:

1. Preliminary statement: (a) emphatic (allegro); (b) calm (larghetto)
2. A gayer and more impudent view (vivace)
3. A contemplative view (andante tranquillo)
4. A restatement of 1(a) with a brief return to (2), leading to
5. The peroration, and a quiet and enigmatic close.

As in all speeches, there are a few anecdotes and small digressions, but I hope the subject appears sufficiently throughout, in one form or another, to warrant the title I have given the work. It is dedicated to the Louisville Orchestra.

FOUR ASPECTS OF MUSIC

From an interview by Hans Keller, music critic and member of the
BBC music staff 1949–79, broadcast on BBC Radio on
14 November 1966.
Composer, 22 (1966–7), pp. 16–17.

KELLER: *You are one of our leading composers as well as being Master
of the Queen's Musick, and it would be interesting to hear from you what
you want from music, what a creative mind like yours expects music to
sound like.*

BLISS: When you asked me to come and talk to you about this, I began
to review my long life in music, and to jot down various things that I myself
demand if I'm going to enjoy music at all. There are four main points which
I'd like to discuss with you. First of all there is the question of the quality of
sound, then the question of the logic and the flow of the musical thought,
and then what kind of communication you get from specially modern
music, and lastly the value of the distinct personality in music.

If we might just take these in turn, going back to sound, to me the sound
of music must be either beautiful or arresting or strange. However logical
the thought, it can't be coarse or ugly. I know that these terms 'beautiful'
and 'ugly' are very difficult to define, but I think we all know what ugliness
is in buildings or in a person's voice or behaviour, and you get, I think,
sometimes in contemporary music sounds which are deliberately ugly in
themselves; however subtle I think the thought behind it is, I am unable to
listen.

As a young man I myself experimented in all sorts of sonorities. I
remember in 1921, when I wrote music for *The Tempest*, I had a quartet in
the pit of trombone, trumpet, a tenor voice, and a bass voice vocalizing
together, and for the storm a piano, four timpani, a gong, and an anvil. One
tried to get certain sonorities; and even today, I am thrilled when I listen to
something that is new and arresting in sound. I would like to give you an
example of that. Last year I was in the Abbey at Bath. Suddenly the organ
began, and I was immediately arrested by the most beautiful sound. I
couldn't think what it was. I was so moved that I tiptoed up to the organ loft
and there was a visiting organist—from Poland, I think—playing one of
the *Méditations*[1] of Messiaen. It was just a question of the superb

---

[1] The *Méditations sur le mystère de la Sainte Trinité* are assigned to 1969, four years after the
occasion Bliss mentions, and no other Messiaen organ work appears to have this word in its title.

registration: on getting a copy of the *Méditations*, I found that I wasn't so interested in the actual notes themselves, but I was absolutely thrilled with the sound they made; and that is one of the things that I feel essential in music.

The second is flow. One ought to listen to music as one views the earth, shall we say, from an aeroplane: it must proceed logically from place to place, arriving at its destination punctually. It must not be static; there again I find in quite an amount of contemporary music the feeling of going round a gallery of abstract pictures, pausing at each one as it were. However interesting it is, there are hold-ups, and there is not this logical flow from place to place.

The third point is communication. The music must convey to me some state of mind, or some emotional or intellectual stimulus. Some part of me must be moved by feeling I'm in contact with a superior mind that wishes to express itself to me, and there again in certain music I feel that the composer is addressing himself to a very small group or clique who in order to admire and respect his music must know certain personal allusions or watchwords. However fascinating their scores *look*, some composers today, when you *hear* them, have a quality unintelligible to me. I think—what on earth is this language, what is he trying to say to me? I can get a score; I can possibly play it. I certainly can read it, but behind that I don't find any communication. Of course, being an old man, that is probably my fault, but I think it's not *entirely* my fault, and I'm not at all denigrating those who *seek*—because after all, how can I follow the flight of an advanced mathematician? Of course, there are certain scores I can't read; I mean I cannot read musical diagrams where the composers have dispensed with notation.

The last thing, which I think is a rather fascinating subject, is—does one need to recognize a distinct musical personality in order to get the uttermost enjoyment? I feel *I do*. I remember with what a thrill I used to go to the first performances in my youth of Elgar, the Violin Concerto and the Second Symphony, simply because I heard a personal utterance, of someone who shaped a phrase which alone belonged to him. The other day, at the end of a television nature film, there came out some very majestic music; although I don't know what work it comes from, I'm absolutely certain only Vaughan Williams could have written it: I find a quality of enjoyment in that. I want tremendous variety in the world in all its manifestations, and especially in music.

There's one great benefit our composers have given to this generation, I think, and that is that they've added immensely to the virtuosity of players and singers. When I see, for instance, what singers or even a trained choir have to sing, and the correct intonation they have to maintain, in craggy and chromatic passages, I am overwhelmed with admiration for them, and that has been done by composers. They have compelled this virtuosity.

———

A CRITICISM OF *TOBIAS AND THE ANGEL*

From a draft of *As I Remember*, c. 1967.
Manuscript, Bliss Archive, Cambridge University Library.

I cannot remember now what was written about my musical score; kind remarks are soon forgotten, and only the caustic ones have a way of lingering in the mind. I remember one adverse comment that made me realize to the full that what moves me may have just the reverse effect on someone else. The 14 bars in question, criticized as completely banal, accompany the scene of Tobias's journey to Ectabane when Azarias, the archangel in disguise, is cutting out the gall and liver of the immense fish that has been landed from the river Tigris.

The fish is, of course, a Christian symbol, and the gall and liver prove in the story to have the magic power of restoring Tobit's sight. While Tobias is sitting on the river bank and watching Azarais at work, the latter quietly sings, as if communing with himself:

> The Word came alive while the World was asleep,
> And swam in the ooze of the primal Deep.
> It swam like a Fish through the gates of the Sea,
> And its golden gills were a Mystery.
> It swam till the frontiers of Death were cross'd
> And rescued the World before it was lost.

The young man Tobias then asks him, half mockingly: 'Do you often sing mysterious nonsense?' To me the words that Azarias sings are sufficiently enigmatic in themselves not to need further musical emphasis and I have set them to a very simple melody.

This melody occurs twice more in the opera: firstly at the end of Act I, where Tobias, in anguish at what he has learnt about Sara, with whom he is deeply in love, sinks to his knees to pray. At this moment Azarias, entering unseen by him, approaches and raises his arms in a gesture of divine protection.

The second repeat is at the end of the opera, where Tobit, regaining his sight, looks at Azarias and finds he is gazing into the face of the Archangel Raphael. He alone is granted this vision. He cries:

I thought I saw an Angel!
He was standing just there!
Arranged in all the glory of the Cherubim!

Now what strikes another as banal I, on the contrary, feel is right, and each time this quiet chorale-like melody is recalled I am moved by it. It came like a flash into my mind when I first read the words, and after the passing of years I still hold to its appositeness.

THE CONDUCTOR AND THE ORCHESTRA

A talk broadcast on BBC Radio on 11 April 1969.
Untitled manuscript, Bliss Archive, Cambridge University Library.

The relationship between a conductor of an orchestra and the players in that orchestra is a unique one. It is difficult to describe what it is, but I know what it shouldn't be, and that is the contact between a drill sergeant and his men on the barrack square—and yet there such conductors who as it were drill every note into their players. Mengelberg, I believe, was one such—a great conductor maybe, but he never seemed to allow the individual player the least liberty, and orchestral leaders in every section should have a certain freedom; they are all skilled soloists. If they do not mind this analogy, I should say the relationship between them and the conductor is more like that of the sheep dog to the shepherd.

This last autumn in the Cheviot Hills I watched with fascination a young shepherd with three trained dogs collect hundreds of sheep spread all over the steep hills, guide them down the slopes, and herd them into the enclosures for the night. The shepherd, standing in the valley, directed the dogs simply by his voice signals and they understood him. If they didn't, they just crouched and looked at him till they *did* understand. The conductor's stick is the shepherd's voice.

A conductor should do everything at rehearsal. He must give the clearest indication of what he wants and how he is going to get it. At the concert the performance should then go just as planned. It is not necessary at a concert to stimulate and over-urge players. If your rehearsal has been too scanty, it is then too late to do much.

I find there are two kinds of conductors—those who have two eyes and two ears only for the orchestra, *i.e.* the good ones, and those who have three eyes and three ears, the third being in the centre of their backs, watching and hearing, as it were, the audience's reaction. Those are the bad ones, whose antics and overacting may appeal to the less musical of the audience who want temperament, but are not in favour with the players —they just disturb them. All that our fine orchestras want is constructive direction given by the point of the stick, or by the hands, and accompanied by the musical knowledge of the score and sensitivity.

Let us suppose an orchestra is playing the *Eroica* for the hundredth time. What astounds me is that they can rehearse it differently with conductor after conductor, and on no occasion does a player get up and say, 'Mr So-and-so, or Herr or Monsieur So-and-so, I *can* play this as fast as you are conducting it, or as slow, but I *refuse* your tempo as being unmusical and indeed ridiculous.'

The leader of an orchestra has a heavy responsibility. He is really the interpreter between the conductor and the whole body of string players. Between him and the conductor there should be a complete rapport.

Conducting a chorus brings a different problem—what you give to them in energy they will give back to you—but with orchestral players, exciting yourself does not necessarily mean exciting them, or your audience. Years ago I saw Nikisch rehearse the *Meistersinger* Overture. At the first rehearsal for the mighty start in C major he made a tremendous gesture, at the second rehearsal only half that. At the concert he just made a short quick down beat, and that brought in the first tremendous chord with thrilling surprise. Perhaps a lesson to be learnt by many 'personality' conductors.

HENRY WOOD

A talk broadcast on BBC Radio on 2 March 1969.
Typescript, BBC Written Archives.

I first met Henry Wood in 1912, when I was at Cambridge. He had come up to take a rehearsal, with the University Chorus, of Beethoven's Ninth Symphony, which he was to give shortly afterwards in the Guildhall at Cambridge. It was naturally exciting for all of us to be keenly rehearsed by so famous a man. I remember the pains he took to get the right feeling into the opening notes of the basses, insisting on a warm tone, and singing the notes several times himself. After the rehearsal, he talked to some of us who were taking our musical degrees, and I carried away as a young man the impression of a warm-hearted, generous, great musician.

Shortly after this, I made a special journey to London from Cambridge to hear him rehearse and conduct Schoenberg's *Five Orchestral Pieces* —the first performance of these in England. That was in 1912. Henry Wood was always a pioneer and eager for new musical experiences. And it was Henry Wood who gave me my first chance to conduct at the Proms. In the years following the First World War it was very difficult for young composers, young singers, young players to get a chance to show what they could do. There were no powerful recording companies or broadcasting orchestras to help them. We all looked primarily to Henry Wood. I had written my first full orchestral work, the *Mêlée Fantasque*,[2] and he invited me to conduct it in his 1921 season.

I have spoken of Henry Wood's generosity, and this was plainly shown by the way he gave young musicians all possible time for rehearsal. In those days the Promenade Concerts had just one orchestra and one conductor. It was a real *tour de force* to get through the season—just the morning rehearsal for the evening concert. Henry Wood would skimp the time for the classical symphony and other repertoire works, to allow the young composer or the young soloist a really generous slice of the morning's rehearsal. In the evening, I remember waiting nervously to go on, and Henry Wood, as he did to so many others, would utter a word of encouragement, and then say, 'Wait a minute, till I get to my seat in the circle: I want to hear this.' That was a tonic for one's nerves.

I also owe him the first well-rehearsed performance of my *Colour Symphony*. I'd produced rather a travesty of this at the Gloucester Festival in 1922. The score was very difficult, the rehearsal time scanty, I was inexperienced as a conductor, and the platform in the Cathedral was not large enough to contain my huge orchestra. I knew beforehand there would something of a disaster. Well, that morning *before* the performance I got a telegram from Henry Wood: 'Please let me have *Colour Symphony* for my symphony concerts next season.' I can't tell you what joy that unexpected and encouraging message gave me.

I met Henry Wood at concerts many times in later years, both here and in America, and however famous an international figure he became, he was always the same eager, friendly, encouraging, great lover of music.

---

[2] This was in fact his second work for full orchestra, the first being *Two Studies for Orchestra*, of which he gave the first performance at the Royal College of Music on 17 Feb. 1920. He conducted *Mêlée Fantasque* at a Promenade Concert on 13 Oct. 1921.

─────

ANGELS OF THE MIND

Programme note for the first performance, by Rae Woodland
(soprano) and Lamar Crowson (piano), at the University of Lancaster
on 2 December 1969.
Manuscript, Bliss Archive, Cambridge University Library.

For a long time I had wanted to set some of Kathleen Raine's poems, but they seemed to me as delicate as flowers or shells, and I hesitated to spoil their fragile beauty.

And then came an occasion five years ago when I had to collaborate with this poet. We both have associations with Cambridge, and in 1964 the University was celebrating the 500th year of the first degree ever given in music. Professor Thurston Dart, then Professor of Music in Cambridge, asked us to combine in writing a choral work to be sung on this occasion. We did so, Kathleen Raine writing eight poems for me to set, which formed a sequence in praise of music and which we called *The Golden Cantata*.

This emboldened me, and early this year I chose seven poems from her collected works written during the years from 1935 to 1949. They are all mystical poems; no wonder she admires and writes so understandingly about Blake. They are charged with human emotion, as if the poet had undergone a deeply affecting experience. She allowed me to call this song cycle *Angels of the Mind*, because she writes of angels, both terrible and comforting, in the same spirit as Rilke did. The seven poems are called 'Worry about Money', 'Lenten Flowers', 'Harvest', 'Seed', 'In the Beck', 'Storm', and 'Nocturne'.

═══

CONCERTO FOR CELLO AND ORCHESTRA

Programme note for the first performance, by Mstislav Rostropovich
and the English Chamber Orchestra conducted by Benjamin
Britten, at the Aldeburgh Festival on 24 June 1970. Bliss initially
called this work a 'concertino', but was persuaded by Britten to drop
the diminutive.

I have always wanted to write some music for solo cello and orchestra, ever since as a young man I played through the classic repertoire for the instrument with my cellist brother, Howard. But it is only now that the decisive impulse has come, as a result of a suggestion from Mstislav Rostropovich. I sketched out the music in the spring of 1969, and on his acceptance of the dedication, 'To Mstislav Rostropovich with admiration and gratitude', made the final full score this March. It is a light-hearted work, at any rate in the first and third movements, and is scored for a Mozartian orchestra, with the addition of harp and celesta. There are no problems for the listener—only for the soloist!

═══

PERFORMING RIGHT SOCIETY
ANNUAL LUNCHEON

An address by Bliss as President of the Performing Right Society on
1 July 1970, with HRH the Prince of Wales as guest of honour.
'The Annual Luncheon', *Performing Right*, November 1970, p. 3.

Today is a unique occasion in our fifty-six years of existence. At our annual luncheons, to which so many of our members come, we always try to secure as our Guest of Honour someone of special distinction. In the past we have had three Prime Ministers. We have had Lord Chancellors, Ministers of State, High Commissioners, Ambassadors—the whole glittering lot. But we have never had a member of the Royal Family.

At this moment in our history we have a great number of young writer members, many of whose tunes and lyrics have been world successes; so your General Council thought it would be very appropriate if we could have a *young* man this year as our honoured guest. We all agreed that there was only one young man that we wanted, and thanks to his kindness we have got him.

Besides his youth, there is a further reason why he is so welcome. If one studies the long succession of our kings and queens, one thing must surely strike the musician. They were almost all tone-deaf: hardly one took any interest in the art of music.

It is true that Henry VIII composed a few tunes, when not otherwise engaged. Queen Elizabeth the First was said to be able to take part in a madrigal, but it was probably wiser for a courtier to say she could. Charles the Second had a good ear for lively tunes, liked gay music in church, and when the French string players that he imported from France played anything with a special lilt he used to wave his royal hand to the beat.

Coming nearer to our own time George IV is rumoured to have played the cello in the Chinese Music Room of the Royal Pavilion in Brighton, and, of course, Queen Victoria and the Prince Consort were kind to Mendelssohn and Wagner on their visits.

But none of them did what our present Queen has done to encourage music, by frequent attendances at concerts and musical functions, and now we have a Prince of Wales who enjoys playing the cello and the trumpet.

I believe he prefers the cello in Great Britain, and the trumpet in Australia, which shows a nice feeling for the relative size of the two countries.

I am sure he will modestly say that he doesn't play either of them very well, but many of us, including myself, do not play an instrument very well, so in that respect too he represents a large number.

He must surely be one of the most sought-after young men in the world, so we are all the more grateful to him for taking time off (I almost said from his practising!) to come and be with us this afternoon.

On this special occasion many distinguished guests naturally have accepted our invitation, but I know that they will agree that there should be only one toast. So I ask them to rise with us all and drink to the health and happiness of our Guest of Honour, the Prince of Wales.

═══

TRIPTYCH

Programme note for the first performance, by Louis Kentner, at the
Queen Elizabeth Hall on 21 March 1971.

With this *Triptych* written last year I return to my first love, the piano. My
very first published works were a jejune Intermezzo, a Suite, and a set of
Valses Fantastiques written when I was at Cambridge, and now luckily
unobtainable.[3] In the twenties, while in California, I wrote twelve short
and varied pieces for the piano;[4] a Concerto for two pianos followed in
1924, a full-length Piano Concerto in 1939, and a Sonata in 1952.

The three pieces forming the *Triptych* are a 'Meditation', a 'Dramatic
Recitative', and a 'Capriccio'. The 'Meditation' is naturally reflective, but
not unduly introspective; the drama in the 'Recitative' rests on the contrast
between rhetorical statements and bravura passages; the 'Capriccio' is
carried on a vivacious rhythmic pulse and ends with brilliance.

It is dedicated to Louis Kentner 'with admiration and gratitude'—the
admiration is for his playing, and the gratitude for the help he gave during
the recording of my Piano Sonata by Marguerite Wolff.

═══

THE MUSICAL PROFESSION

A speech given by Bliss, an honorary Fellow of the Royal Academy of
Music, at a dinner held by the Royal Academy of Music Club on
10 June 1971.
Untitled manuscript, Bliss Archive, Cambridge University Library.

I am more than pleased to be able to talk to this gathering of fellow
musicians, for it gives me an opportunity to express certain opinions about
the art we all share and love.

---

[3] The Intermezzo and Suite (both *c.* 1912) and the *Valses Fantastiques* (1913) were all later
withdrawn. Two movements from the last of these were later used in *A Wedding Suite* for piano
(1974), written to celebrate the marriage of Bliss's half-sister, Enid.

[4] Eleven pieces can be identified: *Masks: Four Pieces for Pianoforte* (1924); Suite for piano
(1925), in four movements; Two Interludes for piano (1925); and Toccata for piano (*c.* 1925).

The Musical Profession

I think I am pretty safe in suggesting that at no time in the history of our civilization has music played so prominent a part in our daily life as it does today. In my own field of composition, for instance, it may astonish you to learn that nearly 5000 composers are now elected members of the Performing Right Society. You know better than I do how many others aspire to be solo pianists, or instrumentalists, or singers, or conductors. Our concert halls, certainly those in London, are often booked a year or so in advance, so great is the demand for recognition. Opera now flourishes in the most unlikely places, competitive festivals grow in size, music departments in universities and schools, many of them of recent origin, are now regarded as indispensable adjuncts to education. This tremendous activity is to be commended if it enables the young to construct rather than to destroy, to learn how to express themselves rather than to live in nagging frustration.

How has this come about? I believe two dominating and certainly new incentives have contributed to this increasing wish to enter the musical profession. I am not saying that they are the most altruistic ones, only that they have injected a new element into the musical scene. One is money, and the other is glamour.

May I take the question of money first? I remember so well Elgar telling me rather bitterly of his struggles in his early years due to lack of means, and indeed, at the start of this century any young man or young woman who aspired to be a composer without a private income was regarded either as mad or suicidal. In spite of a Beethoven and a Schubert, a squalid garret is no place for inspiration—except in novels.

Today, owing to performing fees, commissions, prizes, films, etc. and the relative ease in getting his music heard, a gifted young composer with a modicum of luck can make a living by his own talents, often a very considerable one. This feeling of relief has been a blessing to many composers today.

Now let me take the second new incentive—glamour. By the help of television, broadcasting, recording, international competitions, a young musician can easily find himself or herself famous, literally overnight. Unlike the poet, painter, or sculptor, the musician alone has the chance of a film star's meteoric rise.

Now like all, at first sight, apparent advantages, these two glittering ones, wealth and glamour, bring their own disadvantages with them, certainly in the artistic sense. I mentioned earlier the huge total of 5000 composers listed in this country. Of course only a small minority of these can be called serious composers. Most of them write pop music (often in groups) or mood music to be heard as a soothing background in airports, factories, bedrooms, etc., or jingles in advertisements. The continuous spray of music on Radio 1 is the result, and it is in many cases, though not always, just like a sky sign spelling out the letters MONEY.

I am reluctant to use the word 'serious' music, and it is regrettable that for convenience sake we now divide creative achievement into the three categories of serious, light, and pop—because, in reality, all worthwhile music is the result of hard concentrated work and the desire for as perfect a result as possible. Anyone who attempts to construct something in sound, paint, stone, or whatever without seriousness of purpose is simply not an artist at all; he is just a dilettante.

Composition today is in a strange state, with multifarious styles colliding each with each, with some favouring this 'ism', and others that 'ology'. The stage seems set for some kind of do-as-you-please, free-for-all combat. The glamorous rocket-like ascent of some composers, due to sensational work, immediately leads to others attempting even more ear-catching, and sometimes eye-catching, 'happenings'.

Side by side with masterworks written since the last war are pieces of extreme silliness, often insulting to an adult audience, and certainly an outrage to musical instruments.

It *is* necessary for every new generation to protest and rebel—we have in our time all done it—but it is no use protesting and rebelling when *everything is permitted*. You cannot rebel, with satisfaction, against anarchy, only against some kind of order which you dislike. Now some definition of order is at the very basis of composition. When Nadia Boulanger, for instance, insists that her pupils feel the importance of every note, I applaud. When she teaches them order by the keen scrutiny of past masterpieces, I applaud that too. It must be difficult to teach composition today when the student finds himself unwilling, or indeed unable, to subject himself to disciplined routine. He won't understand that the disciplined routine will give him all the necessary technique and facility, and also give him just the irritant against which he can then rebel.

What I think music most needs today—and it is to influential teachers and far-sighted critics that we look—is a reaffirmation or reassessment of values—and by values I imply that something, fundamental and constant, by which we instinctively feel the presence of great art. Teachers and writers on music have surely the duty of 'pricking their pupils' minds awake'. Awake to what? Well, to the cleavage between the permanent in value and just the ephemeral and phoney.

This assessment of values can be more important than it first appears. 'A change in the music of a state', wrote Plato, 'will be followed by changes in its constitution.' It is possible that the Soviet Union has pondered this axiom. While there is undoubtedly a great amount of creative talent in this country, I think a student would be wise to resist the temptation to start straight off at Omega (*i.e.* the latest avant-garde work, heard perhaps over the radio) and instead, first lay his foundations at Alpha.

It is very tempting to adapt yourself immediately to the taste of the day, and outdo your predecessors in extravagance of sound and idea, but I think it often leads to disappointment. Someone said 'we are born imitators'. Probably true, but what is important is *what* we imitate.

Works of value grow slowly, and, as it were, in the dark, like bulbs. With today's incessant excitements in life (life with a big L) the necessarily right soil becomes harder and harder to find. Let me quote from a letter written by an eminent artist: 'That undisturbed, direct manner of working, almost like a sleepwalker, which alone can lead to greatness, is almost impossible now. All our talents are broadcast in the market place. Critical reviews appear every day in fifty different places and the gossip they spread abroad stifles all healthy growth. Whoever does not keep away from it all and insists on isolating himself is lost.' That was written in 1824 by Goethe, and a hundred and fifty years later it carries the same weight and warning.

I have kept to the end mention of the strongest reason why the young want to be musicians, and that, of course, is for the sheer love of it. To an outsider on some other planet it might appear extraordinary that a man or woman could devote their whole lives just to musical sound, but so compulsive is the pull, on this earth, that here we are—all doing it.

This dedicated devotion results in a strong camaraderie among musicians. They are in their way like gardeners in their conception of sharing and giving. No gardener, even if he is a stranger to you, will refuse to give you a cutting from some rare plant, if he realizes what it means to you. He is not going jealously to keep it for his sole pleasure.

In my long life I have seen in our profession countless acts of generosity —teachers giving of their hard-won spare time, players freely giving their services, unadvertised kindnesses bestowed on a fellow musician fallen on ill times. It is natural then that such a club as this should have come into being, and have existed for so many years. It is easy to propose its health, because of the knowledge that it will continue to prosper. I am proud to be able to write the three letters RAM after my name, and secretly rather self-satisfied, as I know that I have acquired this honour without having done anything in particular to deserve it.

ROYAL COLLEGE OF MUSIC PRIZE-GIVING

Illness prevented Bliss from attending the ceremony on 18 July
1974. His address was delivered by the Director of the College,
David Willcocks.
RCM Magazine, 70, 3 (1974), p. 82.

It is a bitter disappointment to me that I cannot be with you all this afternoon, but one's doctor has the last word and he must be obeyed. It is a great disappointment, partly because coming to the College always has a warm rejuvenating effect, but also because I should have so liked to scan the faces of those who will be the leading musicians of the next generation. I also like handing out prizes, but am so proud that the Director has invited my wife to do this in my place, as she will do it so much better.

Firstly, let me congratulate this year's prize-winners. Competition is always fierce here and they can feel really pleased at their success. But of course this is only a strong incentive to go on and work harder. When the charming Isobel Barnett in 'What's My Line?' asks 'Is there an end product?', all musicians should cry 'No, Isobel, there isn't.' For the only end product in music is to approach as close to perfection as possible. This is a decade of quite extraordinary and indeed unequalled professional talent in all branches of music. Keep that fact well in mind, prize-winners.

As for the majority who have not yet attained prize or scholarship level, don't be in the least disheartened. Many, for instance, are later starters. I certainly was one. I did not leave the starting post till I was 27. The odds at that time against my doing anything must have been about a thousand to one, but I said to myself, 'Stop whining and get down to solid hard work', and indeed for the next three years I *did* work and, as Americans say, I'm telling you!

Finally, I want to emphasize that whether ultimately successful or not, we are among the lucky ones. We deal daily with the mysterious, magical world of sound. Much happiness, friendships, and other delights come from making music together with others, singing the music, and communing thereby with some of the greatest spirits that ever lived, and, if we are composers, we have the exciting joy of trying to extend the boundaries of our art. I think it was Donald Francis Tovey who said of Beethoven that when we are listening to him or playing him there come some rare moments when we seem for an instant to be standing at the same high inspirational summit. The sad difference between Beethoven and us is simply that while he can remain there, we cannot. A fair statement, I think.

In absentia, I wish you all in your own various ways much happiness from life, for if we are not born initially to have a good proportion of *that* as our birthright, what on earth are we doing here?

Good luck.

METAMORPHIC VARIATIONS

Programme note for a concert of Bliss's music broadcast on BBC
Radio on 22 April 1975, shortly after his death.
Manuscript, Bliss Archive, Cambridge University Library.

These variations for a large orchestra were completed in December 1972, and are therefore a comparatively recent work. They were written for the Croydon Arts Festival of 1973 and received their first performance that spring with the LSO conducted by Vernon Handley. I have added the word 'metamorphic' to the title, because the three themes that constitute the opening section of the work, called Elements, undergo a greater transformation during the forty-minute work than the simple word 'variations' implies.

The three elements on which the succeeding sections or variations are based are these:

(a) a long lyrical cantilena for solo oboe, which opens the work;

(b) a two-bar phrase, first heard on the horns, and then on the strings;
    and lastly

(c) a cluster pattern of four semitones close together introduced by the
    woodwind.

The succeeding 14 sections all have a title which indicates the general mood of that particular variation. They are difficult to remember without a written programme note, but I name them in their order just to show the variety to which these elements are subjected. The titles are as follows: Ballet, Assertion, Speculations, Interjections, Scherzo I, Contemplation, Polonaise leading to Funeral Processions (these last two, Polonaise and Funeral Processions, are easy to spot). After the Funeral March comes what I call 'Cool Interlude', woodwind playing softly to a solo viola, then solo cello, then solo violin obbligato. This is followed by Scherzo II, with prominent wood blocks supporting the brass, and next a Duet for solo violin and solo cello accompanied by soft pizzicato chords (this too is easy to spot). The last two sections are marked Dedication and Affirmation. The Dedication (for brass alone) confirms the dedication at the top of the score—'To George and Ann Dannatt[5] in token of a long and cherished friendship'. I make use of their initials, G.D. and A.D.

The last section, Affirmation, starts in the grand style, but the work does not end in the same mood. It fades quietly away after a climax, marked by a stroke on the tam-tam, and at the end there is a repetition of the opening solo oboe cantilena. Its high B♭ is heard pianissimo, alone, and withdraws into silence.

SHIELD OF FAITH

Programme note for the first performance, by the Bach Choir
conducted by David Willcocks, in St George's Chapel on
23 April 1975.
Manuscript, Bliss Archive, Cambridge University Library.

This cantata for soprano and baritone soli, chorus, and organ was commissioned by the Dean and Canons as part of the musical celebrations in honour of the Quincentenary of St George's Chapel, Windsor, and tonight receives its first performance. The title is taken from the Sixth Chapter of St Paul's Epistle to the Ephesians, verse 13, which starts: 'Wherefore take unto you the whole armour of God . . . above all taking the shield of faith.' The symbol on the cover of the vocal score is a Christogram, made up of the first two letters of Christ in Greek, χ and ϱ. It was additionally the symbol of birth and resurrection.

The poems set in this cantata were selected for me by Canon Stephen Verney, one from each of the five centuries. The first, by William Dunbar (1460–1520), is a triumphal battle hymn exulting in the defeat of the Devil and the resurrection of Christ. At the end of this the two soloists, unaccompanied, declaim a setting of the words *Gloria in excelsis Deo*.

The second poem is by George Herbert (1593–1633). This beautiful poem[6] must have been set by many. Luckily I do not know them, or I should not have felt so free to try one myself. The guilty soul is pardoned, and invited with Love to partake of the Sacrament.

---

[5] George Dannatt (1915–), music critic and painter, who discusses their friendship in his Introduction to the *Catalogue*. Bliss found a certain inspiration for the *Metamorphic Variations* in a series of Dannatt's abstract paintings, though the title also reflects Lady Bliss's interest in geology.

[6] 'Love'.

In the third poem, an extract from *An Essay on Man* by Alexander Pope (1688–1744), we enter the region of scepticism. Is man a god or a beast? Pope gives a scathing account of man's life; there is no 'shield of faith' here, only the cold comfort that God is wiser than we are.

In the fourth poem, from *In Memoriam* by Tennyson (1809–92), we seem to glimpse 'the dark night of the soul'. I asked Canon Verney to provide me with something of an agnostic nature here, as a contrast to the blazing faith of the final poem. I feel that the hopeless 'Behold, we know not anything' gives the right feeling. Tennyson indeed hopes for reassurance 'at last—far off', but the whole excerpt seems to suggest that the hope is in vain.

The fifth and last poem comes from 'Little Gidding', the fourth of the *Four Quartets* by T. S. Eliot (1888–1965). It forms the coda to the whole sequence of the *Quartets*. Little Gidding in Huntingdonshire was, in the second quarter of the seventeenth century, the home of Nicholas Ferrar's religious community. Charles I visited it in 1646 shortly before he surrendered to the Scots army at Newark. He had been there before and in his troubles he lamented the peaceful hours he spent there. 'Very privately, in the darkness of night he came once more to Gidding' (Carter, in his *Nicholas Ferrar*). I paid a visit to the chapel some ten years ago. It is very remote and quiet. An aroma of sanctity still clings to it.

I have read these *Quartets* (mostly aloud) many times. I do not presume fully to have their meaning, but their magnificence expresses itself in a rapturous acceptance of belief, ending in the Dantesque vision of the union of divine and human love.

A TESTAMENT

In April 1974 Granada Television recorded archival material
of Bliss introducing *Meditations on a Theme by John Blow* at the
piano. The following extract was published posthumously.
'Arthur Bliss (1891–1975): A Testament', in *British Music Yearbook
1976*, ed. Arthur Jacobs (London, 1976), p. 39.

I think most people like to feel that they leave behind them a remembrance of a definite personality—hence the photos, portraits, biographies, autobiographies; but in the case of an artist it's a little different, because what he wants to leave behind is his work—the poet his verses, the sculptor his works of art, the painter his canvases, the musician his scores;

and of course, there is a reason for this, because with an artist, very often the outer persona that he shows to the world is very different from the inward man at work on his art.

There have been, of course, major exceptions amongst great composers. For instance, reading the scintillating letters of Mozart, sparkling, full of vitality, with underlying melancholy and sometimes tragic mood, you feel if you met him that he'd be exactly like his music; and also, if you read the reminiscences of the friends who visited Beethoven—no question in their mind, each one of them caught a facet of the real man who wrote the symphonies, the sonatas, the quartets.

And then of course you get the other thing. It's almost astonishing to feel that Wagner in middle life, pampered with satins, silks, perfumes, could compose the young, virile *Siegfried*—so there's no rule; but in many cases the composer is a man of two beings—one which perhaps, for self-preservation, he shows the world, the other he keeps hidden and it is only behind the closed door of his workroom that he is really himself, and possibly only his nearest and dearest, in this case my wife, for instance, can blend the two. I have indeed written an autobiography detailing my life to the age of 75, but whoever wants to know the *real* me must listen to my music.

You remember that Elgar wrote on the score of the *Dream of Gerontius* 'This is the best of me', by which I think he meant 'This is the *real* me'. I have therefore chosen as a portrait a characteristic work of mine written at the age of 64. It is music that I should wish to have survive me. In Elgar's sense I can write in this work, *Meditations on a Theme by John Blow*, and in my choral symphony *Morning Heroes*, 'this is the best of me'.

APPENDIX A
The Apple of Discord

A synopsis of an opera based on an episode from the *Odyssey* which
Bliss planned to write with the poet Stephen Spender *c*. 1943–5.
Spender, however, 'was too busy with his own medium of poetry
and with public obligations to be able to give the time, and also he
did not, I think, react enthusiastically to the excitement of the
theatre' (*As I Remember*, p. 168).
Typescript, Bliss Archive, Cambridge University Library.

The scene is the wedding feast of Thetis and Peleus. Thetis, a sea-nymph and
daughter of the sea-god Nereus has been wooed both by Jupiter and Neptune: to
avoid a conflict between the gods, it is decreed that she shall marry a mortal,
Peleus, king of Phthia. Thetis only consents when Jupiter promises that he and the
other gods and goddesses will attend her marriage feast. This takes places on a
night of full moon near the coral caves of Nereus.[1]

The gods bring Thetis gifts to celebrate worthily the marriage from which was to
come the greatest hero of the Trojan war, Achilles. Thetis gives thanks and makes
obeisance. When the ceremonies are at their height, lights darken; an uninvited
guest, Discord, appears, and throws into the midst a golden apple on which are
traced the words 'To the Fairest'. A dispute immediately arises between Juno,
representing Power, Minerva, representing Wisdom, and Venus, representing
Beauty. Thetis and Peleus beg Jupiter to end the dispute. Jupiter refuses to decide
himself, and sends Hermes to fetch Paris, the young son of Priam, who is tending
sheep on Mount Ida.

Juno, queen of heaven, in royal robes and insignia, offers Paris unlimited wealth
and power; Minerva, in glittering armour, offers the bribe of supreme wisdom and
conquest in war; Venus, in her magic cestus, offers a bride as fair as herself, and
shows him a vision of Helen. Paris gives the golden apple to Venus. Juno and
Minerva vow vengeance, and on the backcloth is seen a vision of Achilles' death in
front of the burning towers of Troy.

---

[1] Gods sit enthroned, as curtain rises. [AB]

APPENDIX B
Sonata for Viola and Piano

An analysis originally intended as the conclusion of 'Aspects of
Contemporary Music' (see p. 102, n. 35 above). The sonata,
dedicated to Lionel Tertis, was written in 1933 and first performed
by Tertis and Solomon in a BBC broadcast on 3 November 1933.
Typescript, Bliss Archive, Cambridge University Library.

I have used both these two devices in my Sonata for viola and piano that you are
going to hear this afternoon. It consists of three contrasted movements, each quite
separate from the others, with a coda or epilogue at the end, in which the musical
ideas of all three movements are united and summed up.

The first movement is rather restless and dramatic, in which two opposing ideas
are at work; the second is lyrical with long lines of melody, with one big climax in
the middle of it to which the lines gradually tend; the third is fierce and rhythmic,
growing from one single rhythmic pulse; and the coda which follows with but a
small pause reviews, as it were, the contents of the three movements that precede
it. I am now going to play you the principal themes upon which the whole sonata is
built.

Now one note on the viola as an instrument.

Every phrase I have played to you from my sonata has had a definitely romantic
quality. This is just as it should be, since the viola is the most romantic of
instruments—it is a veritable Byron in the orchestra. The dark sombre quality,
now harsh, now warm, of its low string, the passionate rhetoric of its highest
string, and its whole rather restless and tragic personality makes it an ideal vehicle
for romantic and oratorical expression.

Its career as an instrument has been rather a chequered one. It is the oldest
member of the violin family, and in the late sixteenth and early seventeenth
century held much the same position in the orchestra that the first and second
violins occupy today. Gradually, however, it was ousted from this leading
importance by the coming of the true violin, smaller in shape and higher in pitch.
It was relegated to a subordinate position in the middle of the ensemble, where in
the time of Haydn interesting parts were few and far between. It became an
instrument which inferior violinists took up. If all else failed they could always play
the bass part, and this resulted often in an unnecessary and uncomfortable
three-octave bass, such as we find, for instance, in Pergolesi's *La serva padrona*.
With Mozart and later Beethoven a great improvement took place. Both these
composers could play the viola a little, and both exalted the instrument, as they
did others in the orchestra. Berlioz, however, was the first composer to exploit its
particular tone colour, and this was followed by other French composers, notably
Debussy, whose personality was very sympathetic to the viola's special tone
qualities.

But what the instrument has been awaiting is a great virtuoso who should do for the viola what Paganini did for the violin, Liszt for the piano, and Bottesini for the double bass. We are indeed fortunate to have in England that master player, in the person of Lionel Tertis, who has in one bound extended the viola into a solo instrument of exquisite expression and variety. His name will assuredly go down to posterity as the creator of modern viola playing, and the inspirer of most of the recent literature for the instrument.

I am doubly grateful that I have two great artists like Solomon and Tertis to play this work now to you, for quite apart from the music itself, you will have a half hour's experience of unrivalled playing.

Index

286

Index

Index

289

Index

Index

Index